Marion County HISTORY

Volume XV

Compiled and edited by Sybil Westenhouse, Adele Egan
and David Weiss

Graphic design and composition by Suzanne Stauss,
Exhibit A Graphics, Inc.

Marion County Historical Society
Salem, Oregon

MISSION STATEMENT

The Marion County Historical Society, a community resource, advocates and promotes an appreciation of regional history by present and future generations. The Society connects the past to the present by preserving and interpreting the county's cultural and natural history.

The Marion County Historical Society disclaims responsibility for statements of fact or of opinion made by contributors.

Copyright © 1998 Marion County Historical Society

ISBN: 0-943297-02-8

Marion County HISTORY

Table of contents

Marion County HISTORY

Volume XV ❖ Preface

The Marion County Historical Society has, among its several goals, the preservation of local history. Consequently, the publishing of history becomes an important step toward attaining this goal. To put history into the hands of the reader, whether a dedicated researcher or a casual browser, is the purpose of this Volume XV.

The articles and photographs fall into two groups: some have been previously published in *Historic MARION*, others are being published for the first time. Those from *Historic MARION* are of sufficient value to be republished in a more permanent medium. Both groups of articles have been edited to a high standard for quality and readability. This is Marion County history worth passing on.

As a "Thank You" to the many contributors, a short biography, and for most a photograph, is included for each author. The Society is indebted to these writers and those who edited and prepared the material for publication.

To David Cushing Duniway

David Cushing Duniway
1912-1993

MCHS COLLECTION

Descendant of a famous pioneer family, both historians and makers of history.
Devoted his life to studying and preserving history.
Shared his extensive knowledge in a most selfless way.
A founding member and first president of the Marion County Historical Society in 1950.

He knew that publishing stories and articles is important for preserving historic information.
Marion County Historical Society published his collection of articles in *South Salem Past*,
and *Dr. Luke A. Port, Builder of Deepwood*.

Marion County HISTORY, Volume XV is dedicated to our longtime friend and mentor.
Thank you, David, for the long, fruitful and happy association.

David Duniway

By Alfred C. Jones

David as Mission Mill Museum Association's first administrator.

An interest in local history is not just a fad. It can open related paths to fascinating stories and facts.

That was how David Cushing Duniway regarded historical research: "a sunrise for the brain" to add meaning and enlightenment to one's current existence. Such discovery brings a new respect for old objects, accounts, photographs and old timers' stories.

Every nation, state, county and city needs persons like Duniway to lead the way as he did for Oregon, Marion County and Salem until his death in 1993 at age eighty-one. One significant highlight of his career was being the first president of Marion County Historical Society in 1950. He was quick to see the tenuous connections between the Oregon Trail, missionaries, education, commerce, politics, Gold Rush...and more.

One of the first clues about his arrival in Salem was this item in the *Oregon Historical Quarterly* of March 1946:

The Oregon State Library announces that David Cushing Duniway has been appointed Oregon State Archivist and assumed his duties on January 5, 1946. He inaugurates the State Archives, created by act of the 1945 Legislature, under a current biennial appropriation of $15,000. Mr. Duniway holds a Library Certificate granted by the University of California, 1937. He was for seven years connected with the National Archives, Washington, D.C., and served as archivist consultant to various war-time agencies on the west coast.

Duniway quickly saw the need to save official records and items that were in peril "just because they are old" or on microfilm or "taking up space needed for other stuff." When it's gone, it's gone, he realized, and he encouraged government to preserve both historical records and historic buildings.

As a voracious reader with powerful memory, Duniway could see significant and subtle connections between persons, buildings and documents. Somehow he could see how they fit together like a jigsaw puzzle.

An example was the Holman Building on the northwest corner of Commercial and Ferry Streets. It had been Oregon's substitute state capitol from 1859 to 1874, after the old wooden capitol burned on December 30, 1855.

Its builder, Joseph Holman, had all kinds of connections to Oregon history, having arrived via the Oregon Trail in 1840, at age twenty-five, to be a Methodist Mission carpenter and teacher. It didn't take him long to marry Almira Phelps, who had arrived in 1840 on the *Lausanne* as part of the Great Reinforcement.

Holman's busy life led to his involvement in sheep husbandry and wool manufacturing, superintending construction of the penitentiary and the capitol, owning a flax seed oil plant, and being on the founding board of the Oregon Institute (Willamette University).

Joseph and Almira's only son, George Phelps Holman, was the first white child born in Salem or the county. The Holman's daughter married John H. Albert of the Capital National Bank.

That's how the thread of history's colorful fabric became a joy to trace for Duniway, who advised persons not to accept only one source as the gospel truth, but to explore all sources and records.

He felt that he had been lucky to have a father like Clyde, who was a historian and educator, and the famous grandmother, Abigail Scott Duniway, who led the suffragette movement.

David, as a state archivist in the northwest corner of the third floor of the State Library from 1946 to 1972, began preserving history. One of his first projects was to gather and publish *Members of the Legislature, State of Oregon, 1860-1949.*

He collected materials from all over, taught others how to use the reference services, wrote prolifically and well, helped found the Salem Art Fair, helped initiate the Oregon Microfilm Service, and wrote biographies of persons honored in the Mission Mill Museum's *Panegyric* booklets.

David was a founding member of the American Association for State and Local History, and the National Trust for Historic Preservation. He was a leader in restoring the 1894 Deepwood House, built by Dr. Luke Port, and he researched and wrote at length about Dr. Port's career.

With Professor Kenneth Holmes, Duniway edited *Covered Wagon Women*, letters written by pioneer women.

David knew the dates when certain buildings were constructed or burned or torn down. With his knowledge of downtown buildings and leading Salem families, he was a natural volunteer to spend many hours at the Oregon Historical Society identifying photo negatives from the Cronise Studio in Salem. More that fifty thousand images were bequeathed to Oregon Historical Society in the Cronise will.

It also was natural for David and wife Frances to restore the 1865 McCully-McMahan house, once occupied by early community leaders. In that home, in his retirement, the phone often rang as people asked for answers to historical questions.

David's daughters, Malissa and Sancha, shared in his eternal quest for answers to "Who are we?" and "Who are we becoming?" His passions were to answer these questions, and to add to his list of humorous puns.

The heritage that David left behind can reveal our roots and increase our understanding of the present and our future.

(The eulogies on the following pages were presented at the memorial service for David Duniway on September 19, 1993, and were originally published in *Historic MARION.*)

ᛗ

David At Home

From the Family Viewpoint By Malissa Duniway Holland

Thank you on behalf of the family for joining us for this celebration of the life of David Duniway. The David all of you knew is the David we knew at home too.

He loved a good story and delighted in telling them. His love of literature was shared with us and is one of our earliest memories. The stories we read and were told are now shared with our children and my students.

Like the animals in *Badger's Parting Gifts* we remember some of the things he taught us.
• "Dust is a good preserver of paper." Translated: don't dust my books.
• Honesty. Even as small a thing as the use of state pencils by a state worker's child could not be tolerated—ever!
• Listen! You never know when a mature person will impart an important piece of information.
• Look. The world is a colorful and exciting place to be, and
• Be kind. Not everyone has your same values.

Sancha remembers the "state occasions." We were dressed in scratchy lacy dresses, white gloves and patent leather shoes. We stood through official introductions and ceremonies knowing that they represented something important to our father.

Before Sancha was born, I remember trips to the country to sketch with my father. His group, the Creative Art Group, became the revived Art Association. After Sancha was born I had to be extra careful with my clothes after these outings because she might catch poison oak from me. But during our summer beach trips, Sancha, too, became part of the sketching frenzy. She and our friend Martha DeWeese climbed onto Dad's shoulders while I sat with my hands and feet in his lap, and he drew "Hands and Feet."

In the early years of the Art Fair, this was after the saving of Bush House, we were all part of the activities. I was in charge of endless puppet shows for kids. Dad and Mrs. Brenner put up the chicken wire fence (this is no reflection of Dad's mechanical abilities) on which the art was shown. It was a long way to the dream that Fran helped create—an exhibit hall and classes for the community.

Dad's big dream of a living history museum in Salem was hard to believe. Tom Kay says that he thought Dad was crazy but let him store the Lee House on the grounds. One of my memories is heading to the almost roofless warehouses with a shovel. I was to assist Fran in bagging up the pigeon droppings in preparation for the Fourth of July celebration and sale. Fran worked miracles and transformed the entrance of the most intact warehouse into a store. There was a barbecue outside and people came! It really was becoming a museum.

Dad's legacy includes his concern for refounding of the Unitarian fellowship. Originally it was a discussion group that grew into a church and joined the Universalist Church to become the first Unitarian Universalist Society. He taught Sunday School (the Youth Group) and served on the board. He insisted that the words "interdependent web of life" be inserted in our statement of beliefs on the cover of the order of service.

He carried a small newspaper clipping listing seven sins, by Gandhi:
1. Wealth without work
2. Pleasure without conscience
3. Knowledge without character
4. Commerce without morality
5. Science without humanity
6. Worship without sacrifice
7. Politics without principle

Thank you to the many caregivers who eased David's last ten months. Thank you to Dr. Hughes, Danny, Home Care, and Hazel, our hospice volunteer companion. A special thank you to faithful bathers Ken and Nancy, also Susan, Dixie, Rita, Cecilia, May Ellen, Evelyn, Kaylyn, Peggy and Caroline. You truly eased our way and aided in our caring for David.

I know that he talked with all of you. You all remember him, his caps, his walks, his dogs, his bolos, and his jokes. He talked with everyone he met with the same gentlemanly respect. He knew the town's chiefs and it's eccentrics. He knew their history and contributions. He believed in the value of every person and their story.

It will be for his dream that Dad will be remembered. He convinced us all that we could have parks, art museums, historic buildings, and living history museums. Our greatest tribute to him will be to continue working to unite our city as an open and accepting community of respectful people.

We as a family challenge you to carry on his work and vision for Salem, Marion County and the world. Not everything that is old should be torn down; not everything new is good. That which is passé today may be invaluable tomorrow.

David the school boy about 1925 after a year in England.
MCHS COLLECTION

David, The Unitarian

Memorial By Barbara Hanneman

I was honored to be invited by the family to speak in behalf of our Unitarian Church. To have lost two such stalwarts as David Duniway and Carlisle Roberts within weeks of one another has certainly left a deep void in our small congregation.

David and I were two of the remaining three charter members of the Salem Unitarian Fellowship, the other being Dr. Margaret Dowell, a pediatrician who later married Professor Arthur Gravatt of Willamette University. They were our first church romance and it has been a long and happy one. They now live in Portland and would have been here today except that Margaret has had some surgery.

When the Salem Unitarian Fellowship was formed in September of 1949, a minimum of ten persons was required to become affiliated with our denomination. That was exactly the number who signed the Charter at the old Senator Hotel when we met with the minister from Boston, so we all felt important and needed—as indeed we were.

David was that rare being—a born Unitarian. My late husband, Gene, and I were merely youthful seekers, but it was altogether a hardy, committed little band that held their Sunday evening meetings in the basement of the old "Y". We got to know one another very well through the years, as people do in smaller groups.

David's impressive knowledge and love of history and of his Unitarian heritage was a rich resource for us. We did not have a minister in those early years and he could always be counted on for a thoughtful sermon on short notice. He taught in the church school, served on various committees and as president.

The contemplative David.   MCHS COLLECTION

Our children grew up together in the church school and attended one another's birthday parties. Malissa told me the other day of an incident I had not known about. She said, "You know, of course, Barbara, that Dad was not particularly athletic, but he did love to crawl around on the floor with kids on his back. I remember putting both Laurie and Linda (my twin daughters) on his back at one time, and I can still see them all laughing as they urged him on."

Thank you for sharing that delightful memory Malissa. You and Sancha were so dear to your dad.

Among his many favorite authors, I know that David loved Thoreau and this week I reread *On Man and Nature*. I would like to share two quotations from the book because I think they are appropriate for this day, in David's memory.

Everyone has heard the story which has gone the rounds of New England, of a strong and beautiful bug which came out of the dry leaf of an old table of apple-tree wood, which had stood in the kitchen for sixty years, first in Connecticut and afterward in Massachusetts—from an egg deposited in the living tree many years earlier, as appeared by counting the annual layers behind it—which was heard gnawing out for several weeks, hatched perchance by the heat of an urn.

Who does not feel his faith in a resurrection and immortality strengthened by hearing this?

On the death of a friend, we should consider that the fates, through confidence have devolved on us the task of a double living, that we have henceforth to fulfill the promise of our friend's life also, in our own, to the world.

A Tribute To David

By Elisabeth Walton Potter

It is an honor to join with others here in offering remembrance of David Cushing Duniway, a gentle and learned man, our great friend and guide to community history.

In remembering David, it is impossible not to think first of his cordial and generous nature. He seemed to enter into the matters he undertook joyfully, so great was his desire to learn and lead others to discovery. Never grudging of his time to those who sought his counsel, he was a genuine authority. His views were founded on solid scholarship, wide-ranging interests and constant inquiry. What an example he was for men and women in public service.

As one so often aided and enlightened by Oregon's long-tenured State Archivist, I would like to pay tribute to his professional life, in particular.

As the son of a distinguished educator and the grandson of a leader in the woman suffrage movement, David so well fulfilled his family heritage. It is generally known that he was educated at Carleton College in Minnesota, where his father chaired the department of social sciences. He gained his Master's degree in history and was certified in library science at the University of California at Berkeley. Thereafter, he entered professional life at the National Archives in 1937. He rose quickly in his branch of the federal government and was well connected in his professional circles nationally. He participated in events looked on today as benchmarks in the developing field of state and local history. He was a founding officer, at age 28, of the American Association for State and Local History, organized in 1940, and was a founding member of the National Trust for Historic Preservation, which was chartered by Congress in 1947.

David was recruited from a National Archives field supervisory position in San Francisco to head the newly created Archives Division within the Oregon State Library in 1946. He served the state with distinction for 26 years. By the time of his retirement in 1972 he literally had built an institution. It was his responsibility to review all obsolete records of state and county governments to identify that ten percent having historical significance. He issued the rules that put a stop to indiscriminate disposal of public records and turned up priceless documents. Among the many initiatives he directed was the Oregon Microfilm Service program authorized by the Legislative Assembly in 1955. This program, regarded as a model for other states, applied current technology to duplicating records marked for disposal and it produced security copies of "the oldest and most treasured" government documents that would be saved in original form.

David worked to advance his profession by teaching, mentoring, and organizational work— a sure measure of attainment in any field. In the 1969-1970 academic year, he sought a leave of absence from the State Archives to become a key adjunct faculty member in the University of Oregon's School of Librarianship. He was prominent in the advisory councils of the Pacific Northwest Regional Archives and the National Archives. His service to the profession was recognized in his election as a Fellow of the Society of American Archivists as early as 1959. David was a great repository of facts concerning the capital city. The figures of early Salem and Oregon history were his familiars. He knew them from their papers, journals, published writings and the documents they signed. Who better to write the entry to "Salem" for the 1964 edition of the *Encyclopaedia Britannica*? Throughout his long career here he never ceased being an organizer, spokesman and educator in the cause of history. He was at, or close to, the root of every notable historic building preservation project from 1948 onward. That year of 1948 was significant, for it was then he served as president of the Salem Art Association and helped lay the groundwork to bring the Asahel Bush House, Salem's first historic house museum, into the public domain. After its doors were opened in 1953, the Bush House became the precedent for later successes such as the Mission Mill Museum Association, which he helped organize in 1964 and served as first professional administrator following his retirement from state service. It was in 1948, too, that he had campaigned to save the Holman Building, which stood at the corner of South Commercial and Ferry Streets and was the interim home of the Oregon Legislature for some fourteen years from 1859 to 1874. Though it did not meet with success, David's effort on behalf of a state document of the architectural sort was a catalyst for cofounding the Marion County Historical Society with City Librarian Hugh Morrow and others in 1950. David was the Society's first president and remained one of its guiding spirits.

His published works include dozens of articles in professional and historical journals. Some of these have given us our basic understanding of Salem's growth and development. His guide to the Capitol Mall and City of Salem, brought out in observance of the centennial of statehood in 1959, has not been surpassed to this day. It was David who compiled the pithy biographical sketches of the city's leading citizens, past and present, appearing in the programs of the annual galas to benefit the Mission Mill Museum. He wrote definitively about Dr. Luke Port, builder of Deepwood, and he produced a series of articles on noteworthy places in community history (for South Salem News) that was gathered and published as *Glimpses of Historic South Salem* and *South Salem Past.*

Together with Alfred Jones, he volunteered hundreds of hours to identify images in the immense collection of historic views of Salem making up the Cronise Photographic Studio collection that was bequeathed to the Oregon Historical Society. He directed the long sustained volunteer project for indexing Salem's historic newspapers, a legacy of inestimable value to

The lighthearted David with Mary Eyre at opening of MCHS Museum, April 26, 1984.   MCHS COLLECTION

researchers of the future. His latest work centered on editing diaries and letters of overland pioneer women, that heroic group which included his grandmother. With Professor Kenneth Holmes, he was associated in the compilation and editing of *Covered Wagon Women*, part of the Oregon Trail series recently published by the Arthur H. Clark Company.

With his wife, Frances, he restored the historic McCully-McMahan House, which became their home, and he collaborated with her in the betterment of Deepwood. His role, as customary, was to promote understanding through writing, and he supported Frannie in her restoration of the 1920s landscape developments by Elisabeth Lord and Edith Schryver for their knowing client, Alice Bretherton Brown Powell.

It is pleasing to think of the gracious hospitality extended in this setting over the years. A number of the most recent occasions celebrated David and his good friends Mary Eyre and Cecil Edwards. Among the occasions I treasure most is a visit with David, not at Deepwood, but in his historic home. It occurred last July, around the time of his eighty-first birthday, and it comes to mind because it epitomizes the lifelong value he placed on learning. With the loving care of his wife and daughters, to whom he was devoted, he was settled for the most part in his library. There in the healing environment of his books and favorite paintings, our conversation turned to the tradition of attaching seals to important documents down through the ages. Realizing that I was lacking in the understanding of the earliest forms of the practice, he had me fetch from the shelf a lacquered box, which he opened to reveal a fine collection of antique wax seals, some of them displaying still the faded fragments of ribbon which once attached them to a document requiring a dignitary's imprimatur. Dismissing what it might cost him in effort, David proceeded to impart to me one last lesson in history, making it, as always, a nugget of discovery.

We are one in our warm thoughts of the Duniway family this day. Frannie, Malissa, Sancha and all, I wish you much joy of your memories of David. Such fine memories as you have will be a power to draw on for a long time to come.

Editor's note: This eulogy given by Elisabeth is based in part on a nominating letter she drafted for use by Marion County Historical Society when David Duniway was proposed for the merit award conferred upon him by the Association for State and Local History in 1988.

Hager's Grove

Marion County prehistory

By Dr. Leland Gilsen
Previously published Summer 1996, Vol.34, No.2

Hager's Grove is within the tribal territory of the Santiam Band of the Kalapuya Indians. Richard Pettigrew excavated archaeological sites 35MA7, 35MA8 and 35MA9. *All reported archaeological sites get a Smithsonian number. The 48 states are in alphabetical order and given a number. Oregon is the 35th state, so all Oregon sites start with "35". Each county has a letter code. Marion is "MA" while Linn is "LIN" and Lincoln is "LNC". Then each site has a number based on when it was recorded. Thus, 35MA8 was the 8th site recorded in Marion county in Oregon.*

Excavation site 35MA7 encountered pits, hearths and clusters of fire cracked rock from earth ovens used for processing camas. Plant specimens included camas, hazelnuts, onion, acorn and cherry. Site 35MA8 was not excavated because tests indicated it contained few deposits. Site 35MA9 revealed a living-floor with associated earth ovens, pits and fire cracked rock clusters. Only one charred hazelnut was recovered from this site.

Projectile points ranged from earlier dart (atlatl) types to later arrowheads used with the bow and arrow. *The atlatl is a dart throwing stick.*

Radiocarbon dates suggest that the sites were occupied in a series of short episodes starting around 1800 B.C.; another one about 800 B.C.; perhaps several during the A.D. 600-900 period; and ending with one about A.D. 1550. These dates range through the Middle and Late Archaic Periods. *The Middle Archaic ranges from around 4000 BC to roughly BC/AD and the Late Archaic after that. The Middle Archaic is characterized by the use of atlatl dart points while the Late Archaic contains bow and arrow points. Both Periods are based on a gathering and hunting economy. The Middle Archaic is marked by the beginning of the systematic burning of the valley to expand valued plants and animals exploited by the Indians (camas, tarweed, oak, deer and elk).*

The sites suggest that reuse was probably based on natural resources. This was a fairly good place to camp and was used over and over. Reuse disturbed previous occupations. Thus, features such as hearths and ovens were easier to see and find in later deposits. *Feature is a term for any non-artifactual remains in the ground. Arrowheads are artifacts. Examples of features are pits, hearths, post molds, house pits, cache pits, and clusters of artifacts suggesting activities or living surfaces.*

Pettigrew believed that the sites were warm-season camps for a few families. Camas was the primary resource at the latter end of the occupations, but there was not as much evidence for plant use in the earlier occupations. The presence of dart points, followed by arrow points, scrapers, knives, drills and flakes, indicates that hunting was important along the stream channel forests which were surrounded by burned off grasslands. The annual burning created what is called a grassland/oak mosaic, with forests along the rivers and streams resisting the fires. Thus, the valley streams had what are called gallery forests of varying width which contained habitat for many other valued plants and animals.

There was a change from dart points to arrow points during the periods, but no fundamental changes in the activities over nearly 3500 years.

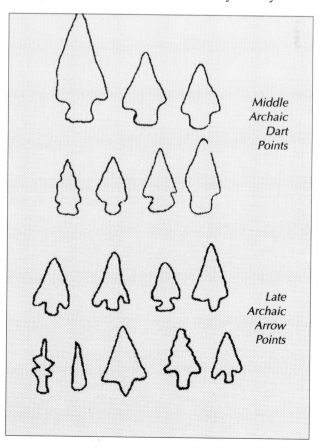

Middle Archaic Dart Points

Late Archaic Arrow Points

In general, the archaeology of Oregon is divided into major time periods.

PALEOINDIAN: This period is characterized by the presence of the large animals that lived in the last ice-age and the technologies developed by humans to hunt these animals. The best known point types associated with such groups are the Folsom and Clovis dart and/or thrusting spear points. Some archaeologists place Windust points in terminal Paleoindian, and others into the Early Archaic.

EARLY ARCHAIC: This period involves adaptation to essentially modern animals. The first clear evidence for large scale plant gathering and processing and fishing appears. The Cascade point and large side-notched dart points are characteristic aspects of the hunting. Some housepits are assigned to this period as well.

MIDDLE ARCHAIC: As populations expanded, more intensive gathering and hunting developed. The first evidence occurs of valley and upland forests burning to reduce plant matter in trees and expand valued plants and animals. Pithouse villages are more common. Fishing technology is very sophisticated and the earliest fish weirs and traps are found. Coastal shell middens become very common. Trade networks expand. The atlatl and dart is still in use, but decreases in average size.

LATE ARCHAIC: The atlatl and dart is replaced by the bow and arrow. Trading centers develop at strategic locations such as The Dalles and Willamette Falls. The Chinook essentially govern from the mouth of the Columbia River to The Dalles and control trade between coastal, valley, plateau and plains groups. Long range trade networks are in place. Systematic burning has opened up the Willamette Valley into a grassland/oak mosaic. High elevation burning has opened up forested areas.

The pre-contact influx of Euro-American goods and horses changes political and economic patterns. The impact of disease devastates entire political and social groups, causing the extinction of some.

NOTE FROM THE AUTHOR

I thought that the members of the society would like to have a summary of archaeological work that has been done in the county over the years. Once some of the background work has been presented, this is expected to be an occasional series based on reports hot off the press.

As the State Historic Preservation Office archaeologist, I maintain the archaeological site files for Oregon. Currently, we have over 15,000 survey, testing and excavation reports on file. Most of this is known as "gray" literature (unpublished manuscripts). Because it is unpublished, its distribution is marginal. The only publication that summarizes this information is C. Melvin Aikens' book *Archaeology of Oregon*. His book is available in bookstores or through the BLM.

The first time I use archaeological jargon, I will explain its meaning (*in italics*).

Relating To Kalapuya Culture

By Suzanne Stauss
Previously published Winter 1996, Vol.34, No.4

 Archaeological research indicates that the Kalapuya Indians lived in western Oregon for six to ten thousand years before the arrival of early white settlers in the Willamette Valley. One of the first EuroAmerican records of contact with the Kalapuya was by fur trader Alexander Henry in 1814, although there was evidence that the Kalapuya had traded with EuroAmericans since the mid-1700s.

Origin of the Kalyapuya is not certain, but materials from archaeological sites indicate an emphasis on root crops which could determine that our original Native Americans may have migrated from the North American Plateau region.

Although the different bands of people spoke diverse dialects depending on where they lived in the Willamette Valley, all Kalapuya languages were related to the Penutian stock language. The natural boundaries of mountains and river basins divided the Kalapuya language into three major dialects. The Tualatin-Yamhill dialect was the language of Kalapuyans who lived in a small portion of the lower Willamette Valley upstream from Oregon City. Santiam dialect was common in the middle and upper Willamette Valley and Yoncalla was the dialect of the upper Umpqua basin, south of what is now Cottage Grove.

But unlike language, characteristics of Kalapuya culture and their relationship to animal mythology were consistent throughout the region. Coyote created many of life's essentials, including the earth. Shamans were the spiritual women or men who served as ceremonial leaders and healers. Permanent winter villages were established for collective habitation and then bands divided into summer camps to gather food, hunt and fish. Otter fur was included in the typically braided hair. Otter fur, feathers, porcupine quills and beads derived from salmon backbones and shell fish composed the necklaces, nose or ear plugs and arm bands that depicted social status.

Chronicles by early settlers indicate that the Kalapuya were influenced dramatically to simulate EuroAmerican culture. Epidemics raged through Kalapuya settlements in the 1830s, killing up to 90% of the population. The treaties of 1854-55 relocated the remaining Kalapuya to the Grand Ronde Reservation. Since then, newspapers have published at least four different obituaries that declare the deceased to be the last of the Kalapuya.

Although most of Kalapuya culture has been thoughtlessly lost or destroyed, we can still relate to a known element of Kalapuya heritage. The Kalapuya year was divided into 12 lunar months that reflect their culture and lifestyle from prehistoric times. The New Year began with the first new moon in late August or early September.

The Kalapuya Calendar Year

September begins the **Kalapuya New Year.** Prairie burning commences for tarweed seed harvesting while groups are living in summer camps throughout the Willamette Valley to harvest acorns, berries and camas roots.

October is the month when **Hair (leaves) Falls Off**. While Kalapuya camps in the northern Willamette Valley relocate near lakes to begin wapato harvest, southern valley camp residents complete camas harvesting.

November is **Approaching Winter** and the Kalapuya people prepare their winter village homes.

December is **Good** month when people are settling into winter villages before the hard winter weather arrives.

January is the month of **Burned Breasts** because senior Kalapuyas singe their chests by sitting too close to the continual inside fires to overcome the cold temperatures outside. The winter dances are beginning.

February is **Out Of Provision** month because food supplies are running short although hunters are trying to replenish the supply with fresh game.

March is **First Spring** as people begin short camping trips to gather food, especially the fresh shoots of camas.

April, **Budding** month, is the time when the Kalapuya make more extensive trips to the Willamette Valley floor to gather camas roots.

May is **Flower Time** because the camas is in full blossom while the people exit the winter home to begin summer camps. Salmon have begun their annual run up the Willamette River and tributaries.

June is **Camas Harvest** as women begin their three-month-long role to gather bulbs from the fully ripe camas and dry them for winter food. Fish and berries are also plentiful to glean and preserve.

July is **Half Summer-Time** and the Kalapuya collect caterpillars and hazelnuts during the hot, dry weather.

August represents **End Of Summer** while the people continue to gather berries, nuts and roots in preparation for winter.

Cooking Up Camas

(camassia quamash)

By Jordis Schick
Previously published May 1992, Vol.30, No.4

The beautiful blue blooms you see in the fields and meadows in the Willamette Valley in early spring is the camas—a staple in the diet of the Kalapuya Indians.

A type of lily, the camas was (and still is) readily available in the wild. The bulbous root resembles the onion in shape and consistency but is considerably more bland in taste.

Camas has also been called a wild hyacinth. Harriet L. Smith, who wrote an Oregon vignette entitled *Camas, the Plant that Caused Wars*, says the name appears in Greek mythology, which tells of a plant started from the blood of a beautiful Spartan youth, Hyacinthus, whose death was caused by jealous Zephyrus.

According to the journals of Merriwether Lewis, the Indians either ate the quamash "in its natural state, or boiled into a kind of soup or made into a cake, which is then called pasheco. After the long abstinence this was a sumptuous treat."

Other sources say the Indians dried the root in a very specific procedure after harvesting. They started a fire at the bottom of a hole they had dug and let it die down to hot coals. Then they spread the coals over the bottom of the hole, covered them with dirt and leaves, placed the camas on top, added another layer of dirt and leaves, and built another fire on top of the whole thing. They cooked the camas for 24 to 48 hours to preserve it for consumption in the winter months.

The camas thus prepared was ground into meal in a large stone mortar with a pestle. To cook it, sometimes water was added to the ground meal to make a batter which was then fried on a large flat rock to make something similar to a pancake. Or often the meal (and a small amount of water) was formed into large bricks weighing up to ten pounds which were cooked in stone kilns that quickly seared the outside while leaving the inside moist for future use.

Camas flower

The Battle Creek Affair

By Jim Martin
Previously published November 1994, Vol.32, No.4

Many people have heard about the Texas Rangers, but how many know of the Oregon Rangers, and their first encounter with Indians—called the Battle Creek Affair—near Salem?

The Oregon Rangers were formed after a "goodly number" of men attended a meeting in May 1846 at the farm of Daniel Waldo.

There had been several previous attempts to organize militia companies in Oregon, but all failed, wrote historian Joseph Henry Brown in 1892, mainly because of the "sparseness of settlement."

The meeting, chaired by T.D. Keizer, agreed that *Whereas, The people of Oregon territory are situated remote from, and without the protection of, any Government, we, therefore as members of a free and enlightened community, wishing to preserve the principles and institutions of a free and republican form of Government, and being well aware that the body of the people is the only power capable of sustaining such institutions, therefore we deem it advisable to form ourselves into military bodies, for the purpose of preserving peace and order at home, and preventing aggression from abroad...*

The Oregon Rangers, a company of mounted riflemen, was formed by 45 men who signed a code of bylaws regulating the group's conduct.

Elected as officers of the company were Charles Bennett, captain; A.A.A. Robinson, first lieutenant; Isaac Hutchins, second lieutenant; Hiram English, third lieutenant; Thomas Hold, orderly sergeant; Thomas Howell, second sergeant; S.C. Morris, third sergeant; William H. Herron, fourth sergeant; P.C. Keizer, first corporal; Robert Walker, second corporal; B. Frost, third corporal; John Rowe, fourth corporal.

A month later, in June 1846, a party of Wascopam Indians, from The Dalles or Warm Springs in Wasco County, appeared in southern Marion County and camped for a time northwest of Looney Butte in the lower Santiam Valley. The Indians' "numbers and their rather free and easy behavior" were noticed by the scattered settlers, reported one observer.

Hamilton Campbell, a member of the recently dissolved M.E. Mission, had become owner of the cattle of the mission by purchase, this observer stated, *and these cattle ranged on the hills between the Santiam river and Mill creek to the north where the mission was and Salem is now located.*

A rumor was started in the settlement that the Indians were killing and eating from the cattle ranging in the vicinity of their camp, he continued, *and upon that rumor a young man was sent to ask the aid of Captain Bennett's company of rangers, who met for drill every Saturday at the farm of Daniel Waldo, in the range of hills now bearing his name.*

Lt. Robinson, temporarily commanding the detachment in Capt. Bennett's absence, led a 14-mile gallop to where the Indians were presumed to be.

But the unsuspecting Indians had moved about four miles north, toward Salem, and the Oregon Rangers, on the trail between Salem and the Santiam settlement, rode headlong into the new Indian camp. The Indians, alarmed by the troopers' sudden appearance, took what cover they could in a little fringe of brush.

Shots rang out, and an Indian fell. No whites were wounded, however, as the Indians generally had only pistols—although several were armed with "fu-sees", rifles obtained in trade with the Hudson's Bay Company.

The shooting soon stopped, and the Indian chief asked why his people were being fired on. The chief was told the troopers were checking information that the Indians were killing and eating white-owned cattle.

"This the Indians stoutly denied, and the proof of the charge was not made," an observer later wrote. *No further shooting occurred, and the casualties were one white man badly frightened (it required a wet-nurse application of water to restore the victim to normal condition), and one Indian shot through the fleshy part of both thighs. As everything could be settled with the Indians for a property consideration, this man's case was no exception. A gift of a pony and a pair of blankets settled the trouble, and the trouble and the name of it settled Capt. Bennett's company of Oregon Rangers. It needed no instruction after the affair of Battle Creek. Public spirit wilts under ridicule. The effect of a prospective fight had such an effect upon one of the Rangers as to bring the action into ridicule. The Indian recovered from his wounds; the rangers never recovered.*

This incident, concluded historian Samuel A. Clarke in 1905, looked "very much as if the Oregon boys were more impetuous than the occasion called for."

Willamette Mission State Park

A treasure that needs more attention

By Jordis Schick
Previously published May 1993, Vol.31, No.2

Within this county's boundaries are many treasures, but one of the least heralded and most deserving of more attention is the uncut jewel—Willamette Mission State Park.

The park deserves greater notice not only because it is so well-situated to historically commemorate the early Jason Lee Mission and its influence on the settlement, government and economic development of the Willamette Valley, but also because it is a lovely spot that offers many opportunities for a wide range of recreational activities.

Willamette Mission State Park is one of Oregon's largest at 1,682 acres. It used to be called Lone Tree Bar State Park with most of the land belonging to the county. Acquisition by the State began in 1971 and, after the State Legislature of 1973 authorized five river-oriented parks to serve public recreational needs along the Willamette River, acquisition continued until essentially completed in 1978 when the development of park facilities began in earnest.[1]

The park is located 12 miles north of Salem with land on both shores of the Willamette River in both Marion and Yamhill Counties. Wheatland Ferry is near the park's geographic center. Paved county roads provide access in all directions.

An expanded archeological survey of the Mission Lake locality within the park was authorized by the Oregon State Historic Preservation Office in April 1980 after two preliminary studies (which identified the specific locations of the main house and blacksmith shop) still left unanswered questions as to the size of the compound and also the integrity and interpretive potential of the site.

As a consequence, a total of 190 square meters of the site were excavated and 9541 artifacts were discovered, which were then extensively examined.

This effort culminated in a wonderful document for history, archeological, and even horticultural buffs, entitled *Willamette Mission Archeological Project, Phase III Assessment.*[2]

According to the Assessment, the mission farm, one mile south of the mission compound, was surveyed by Jesse Applegate and sold to Alanson Beers in July 1844. The "old mission place" was sold to a Mr. Campbell in August 1844 for 700 bushels of wheat.

Another early settler, Daniel Matheny, arrived with his wife and seven children in 1844 and purchased a section of land on the west side of the river, on the former homesite of Rev. David Leslie, across from the original mission. He acquired a newly built ferry boat at the same time and began operation of the Willamette River's first ferry.

Encampment on the banks of the Willamette with the Methodist Mission on the opposite side of the river—Oregon Territory, September 9, 1841, illustrated by Henry Eld, Jr.

In 1851, ten years after the mission had abandoned its site and moved to Salem, the actual house site became part of the Donation Land Claim of William Matheny (*State of Oregon,1865 Donation Certificate 2448*). Matheny sold the west half of his claim to Blake Greenville in 1869. He sold the east half, with the mission site, to Alexander M. LaFollette on October 10, 1872.

In April 1930, the LaFollettes deeded 6.57 acres to the State with Willamette University as trustee. The deed stated:

"The parcel was to be held in trust for the people of Oregon as a perpetual shrine in memory of the Jason Lee Mission. The property should be fenced and never be used as a site upon which to conduct business for profit." (State of Oregon 1930, Marion County Deed Records 107:134.)

A large rock with a bronze plate was placed at the site in 1930. The exact location was known at that time from the work of Willamette University historian Robert Moulton Gatke, one of the principal sources for all information on the site.

The inscription recorded the date Lee arrived in the Oregon Country and the names of the LaFollettes and Aspinwalls who donated the plaque. (This plaque was later stolen, but the rock remains in position.)

Willamette University lacked adequate funding to maintain the property so they deeded it back to the LaFollettes in 1956. In the early 1960s the Marion County Parks & Recreation Committee got into the act by negotiating an agreement with the LaMars (Beryl LaFollette LeMar had inherited the property) to establish the area as a Marion County Park with the county as trustee for the people of Oregon.

The park was formally dedicated on December 9, 1963, by the Marion County Board of Commissioners for park and recreational purposes for present and future generations.

The Willamette Mission acreage and additional park parcels were acquired and developed by the State of Oregon as part of the Willamette Greenway System.

———————— M ————————

[1] From *Master Plan, Willamette Mission State Park*, January 1979, Oregon Parks & Recreation.
[2] By Judith A. Sanders, Mary K. Weber, and David R. Brauner.

Willamette Mission Park Specifics

By Oregon Parks & Recreation
Previously published May1993, Vol.31, No.2

Willamette Mission State Park occupies the Willamette River site used by missionary Jason Lee and his followers in the 1830s. A road cutting through the northern section of the park leads to Wheatland Ferry, one of only three ferries operating on the river.

The park includes Mission Lake and Goose Lake, as well as the Wheatland boat ramp next to the Wheatland Ferry. Grand Island is also part of the park, to the north from where the ferry crosses the river.

Willamette Mission Park offers picnicking facilities; fishing; boating; wildlife viewing; and miles of hiking, bicycling, and horseback riding trails. It also contains the nation's largest black cottonwood tree—measured at 27.5 feet around.

While a large portion of the park is as yet undeveloped and much is also presently leased for agricultural usage, there are two good-sized areas for day-use, both with restroom facilities. One is known as the Walnut Grove or Mission Lake area and one is called the Filbert Grove.

In the Mission Lake area there are 24 tables, a kitchen shelter with electrical outlets and sinks, sports field, hiking trail, trail leading to the Jason Lee Monument, and Mission Lake access. The lake is generally too stagnant for swimming, but it has a fishing dock, a boat ramp, and boat dock. Fish in the lake are Crappie, Blue Gill and Bass. The public can pick walnuts in this area about the end of September or early October.

The Filbert Grove has two group areas, a shared kitchen shelter with electrical outlets and sinks, a four-mile long paved bike trail and five-mile hiking trail, an equestrian trail, horseshoe pits and other sports activity areas, and river access. The public can pick filberts in this section during the fall.

The Willamette Station

A mission with vision

By Jordis Schick

Information provided by the 1983 Willamette Mission Archeological Project[1]
Previously published May 1993, Vol.31, No.2

It all started in 1832 when the Methodist Episcopal Church of New York City laid the groundwork to authorize the establishment of Indian missions on the western and northwestern frontiers.

Within a year they approved plans for a mission among the Flathead Indians and asked Reverend Jason Lee to be the superintendent. He accepted with alacrity and his nephew Reverend Daniel Lee agreed to accompany him.

Lee engaged Cyrus Shepard as a teacher and P.L. Edwards and C.M. Walker as carpenter and farmer, respectively. They prepared to depart in the spring of 1834 with Captain Nathaniel Wyeth across the continent by land, sending their provisions, tools and supplies on the brig *May Dacre*, bound for the Columbia River.

The expedition arrived at Fort Vancouver in September 1834 and, at Dr. John McLoughlin's suggestion, located in the Willamette Valley. (Historians assume that McLoughlin hoped to keep the missionaries south of the Columbia River in anticipation of a boundary dispute between Great Britain and the United States. But they are also pretty certain the missionaries wanted to avoid the interior Flathead area where the agriculture was suspect and the remoteness would provide little availability for resources).

The Lees began an inspection tour of the Willamette Valley on horseback. The landscape at that time is described as consisting of mixed stands of Douglas fir, Oregon ash, cottonwood, willow, alder, and bigleaf maple with a dense undergrowth of Oregon grape, salmonberry, elderberry, rose, hard hack, nine bark, and cascara (much as today).

The higher terraces were covered with a vast savanna dotted with stands of oak. The savanna was possibly the result of the seasonal burning practiced by the Kalapuyan Indians, which was thought to be a major factor in maintaining their subsistence.

The Lees selected a site 60 miles south of the confluence of the Willamette and Columbia Rivers (despite a declining Indian population in the area) because the river would provide a transportation route and the spot was centrally located for future settlement.

It also happened to be the first available land they came to on the southwestern fringe of the expanse known as French Prairie where approximately twelve French Canadian families were already farming.

The mission compound was built close to the river on an alluvial floodplain. Jason Lee described it himself in 1835:

The house stands a few rods from the river in a very beautiful situation, upon a prairie two miles in length and half a mile in breadth, covered with grass, and here and there is a white oak skirted with timber. In the rear is another prairie, elevated about 25 feet above this, say 50 miles in length and ten broad.

Anna Maria Pittman Lee   Jason Lee

The initial mission structures were located along the eastern bank of the river as shown in the picture on page 10, illustrated by Henry Eld, a midshipman with the Wilkes Expedition which visited the Oregon County in 1841. The first structure (18x32 feet) was made of oak logs hewn only on the interior surfaces and was partitioned down the center. The window sashes were partly carved by Jason Lee with his jack knife. A puncheon floor was made from planks split from fir and hewn on the upper side as were the doors, tables, stools and chairs. It was originally used for living quarters, a schoolroom, and a chapel.

During the winter of 1834 the missionaries relied on previously purchased supplies for food, with staples brought from Fort Vancouver, farm products bartered from the French Canadians, and venison acquired from the Indians.

In the spring of 1835, the missionaries began subsistence farming activities. They plowed, fenced and planted 30 acres of land with seeds furnished by Dr. McLoughlin. He also loaned them oxen, a bull, and eight cows and their calves.

In the summer of 1835 a log barn measuring 30 by 40 feet was completed to store harvested farm produce. The missionaries also enlarged the house with a 16 by 32 foot addition to use as kitchen and combination schoolroom and dining room. This was done so they could begin their religious and educational activities which were in fact started that first winter when they accepted Indian charges (mostly children) as school members. Records indicate they also instructed neighboring settlers' children and conducted church services at French Canadian homes in the vicinity on Sundays.

By 1836 it was apparent that more laymen were needed for the mission to succeed— particularly a physician, blacksmith, and carpenter. Lee also wanted a bigger school, which would require more missionaries and teachers, as well as farmers to enlarge the agricultural base so the mission could ease its reliance on the Hudson's Bay company for provisions.

A meeting, called at the mission house in early 1837, organized a joint stock company to purchase cattle in California. The expedition was conveyed there on ship by William S. Slacum who, at the time, was making a political and physical investigation of the Oregon Country. (He highly approved of the Methodist settlement, the missionaries' American political aspirations, and the Oregon Temperance Society.)

The first reinforcement of additional personnel requested by Lee arrived in May 1837. This group included Anna Maria Pittman, Jason Lee's future wife; Dr. Elijah White and family; Alanson Beers, blacksmith, and family; William H. Willson, carpenter and joiner; and the teachers. Another reinforcement arrived in September 1837 with Reverend David Leslie and family; Margaret Smith (Bailey),[2] teacher; and the Reverend H.K.W. Perkins.

Both groups arrived at Fort Vancouver by ship after a trip from the East Coast around the Horn with many personal possessions and provisions on board, and other supplies picked up enroute.

To prepare for these arrivals the missionaries built new houses and added to existing structures. A round-log house was constructed for Beers and his family with a blacksmith shop, wheelwright house, and shop nearby. A one-story log house was bought from a French Canadian for the Leslie family, but it burned in December 1838.

The mission cemetery was situated close to the main mission houses and it was used for Indian charges as well as personnel. The mission garden was described as the most pleasant spot of all— with herbs, vegetables, fruits, and flowers, and even a row of peach trees.

Soon after reinforcements arrived in 1837, the missionaries looked to higher ground where they built a fine blockhouse for Dr. White's family. In 1838 and 1839 they also constructed a hospital to serve settlers, natives and mission personnel. It is thought that lumber was supplied through Ewing Young's sawmill, operating on Chehalem Creek by February 1838.

But the hospital was never used as such since it was needed for living quarters when additional personnel arrived. In 1841 it was being used as a dwelling by George Abernethy, his wife, and three other families. He was the mission's secular agent and later provisional governor of Oregon.

Old Mission House in 1841, illustrated by Henry Eld, Jr.
YALE COLLECTION OF WESTERN AMERICANA, BEINECKE RARE BOOK AND MANUSCRIPT LIBRARY

When the Charles Wilkes' Expedition visited the site in 1841, Wilkes noted there were also two log homes near the hospital, one of which was the home of Ira L. Babcock, a physician who arrived in June 1840.

A granary had also been built near the hospital to function as a multi-purpose building—granary, schoolhouse, church, and briefly, on May 25, 1843, as a legislative hall to prepare laws for the newly organized provisional government of Oregon.

In March 1838 Lee went east to conduct a two-year tour. His purpose was to promote the mission; request more donations, money and personnel; and inquire about the possibility of establishing other missions. Before he left, the people at the mission formulated a petition to be read by Congress stressing the agricultural and commercial possibilities in the Oregon Country. Since they also wanted to sever ties with Hudson's Bay Company, they also requested an extension of the U.S. government to the Oregon Country.

Clearly they had "visions of Oregon becoming a United States territory and possibly a state."

Lee returned to Oregon on the ship *Lausanne* in June 1840 with fifty-two people on board and a large supply of equipment, clothing, and provisions, enough to endow an enlarged mission family and future subsidiary stations. Some of the goods went to stock the Oregon Mission Store, from which an account book, dated 1838-1841, has survived.

The book shows the missionaries acquired local merchandise such as wheat, beaver skins, bear skins, butter and potatoes, which were presumably resold to Hudson's Bay Company. The Mission Store supplied settlers with a diverse line of standard consumption goods purveyed from American east coast markets and donations. So it appears the missionaries had worked out some sort of network.

Even though the Indian population in the Willamette Valley had decreased during Lee's 1838-1840 absence, he proceeded with plans for expansion. Foremost was construction of a new central station for mission activities to be erected on Mill Creek, ten miles up the Willamette River from the original mission site, with a combination saw mill and grist mill included. The mill was situated on the Chemeketa Plain, which was also the intended site for the Oregon Indian Manual Labor School.

Various explanations have been offered for the shift in locations. One was that a small creek rather than a river was needed to power the mill; another that the original mission house was increasingly difficult to live in because it was infested with "vermin." The main reason, however, appears to be that the main mission site was periodically threatened by floods. There is frequent mention of freshets and floods in historical references.

At any rate, by 1841 the mission family had moved to Mill Creek which would, in time, become the town of Salem. Only a few settlers associated with the mission remained to work the farms at the original site. Meanwhile Jason Lee's ability as a superintendent was questioned and he returned once again to New York to answer the charges. Before he arrived he found he had been superseded by Rev. George Gary. Lee was later exonerated, but the Willamette Mission was dissolved in 1844 for various reasons including internal conflicts within the mission community, financial problems, a low Indian population, and increased Euro-American settlement in the Willamette Valley.

As new superintendent, Gary proceeded to dissolve mission activities and dispose of mission property (by 1839 the missionaries had claimed approximately eight square miles of land at the old mission station).

The rapid decay of all structures except the main building was noted in 1844 by H.K.W. Perkins, one of the reinforcement missionaries at the Chemeketa settlement. However, in the winter of 1843-44, Lindsay Applegate and members of his family made their way across the Willamette Valley: *to Lee's Old Mission ten miles below where Salem now stands, and on the first day of December entered one of the old buildings to remain for the winter.*

Although that was the end of the Willamette Station at the Wheatland site, that the settlement happened at all is a testament to the courage of these early pioneers.

Think about it. In the brief span of seven years they managed to:

❖ Incite the imaginations of thousands of immigrants who followed them to the Oregon Country;

❖ Lay the groundwork for future American statehood and government;

❖ Grasp the potential for the agricultural and economic development in this fertile valley; and

❖ Have enough wisdom to envision the necessity of providing for the intellectual, physical and spiritual well-being of future generations.

We are deeply blessed and indebted, for we are still enjoying the fruits of their foresight today.

[1] *Willamette Mission Archeological Project, Phase III Assessment,* by Judith A. Sanders, Mary K. Weber, and David R. Brauner Authorized by Oregon State Historical Preservation Office.

[2] An interesting book by Margaret Bailey, entitled *The Grains,* has just been republished by the OSU Press. Evidently she had to share a cabin with W.H. Willson and, in the book, makes accusations against him and other early missionaries. However, there is some doubt as to the reliability of her stories.

Henry Eld, Jr., USN

Information supplied by Elisabeth Potter, Oregon State Parks Historic Preservation Office
Previously published May 1993, Vol.31, No.2

 Henry Eld, Jr., the young midshipman on the Wilkes Expedition who drew the illustration in the Willamette Station story, was also credited with being the first man to sight land beyond the ice barriers of the Antarctic.

In 1838 Charles Wilkes was appointed to command an exploring and surveying expedition to the South Seas. Five ships set out; aboard one of them, *The Peacock*, was Passed Midshipman Henry Eld. On January 16, 1840, he sighted and called out "land" from the crosstree of his ship. The discovery of the Antarctic continent dates from this event and Lieutenant Wilkes named the highest peak sighted on this expedition Eld's Peak after the young officer.

The expedition continued five years, from 1838 to 1842, and, in this time, Wilkes not only reached the Antarctic but visited various islands in the Pacific and also explored what is now the Pacific Coast of the United States.

The sketch of the entire Mission encampment is the only known contemporary rendering of the old mission station. It was made during the summer of 1841 after expedition headquarters had been moved to Salem from Mission Bottom.

The sketch was interpreted as an engraving, probably by R.S. Gilbert, and appears as an illustration in Charles Wilkes' *Narrative of the United States Exploring Expedition*.

The Willsons In Salem

By Sybil Westenhouse

Part I: William Willson and Chloe Clark • Early Mission Years

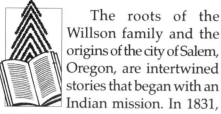

The roots of the Willson family and the origins of the city of Salem, Oregon, are intertwined stories that began with an Indian mission. In 1831, William Holden Willson was a New Hampshire born man living in Massachusetts and Chloe Aurelia Clark was a teenage girl in a comfortably well-off Connecticut family when news spread of the arrival in St. Louis of four "Flathead" Indians asking for the white man's "Book of Heaven." This was thought to mean that the Indians were voicing a desire to learn about

William H. Willson   Chloe Willson

the white man's God, and within a short time the Board of Missions of the Methodist Episcopal Church organized an effort to meet that request and to solicit volunteers for the work. In 1834 they appointed Reverend Jason Lee to head the endeavor.

Lee traveled overland with the fur trader Nathaniel Wyeth. After a respite at Fort Vancouver where he discussed his plans with Dr. John McLoughlin, Lee chose a mission site on the east bank of the Willamette River, about fifty miles south of Fort Vancouver and across from present day Wheatland. Aided by his nephew, Daniel Lee, and by Cyrus Shepard, Phillip Edwards, and Courtney Walker, he set about clearing a spot in the wilderness. Within two years they felled trees, built a log cabin and lean-to, cleared and planted acres of land from which they harvested vegetables and wheat, and simultaneously accepted Indian children into their care for education and nurturing. Reports and letters about the progress of the Oregon Mission were widely circulated and it is likely that William and Chloe each gave them some attention from time to time.

In Oregon, reviewing the many months of unceasing wilderness struggle, Jason Lee realized that the mission was merely surviving, with little time devoted to religious work. He requested from the Board of Missions that a small group of skilled reinforcements including carpenters, blacksmiths,

teachers and a doctor be sent to him, accompanied by some additional missionary families. Lee's requisition was partially filled, and one of the first lay workers was William H. Willson.

William, born in 1805, was 31 years of age, had been a whaling ship's carpenter and was a member of Reverend David Leslie's church in Fairhaven, Massachusetts, when he joined the first reinforcement group. His companions were Dr. Elijah White and family, Anna Maria Pittman, Susan Downing, Elvira Johnson, and Alanson Beers and family. With outfitting and travel expenses paid by the mission board, this small group embarked on the sailing ship *Hamilton* which left Boston in late July 1836, bound for the Sandwich Islands.

William was interested in medicine, and took instruction from Dr. White during the months at sea. He read the doctor's medical books, discussed the causes and treatments of disease, and became familiar with the surgical instruments available. This informal education prepared William for a medical practice which he would follow for many years. His training was not too dissimilar to the formal medical education of the time.

Until the 1880s, the requirements for becoming a doctor were meager: with a high-school degree or frequently less, a candidate could take a haphazard series of "courses" and end up certified in less than two years. As of the 1870s, the exams at Harvard Medical School consisted merely of nine professors spending five minutes each questioning the candidate. To pass, it was necessary only to satisfy five of the nine professors; thus, a candidate could fail four of his nine subjects and still get a degree. [1]

This voyage of the *Hamilton* from Boston to Honolulu took 148 days. The group then spent five months in the Sandwich Islands before getting passage on a ship that would take them to the Columbia River and Fort Vancouver.

On May 18, 1837, the brig *Diana* with the mission recruits aboard, arrived at Fort Vancouver. Dr. John McLoughlin welcomed the missionaries and crew and gave them the hospitality of the fort.

The day finally came when Jason Lee arrived with two canoes, paddling against a strong wind. ... Reverend Lee arranged with Dr. McLoughlin for the storage of the supplies that could not be transported to the mission the following week...

One boat and three canoes were to be used in taking the passengers and baggage up the Willamette River.

Mr. Whitcomb, Mr. Willson, and Mr. Lee were good at the oars, and so were the Indians in the boats. Before long the oarsmen vied with each other. The boats passed and repassed—sometimes so close that the crews could join hands. There was much splashing as the paddles cut into the water, and then were lifted out. Everyone was having an enjoyable time.

When evening came, camp was made upon the river bank in a grove of oak trees. Supper consisted of salmon, potatoes, bread, butter and tea. It is likely that the women did the cooking.

After the evening meal, some of the group took a stroll among the trees. There was much conversation. Later prayer was offered, and then the missionaries bedded down under the oaks. The birds sang for awhile and then they too became quiet.

The next morning the group was up early. After breakfast, they were on their way. By eleven o'clock they reached the falls of the Willamette. Here, the water tumbled over a wall made of basalt. The torrent gushed, leaped, and foamed in a wild manner...In order to get around the falls a portage had to be made. There was considerable time spent in bargaining with the Indians... Finally the price of portage was decided to be five charges of ammunition and a large cotton handkerchief for the chief.

After the portage, the missionaries left the falls, passing Elk Bluff, a precipice 700 feet high. On the second night they camped near Pudding River.

The next morning the group began another journey early...The Willamette by now had begun to narrow, but it still was skirted by virgin wilderness.

They continued to paddle upstream until they reached the landing of Baptiste Desportes McKay at Champoeg, about fifteen miles from the Oregon Mission. [2]

While this enjoyable excursion was in progress, illness had spread among the Indian children at the mission. Daniel Lee rode out to meet the group to request their urgent help. He found them at McKay's at Champoeg. Dr. White, Anna Maria, Jason and a few others went ahead to help with the sick children. William took charge of the canoes for the remainder of this trip, then soon set out again, accompanied by Alanson Beers and J. L. Whitcomb, on the first of their many trips to transport the goods brought in the *Diana*. Crossing the Columbia from Fort Vancouver, then paddling, poling or wading and pushing the heavily laden canoes up the Willamette River some fifty miles took weeks of strenuous effort.

Jason Lee's Mission as it appeared in 1834.

Each person at the mission had a regular duty assignment. Anna Maria and Mrs. White took charge of the cooking and housekeeping. Susan Downing and Cyrus Shepard took care of the children. Elvira Johnson became one of the teachers.

On week days the work output was prodigious. Supplying wood for fires, carrying and heating water to wash dishes and laundry, cooking for twenty or more people three times a day, and tending the children and the ill were routine requirements. A blacksmith shop had been erected so Alanson Beers could make the necessary metal work for the buildings. Houses for the White and Beers families and shelter for the unmarried members had begun. A log schoolroom/church was planned, as were additional storage sheds. However, harvest season interrupted the usual routine as well as the building. Everyone

Jason Lee, first superintendent of the Oregon Mission.

was needed in the fields. Jason Lee swung the cradle-scythe and Dr. White raked and bound after him. Some of the grain was stored for the cattle, but a considerable amount had to be hand thrashed and hand ground for bread making. It was fortunate that the food crops were exceptionally heavy that year because more reinforcements were on the way.

The rudimentary nature of the activities of the mission consumed everyone's time and energy. However, busy as life at the mission was, with buildings under construction, harvesting to be done, land to be cleared, and close, crowded living conditions, the small group found time for religious meetings. On July 4 they held the annual meeting of the Oregon Temperance Society at the mission house. All interested persons were invited. Hudson Bay employees, free trappers, French settlers in the vicinity, Indians, and the mission folk themselves made up the gathering. Short and appropriate addresses were made by Jason and Daniel Lee, Alanson Beers, William Willson, and Dr. White.

On Sunday, July 16, 1837, the first public communion service was held. To begin this propitious day, three marriages were performed. The couples were Jason Lee and Anna Maria Pittman, Cyrus Shepard and Susan Downing, and Charles Roe and Miss Nancy, a daughter of Thomas McKay. These rites were followed by the hymn "Watchman Tell Us of the Night," then

William offered a prayer. Rev. Jason Lee preached the sermon, explained the rules of baptism, and baptized Charles Roe and Webley Hauxhurst. The Lord's Supper followed for fourteen people. Then a time of testimony by some and confession of sin by others was held.

The service closed with a hymn and a prayer. The site for these combined services was a grove of trees near Mission Bottom. Jason Lee noted that he had seldom known the presence of the Lord to be more manifest than on that occasion. The day concluded with a wedding feast for all those gathered together.

In September of 1837, Rev. David Leslie with his wife and three daughters, Rev. H.K.W. Perkins and Margaret Jewett Smith arrived. Housing became even more crowded and William was kept busy as a carpenter after the harvesting was finished. In November, Reverend Perkins and Elvira Johnson were married. Eventually the Perkinses and the Leslies shared residence in a newly built house.

In the months that followed, Jason Lee saw the opportunity and the need for expanding the missionary work by establishing new mission sites at Nisqually, at The Dalles, and at Clatsop Plains. He even considered extending their work along Oregon's southern coast. This expansion would require many more people and much greater funding for equipment and supplies. To get the Mission Board's permission and to raise the funds through speaking engagements and religious meetings emphasizing the work of the Oregon Mission, Lee made plans to personally return to the East.

It was during Lee's speaking tour in the East for financial support of this project that Chloe Clark determined to join the missionary group. Family and friends were aghast at her decision but Chloe stood firm. She was selected specifically to teach the Indian children about Christianity and the rudiments of civilization. That she would also lend a hand wherever needed was undoubtedly understood when one would be living well beyond the western frontier, outside the United States. Chloe accepted her selection as the Will of God and prepared herself mentally, physically, and emotionally as well as she could.

In Oregon, after Jason Lee left to travel east in 1838, William was of help to Anna Maria.

While in another part of the house, Anna Maria heard loud voices in the kitchen. When she arrived she saw a Kanaka (Hawaiian) and an Indian having a dispute. The Indian had a gun and threatened to use it. With no men of the mission near, she knew that she had to do something immediately or there would be bloodshed. Calmly she walked into the room and took the gun away from the Indian. The two continued to threaten each other. Mr. Willson, however, arrived at the kitchen and settled the quarrel.[3]

It probably was William who provided one of the last services for Anna Maria by supplying a home-made casket when she died following childbirth on June 26, 1838. She was a well loved member of the small mission family and the deaths of Anna Maria and her infant son were cause for much sorrow among the survivors. Reverend Leslie and Dr. McLoughlin sent a dispatch with the sad news which reached Jason Lee at Westport, Missouri, as he travelled east.

The Oregon Mission work went on under the direction of Rev. David Leslie. While the others continued with the activities at the Willamette site, David Leslie and William travelled north to Fort Nisqually on Puget's Sound to select a site and begin construction

Rev. Daniel Lee

of the Nisqually Mission. Dr. McLoughlin had been so impressed with Jason Lee's character and purpose that he instructed A.C. Anderson, factor at Fort Nisqually, to provide help in the establishment of the new mission. This was done, and on April 17, 1839, William felled the first tree for the mission. The site was about one-half mile inland from the Hudson Bay Company fort and trading post.

David Leslie returned to the Willamette within a few days but William remained at Nisqually to continue the work. With the help of Indian laborers and men at the fort, whip-sawed lumber was produced to construct a main building eighteen feet wide, thirty-two feet long, with nine foot high walls. A stockade was erected around this, enclosing enough land for a garden plot and space for mission work. The area seemed like an ideal site for a mission because it had a sizable Indian population, and:

Mr. Ezra Meeker says: 'People now traversing what is popularly known as the Nisqually Plains will hardly realize that in the years ago these bare, gravelly prairies supplied a rich grass of exceeding fattening quality and of sufficient quantity to fatten many thousand head of stock. Nearly a half million acres of this land lies between the Nisqually and Puyallup Rivers, an ideal park of shade and open land, of rivulets and lakes, of natural roads and beautiful scenery.'[4]

When William returned to the Willamette mission, more than his carpentry services would be required.

Cyrus Shepard had been a mainstay of the mission during the early years. He was especially important in the work with the Indian children. Though he had been struggling with ill health for several years, he continued to work and started his own family. But by 1839, tuberculosis had weakened him considerably. The disease affected his leg so seriously that, in December, amputation was done in an attempt to save his life. For this surgery, Dr. White was assisted by Dr. Bailey and William. Because the disease had progressed so far, nothing that was done could save Cyrus and he died within a few days. The mission family lost another much loved and much needed member.

Not until the following June would Jason Lee and the new reinforcements arrive to help carry on the work.

[1] Goodwin, Doris K., *The Fitzgeralds and the Kennedys*, p 67.
[2] Mattson, Sylvia, *Missionary Footpaths*, p 44-50.
[3] Ibid. p 98.
[4] "Pioneer Reminiscences of Puget Sound," by Ezra Meeker, p 119, as quoted in *The Conquerors* by Rev. A. Atwood, p 124.

Part 2: The Lausanne Voyage • 1839-1840

The *Lausanne* sailed from White Hall Dock, New York City, on October 9, 1839, carrying Chloe and her companions who would become known as "The Great Reinforcement." The voyage around the horn would cover 22,000 miles and take about eight months. The *Lausanne* was a new, 400 ton, first class sailing ship, with spacious staterooms.

The Lee group of missionaries, lay people, and children numbered approximately fifty-three. In addition to the passengers' belongings, the hold contained a sawmill, a gristmill, all necessary building materials, farm tools and implements, household goods, clothing, and food supplies. The expedition cost $42,000.

Chloe's diary entries during the voyage suggest that she daily spent much time and effort in spiritual self-analysis and self-improvement. Born in 1818, she seems to have been a very serious twenty-one year old woman, determined to mature spiritually and socially as quickly as possible so she could immediately fulfill her responsibilities. Determination, tenacity, independence, introspection and gentility are qualities she possessed. Chloe's own words allow us to see her as she was on the voyage.

Oct. 9th, 1839, was the day in which I left New York and took the last long lingering look of my native land. It was a most delightful day. It seemed that all heaven smiled upon our undertaking. The sky was clear, the ocean calm and our little band cheerful in the prospect of being ere long permitted to point Heathen souls to the Lamb of God...an address from Dr. Bangs...The kindness of friends in New York I shall never forget especially of the Drs family. O may heaven reward them.

...O how blessed it is amid all the bustle and hum of a busy world to feel a calm and settled peace within. . . .

...24th, Trials are mixed with all our pleasures. Today a new and unexpected trial has come up, every day brings its own little burdens, of these I complain not, but only pray, God give me wisdom and grace to conduct myself aright. O for discretion and prudence, I feel that I need much wisdom and grace in order to do right and not give offence. [1]

Though Chloe suffered repeated bouts with seasickness, she aided others more severely afflicted when she was able. She also found time and energy to follow a daily schedule of work.

...from six to seven in the morning is my time for morning devotions. From seven to eight study, breakfast at eight, prayer meeting in our room at half-past eight, from nine until ten studying, from ten until twelve instructing the children of the missionaries, from twelve until one studying music, half an hour for dinner, half an hour after dinner for secret devotions, from two until three for reading, from three until half past four the afternoon session of my school, reading until five, from five until six prayer meeting in our room, tea at six, family prayer at seven, after which we usually have prayer or class meetings or lectures. These with singing school twice a week, knitting, sewing, and writing keep me very busy. I think our school, Sabbath school and Bible class are doing as well as we could expect in such a place and under such circumstances. [2]

Fortunately, a few other accounts of the voyage of the *Lausanne* are still in existence. One such is a letter written by Sarah R. Frost Beggs, who was there as the wife of Reverend J. H. Frost. She provides several interesting highlights of the voyage.

After sixty-five days we arrived at Rio de Janeiro, South America, and as we sailed up the harbor, saw the most beautiful scenes we had ever looked upon. No ladies appeared on the streets unveiled, but we missionary women walked where we pleased and were a great curiosity.

We visited the palace and were introduced to the emperor of Brazil, Don Pedro. He was a fine looking gentleman and was very courteous. We also saw a beautiful Portuguese lady of the court.

Two of our United States war vessels were in the harbor, and during our stay of a week, they sent their gig down and took us ashore and showed us much attention.

Soon after leaving this port we were detained about a month by terrific head winds.

...we arrived in Valparaiso to find that the smallpox was raging as an epidemic in the city. We lay in the harbor for two weeks without going ashore...we sailed for the Sandwich Islands. [3]

The *Lausanne* arrived in Honolulu on April 11, 1840, and sailed for the Columbia River on April 28.

After crossing the bar, but still somewhere near the mouth of the Columbia, they met Captain Duncan of the English barque *Vancouver*. He brought the news to them as he came down the river that Daniel Lee and William Willson were at Fort Vancouver. These mission men, along with many others, were anxiously awaiting the *Lausanne's* arrival.

On June 1, 1840, at 6 P.M., the *Lausanne* dropped anchor at Fort Vancouver. The party debarked on June 2. Dr. McLoughlin kindly provided accomodations for everyone. Superintendent Lee announced their mission assignments. Chloe was to teach Indian children at the new mission site at Nisqually on Puget's Sound. Another new arrival on the *Lausanne*, Dr. J. P. Richmond, was to be in charge there and William Willson was to provide the lay services. This group left Fort Vancouver on July 2, 1840, taking canoes down the Columbia River and up the Cowlitz River to the Cowlitz Landing.

1 Willson, Chloe, "Diary of Chloe Clark Willson."
2 Ibid.
3 Atwood, Rev. A., *The Conquerors*, p 89.

Part 3: Nisqually Mission • 1840-1841

The procedure of moving the small missionary group and their belongings to the Nisqually mission site was greatly aided by Dr. McLoughlin's intervention and support. Starting any new enterprise in the wilderness was difficult at best. Knowing this, he provided for Indian helpers, canoes, and horses to be available where needed throughout the trip. And once the group reached Nisqually, his chief trader made the missionaries welcome and provided them with whatever they required.

Dr. Richmond's account of the trip offers some interesting details and some insights into the preconceptions and expectations of the newly arrived missionary.

Nisqually Mission House

...entered the mouth of the Cowlitz River. We found the current for some miles tolerably smooth; but after that it became rapid, and required the utmost energies of our boatmen to make headway. We, however, had a pleasant time; and in two days ascended the river to the commencement of the portage; and on Sabbath morning, 5th July, we were encamped on the banks of the river, contiguous to the Courlaitz [Cowlitz] farming port, belonging to the Hudson's Bay Company. Here we spent Sabbath as pleasantly as we could; but we had a very disagreeable night, occasioned by the arrival of a considerable number of Indians who encamped all around us, and who annoyed us during the whole night with whooping and singing. We slept but little, one of us being compelled to keep a look out to prevent the Indians from stealing our goods, which otherwise were rather exposed.

On Monday morning we were very kindly invited by Mr. [Charles] Forrest, who is in charge of the farm, to take up quarters at the farm house until we could make the necessary arrangements for the further prosecution of our journey. He accordingly sent a cart to carry our goods to the house, and also horses for our ladies [Chloe and Mrs. Richmond] to ride, the distance being about two or three miles from the landing.

Here we remained until Tuesday the 7th of July; and having, through the kind assistance of Mr. Forrest, secured 17 horses, the number sufficient for the transportation of ourselves and our effects through the portage, when we set out about noon under the guidance of several half breeds, and two Indian women, who took charge of the eldest of my children. We found the roads very bad, and progressed very slowly, sometimes through dense forests, and sometimes over beautiful plains, until the third day after leaving the Courlaitz [Cowlitz], and arrived at our destination in good health and spirits.

We were very kindly received by Mr. [William] Kittson, the gentleman in charge of Fort Nisqually, who furnished us with several rooms within the stockade, and invited us to the hospitalities of his house and table. We remained at the Fort about three weeks, having every attention and accomodation within the power of Mr. Kittson and his excellent wife, to render our situation comfortable. At the expiration of which time, Mr. Willson having laid part of the lower floor on the mission house, we removed and commenced housekeeping for ourselves. Our cooking for several months was done out of doors, and our table consisted of several boxes permanently located in the middle of the floor.[1]

Once settled on the mission site, the work with the Indians began in earnest. William accompanied Dr. Richmond as he visited the numerous Indian camps, using an interpreter to talk with them. All of the Indians were invited to the religious services regularly held at the mission. Fairly soon fifty students had been gathered for Chloe's classes. As time went by, Chloe proved herself to be a faithful and effective teacher.

Chloe and William spent enough time in each others company both at Fort Vancouver and thereafter to develop a fellowship. As had some other newly acquainted couples in the missionary group, they agreed to marry. Dr. Richmond performed the ceremony August 16, 1840, at the Nisqually mission. Through the fall and winter the mission work continued. William was busy with the many jobs that a layworker was expected to do. He worked on the buildings, constructed furniture, cut and hauled firewood, helped with the Indians, and generally kept the life-supporting basic work under control. Chloe, of course, was busy with her teaching in addition to being a dutiful wife with the accompanying responsibilities. Somehow she found time to write and her diary entries begin again in the spring. Though happy in her marriage and her teaching, she continued to be very introspective and intense about her own religious state. The entries for the spring of 1841 describe a very eventful time in her life, the birth of her first child, her own nearness to death, and the Willsons move to Oregon City.

April 4, 1841, I have had the liberty in praying for the heathen, I see them in their lost deplorable condition and feel a desire to live and be useful among them....

April 6, 1841, Laboring under body infirmities but enjoying a quiet frame of mind. I find my time very much taken up with cares and labors of my family and my scholars.

Dr. John P. Richmond   *Mrs. America Richmond*

The task of instructing the youthful mind in the principles of Science and religion is as pleasant to me as ever. No work looks to me so desirable.

May 9, 1841, Since my last date I have been very sick. I have given premature birth to a tender infant. God has permitted us to hold it in our embrace three short days and then in mercy relieved the little sufferer of all its pains and took it to himself...I see the hand of God in my early delivery, had it been otherwise it would without doubt have terminated my earthly cause. Thanks to God for bringing me up from the gates of death.

May 18, 1841...last week two of the ships companies of the Exploring Expedition anchored here under the command of Capt. Wilkes, several of the officers called on us and I am happy to say they are in every respect gentlemen.

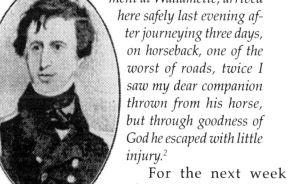

Coulitz June 9th, Set out from Nisqually last Saturday for our appointment at Wallamette, arrived here safely last evening after journeying three days, on horseback, one of the worst of roads, twice I saw my dear companion thrown from his horse, but through goodness of God he escaped with little injury.[2]

Captain Charles Wilkes

For the next week Chloe and William continued south, down the Cowlitz River, across the Columbia, and up the Willamette River to Willamette Falls (Oregon City). It was there they were to await a new assignment from Jason Lee.

[1] Brosnan, Cornelius J., *Jason Lee: Prophet of the New Oregon,* p 170.
[2] Willson, Chloe, "Diary of Chloe Clark Willson."

The location known today as Oregon City was originally called Willamette Falls by the early traders and settlers. The falls were so high as to require portage by all river travellers. Local Indians often provided the service for a negotiated price in trade goods. The water power potential had been obvious to Dr. McLoughlin. He staked out some of the area for a future mill site in 1829, and had a building or two erected there.

When the missionary reinforcement arrived in 1840, one of that number, Alvan Waller, was assigned to establish a mission at Willamette Falls for the several Indian tribes living in the area. He built a substantial residence for his family and proceeded in his work. When William and Chloe arrived in June, 1841, there may have been as many as four houses near the mission and falls. Chloe wrote of life as they found it soon after their arrival from Nisqually:

Wallamette Falls June 19th, 1841, Reached this place on Monday, last. We are waiting here for Br. Lee. I am busy in making shirts for the Indians. They are quite numerous here, more so at this season than any other. This being their fishing season, salmon are taken at these falls in abundance. The Indians here are not as indolent as those with whom we have been laboring the year past. I think this a very prom- ising field.

27th, Br. Waller and Mr. Willson have gone to hold a meeting with the Molaly tribe... [1]

The Wallers and Willsons found approximately 300 Indians gathered along the river during salmon fishing season, from January to August. During that time, the missionaries had to go to the Indian lodges to meet with them. The alternative was to pay the Indians to come to the mission. After fishing season, barely half the Indian population remained in the area.

Also in June of 1841, Jason Lee ordered sawed lumber to be sent from Vancouver to Clatsop. He assigned William to construct a frame house for Rev. William Kone and his family at the Clatsop mission. The Kones had been struggling with very primitive facilities for a year.

While William was at the coast working on the Clatsop mission, Chloe remained at Willamette Falls. There were many responsibilities and new experiences to occupy her hands and mind as she details in a letter to her friend Mary Norton.

July 29, 1841. If my poor scribblings are read by you with interest, think I pray you, with what feelings of pleasure yours are read by one shut out from a Christian world and surrounded by savage, heathen tribes. However, secluded as I am, health, happiness and a contented mind are mine to enjoy. And still to the question: "Does she not regret the step?" You may answer for me, "No, by no means!" I only regret that I am not more useful, more holy.

Several of the natives sit around me as I write. I have been trying to learn some words of their language. You see, we have to be their scholars (or learn of them the language) before we can be their teachers. One great discouragement in learning their language is this: if we get the language of one tribe, say for instance the Wallamette tribe, communicate with them, and then only cross the river to the

Willamette Falls (Oregon City) in 1849.

Molaly tribe, we must learn an entirely different language. And so it is as far as I have learned throughout the country. To think of learning the language of all these different tribes or not be able to do them good seems rather disheartening. However, I know no other way than to be up and at it and always at it.

Another great discouragement is the wandering life which they lead. Collect them for school this week and perhaps before the next week they will be 20-30 perhaps 50 miles distant. The men are generally hunting, fishing, gambling or racing horses. The women and children are gathering berries, roots, wood and bark of which they make their dress if a dress it may be called. Some of them are getting to make dresses of skins. Considering by whom they are made, they are quite passable.

There is not much to be done for them in school unless we can take them in to the house (away from their parents' example which is anything but what it should be), feed, clothe and watch them continually. I have done what I could but it seems little, indeed, to what I hoped to do. I have been engaged with a class rather than a school most of the time.

I accompany Mr. Willson on the Sabbath when I can, consistently, and enjoy the meetings, but not as I should, could I feel that they were our Father's real worshipers. O that the time may come when they shall sit at the feet of Jesus clothed and in their right mind.

The Molaly's seem rather to hold us at a distance than to receive us as their friends. They have threatened our lives, but as yet have not attempted to take them. Our lives are on the alter, the will of the Lord be done! We feel that while in the path of duty, our days are immortal until our work is done.

I made some advancement in the Nasqually language while there, but if I speak it to these, they understand no more what I say than they would if I spoke to them in English.

However, amid all our discouragements, we have much to encourage and cheer us. Perhaps you wish to know what it is. I'll tell you. It is the naked promise of Jehovah. "The wilderness and the solitary place shall be glad for them and the desert shall rejoice and blossom as the rose. Go forth—and I am with you." If such promises are not precious to us, I know not to whom they are. With regard to the heathen, it is emphatically true that we have to walk by faith and not by sight . . . [2]

A year after their arrival on the *Lausanne*, several of the men, laymen and missionaries alike, were also struggling to accept the differences between their expectations and the realities of their endeavors. Among the laymen in particular, frustration led to action. A misunderstanding arose between them and Superintendent Jason Lee. The laymen believed that at the yearly meeting they should have a voice in the management of the secular side of the mission. Lee decided that only the men designated as Conference Teachers should take part. This essentially meant that only the ordained ministers in the group would compose the assembly for both the religious and the secular planning. His plans were compatible with the Methodist Conference system of governance. Nevertheless, a petition was sent to the Board of Missions, citing their disagreement with Jason Lee, and signed by some notable lay workers. They were Josiah Parrish, George Abernethy, W. W. Raymond, Dr. Babcock, Mr. Olley, L. H. Judson, Alanson Beers, William H. Willson, and Mr. Whitcomb. Other than venting their feelings, very little could have been expected to come of this in the near future. Return response by mail took from twelve to eighteen months. The Oregon Mission was a very distant place! In actuality, the board noted receipt of the petition but did not act further.

Chloe wrote in her diary of the following occurrences and observations from her experience in 1842.

April 3. Laboring under bodily infirmities and weaknesses but feeling God within strengthing the soul. My dear companion as well as myself is advancing in the way of heaven.

August 16. Two years ago this day I was united in the closest earthly union to my dear W. who has proved himself to be one of the best of husbands.

September 4. Our prospects for doing good in this land are very dark. Rum is being sold here and we fear very much harm will be done by ardent spirit, and the spirit of the Lord will not long inhabit the same body together.

October 9. My dear companion finds that his bodily infirmity forbids the discharge of his duty to the mission as carpenter. He therefore concludes after much deliberation and prayer to leave the mission and enter a door which a kind providence has opened to him where he hopes to be more useful than he can be in the mission at present. A physician is needed in the settlement and as his knowledge of medicine *enables him to act as such he enters upon the duties of this new relation to the world in the fear of God, praying that while he administers to the bodies of his fellow men, God will administer salvation to the soul and so soul and body both shall be saved. He is in this way enabled to support his family and save the missionary society a great expense. Many may wonder at our leaving the mission and I should wonder too if we were leaving the field to return home. I consider that we are by no means leaving the missionary field. We are only leaving one department for another where we hope to be more useful.*[3]

From this time on, William would be accorded the title of Doctor and would be known as Dr. Willson.

In November of 1842, James Olley, one of the missionary laymen, drowned while rafting logs down the Willamette. His death had future consequences for the Willsons.

By December, 1842, the Methodists began plans for their first church in the Oregon Country. It would be built at Willamette Falls. The building was complete enough for use two years later. That settlement grew slowly because the few American settlers, like the earlier French trappers, scattered over the Willamette Valley on land they could farm. Willamette Falls was on land claimed by Dr. John McLoughlin in 1829. He had previously constructed a small salmon packing house there for Hudson's Bay Company. Seeing the Methodists building at that site and agreeing to their temporary use of the land because it would benefit the local Indians, he laid out the town in 1842. This was in a dense forest of fir trees and underbrush along the east bank of the Willamette River. It was a prime site and major land disputes soon followed.

A company of settlers began building a sawmill on a nearby rock island in the Willamette River. A document in the Oregon archives recorded December 2, 1847, states that on November 23, 1842, a committee from Oregon Milling Company composed of A. F. Waller, W. H. Willson, and E. Lucia (Lucier) agreed to pay Felix Hathaway $450 for his right and title to that island and his house, timber and waterways. (Originally Dr. McLoughlin claimed this island.

Rev. Gustavus Hines

Hathaway and others jumped his claim in 1841.) The Methodist mission building, the salmon packing structure and the island mills along with a half dozen houses made up the settlement of Willamette Falls.

All too often tragedy was a part of the settlers' daily lives, and sharing the burden was an immense help. When early in 1843 a canoe went over the falls, drowning six people, the entire valley community was in shock. Evidence from orders on the stores indicate that three of those drowned, Cornelius and Satira Rogers and Satira's youngest sister Aurelia had been boarding with the Willsons. The two girls were daughters of David Leslie. This tragedy really hit hard at Chloe and William and their friend David Leslie. Sharing their shock and grief and seeking refuge in their religious beliefs helped them overcome the heavy blow.

Meetings for a variety of purposes were frequently held throughout the valley. Many of the same people traveled long distances over trails and unbridged streams to attend each gathering, sharing their ideas, opinions, observations, and news. An opportunity for social intercourse was always appreciated and rarely missed. During that winter of 1842-1843 the "Pioneer Lyceum and Literary Club" was formed at Willamette Falls. It met regularly during the winter months with discussions covering a broad range of topics. One topic of common and frequent interest was the organization of a local representative government. The American settlers were few in number and came from quite different backgrounds and experience, but they were all accustomed to living under the rule of law. Their primary concern was their legal right to the land they occupied, but they also saw a need for laws to regulate and give permanence to other social contracts. The absence of certain desired laws and regulations coupled with some rules and practices imposed on them by HBC and which were resented, led to a petition against Dr. McLoughlin and the Hudson's Bay Company.

The petition that was circulated throughout the Willamette Valley urgently requested the United States Congress to extend the authority of the United States government over the Oregon

Country. The petitioners expressed a belief that Dr. McLoughlin and the Hudson's Bay Company were taking sharp trade advantage in all business dealings with the settlers and that the monopolistic practices were a major detriment to continued settlement by U.S. citizens. Robert Shortess, who came with the Peoria party in 1839, circulated the petition. Among the 65 signers were Methodist mission recruits Alvan Waller, Lewis Judson, Hamilton Campbell, Alanson Beers, Josiah Parrish, and William Willson. The concern about HBC and Dr. McLoughlin may have had as much to do with rights to land claims at Willamette Falls as it did with monopolistic trade practices. Whatever the specific concerns, it was obvious to all that by tenure, tradition, and sheer numbers, the Hudson's Bay Company was then the only powerful group in the country. It was British, it was a monopolistic fur trading company, it existed to make money, and under Dr. McLoughlin's leadership it had controlled the Indian tribes for years. Restless, individualistic, land hungry Americans could find fault with every aspect of the HBC dominion. The request for help from the U.S. government was just one of several ways they would try to thwart the British.

The Oregon Country settlers in 1843 continued to think about and discuss their circumstances in general and their respective individual situations. At Clatsop and in the Willamette Valley people were subject to couger and bear attacks, but most often it was their livestock that suffered. Much of the valley was covered in tall grass. "Up to the pommel of the saddle" was the descriptive measurement. Wild animals easily hid in the grass, waiting for prey. The men organized wolf hunts which fanned out across the prairie. In February, 1843, an informal meeting was called to consider some better way of eliminating the various predatory animals. The group decided to call a general meeting for March 6 at the home of Joseph Gervais. William signed the minutes as secretary of the February meeting and he also served as one of a committee of six men who notified the valley inhabitants about the general meeting.

The American population at this time numbered fewer than 250 men, women and children. Most of the men would have attended the March 6 meeting because each had a personal interest in protecting his livestock. Also, should the question of forming a government arise for discussion, each man had the ever present concern of protecting his land claim. Throughout those early years, claims to land were honored simply by common agreement. There were no laws regarding land ownership because no country had sole authority over or claim to the territory. England and the United States were holding the Oregon Country by right of joint occupancy only.

When the March 6 meeting convened at Joseph Gervais' place, James O'Neal presided. The measures agreed upon to eliminate the wolves, bears, panthers, and other animals preying on cattle, horses, sheep, and hogs would primarily be bounties. They would pay 50 cents for a small wolf, $3.00 for a large wolf, $1.50 for a lynx, $2.00 for a bear, and $5.00 for a panther. An Indian would be paid only half as much as a white. A $5.00 assessment was levied on each member, but because money was nearly nonexistent, the assessment was payable with a draft on Fort Vancouver, the Methodist mission store, or the milling company at Willamette Falls.

To apparently no one's surprise, the next order of business was a discussion about the need for civil and military protection for themselves and their neighbors. A committee of twelve men was chosen to deliberate and make specific recommendations. A few days later this group met and determined that there was enough interest in forming some type of local government that a mass meeting would be called at Champoeg on May 2, 1843.

Now a legislative committee was formed to determine the organic laws that might best meet the civil and military needs of the widely scattered and relatively small community of settlers. William served on this committee along with A. E. Wilson, George LeBreton, Joe Meek, D. Hill, Robert Shortess, Robert Newell, Alanson Beers, T. J. Hubbard, W. H. Gray, James O'Neal, Robert Moore, and William Dougherty.

May 2, 1843, a large assemblage of men gathered near a small house on the open prairie at Champoeg. The missionary and the non-missionary Americans, the French fur trappers who settled on French Prairie, and the British officials of Hudson's Bay Company were there. Once again, Dr. Babcock presided and W. H. Gray, George W. LeBreton, and William H. Willson were named secretaries. After the committee offered their plan of governmental organization, the motion to adopt the plan failed. Much confusion followed wherein either Joe Meek or George LeBreton suggested the large group divide and be counted. Joe Meek encouraged all favoring the formation of a local government to congregate near him. The exact number is not clear, but a majority favored organizing a government.

The pro-government faction reconsidered the report and adopted it item by item, then elected a supreme judge, clerk and recorder, sheriff, treasurer, four magistrates, four constables, a major and three captains, and a legislative committee of nine. William had been an active participant in these several meetings, sharing duties as notifier, secretary, legislative planner, and voter. He was the man elected to be the first provisional government treasurer.

There are two historical questions to be dealt with here. One begs clarification of the actual question voted on at Champoeg. Following is Hussey's lucid explanation:

First, it is not the case, as is sometimes said, that those who voted for organization on May 2, 1843, voted for United States rule while those who lined up against organization voted "in favor of British domination." The question voted on that day was whether or not "to organize themselves into a civil community, and provide themselves with the protection, secured by the enforcement of law and order." When adopted at the meeting on July 5, 1843, the Organic Act declared the purpose of the organization to be "mutual protection, and to secure peace and prosperity among ourselves. ...until such time as the United States of America extend their jurisdiction over us." ...The positive measures taken by conservative leaders of the Provisional Government to protect the lands of the Company after McLoughlin had agreed to join it, demonstrate that the organization was what the chief factor said it was, "merely a union of certain parties, British and American subjects, being divested of all nationality of character, having no national objects in view, and its exclusive aim and purpose being the protection of persons and property."[4]

The second historical question is: What happened to the three sets of notes that should have been written and kept from the three secretaries at the meeting? Some disparagement has been cast upon the secretaries, and since William H. Willson was one of them, the question is pertinent. Hussey again provides some enlightenment.

At the May 2, 1843 meeting at Champoeg, William H. Gray, George W. LeBreton, and William H. Willson were selected as secretaries. Only the notes made by the intelligent, energetic New Englander, LeBreton have survived.

Mr. [David] Duniway had found a fourth, and the earliest known, version of the minutes in Charles Saxton, "The Oregonian or History of the Oregon Territory No. 1 (Washington D. C. and Oregon City, 1846)" 19-20. Mr. Duniway now suspects that the four extant versions of the minutes, all of which are printed, may represent the work of two of the secretaries, who turned them over to the recorder LeBreton, who attested them.[5]

The provisional government treasurer was to receive the money raised by contributions and other means, then pay the bills as specified in the organic law. For services rendered the treasurer could claim five percent of all monies received and paid out, plus two percent of the treasury funds available when he took office and three percent of the treasury funds available when he left office. All of this meant very little because very few dollars were received. The settlers learned that year that funding government by contributions will not work.

The treasurer was to provide a bond of $1500 with at least two securities to the executive committee prior to taking office. The officers elected at the May 2 meeting were to hold office until the second Tuesday in May of 1844.

While William was occupied that spring and summer with his work as physician, lay preacher, and government organizer, Chloe's diary reflects that she continued to be involved with religious activities in addition to her work as homemaker and Sabbath school teacher. She helped establish the Oregon Juvenile Temperance Society of Willamette Falls in early July. At mid month she attended the first Methodist camp meeting held in Oregon for whites. Camp meetings were revival meetings, a favorite evangelistic technique of the Methodist Church because they usually brought forth many conversions. This July meeting site was in a grove of trees about thirty-five miles west of Willamette Falls, on Tualatin Plains. The camp meeting ran from Thursday through Sunday. It was at this meeting that Joe Meek's conversion occurred. This successful camp meeting was soon followed by at least two others. Chloe joyfully attended them both.

During this summer of 1843 Narcissa Whitman spent a few weeks visiting at each of the Methodist missions. In August, Narcissa, accompanied by Jason Lee and David Leslie, returned from a visit at Clatsop and went by way of Willamette Falls to the Chemeketa site. It was here some weeks later that she received word that her husband was returning over the Oregon Trail from his trip to the East. Periodic visits such as hers established friendships among the far-scattered mission settlements. Certainly the Willsons and the Whitmans were acquainted. Marcus wrote of enjoying dinner at Chloe's table on one of his visits to the valley.

The settlement at the falls was alternately referred to as the Falls and as Oregon City for some period of time. This slow acceptance of a name change is just human nature. William and Chloe saw many changes during their three years residence at the Falls, many far more significant than the change of name. One writer in September of 1843 noted that about twenty houses, two sawmills and one flour mill had been built within the year. Another writer left us a detailed description of the place as he saw it in November, 1843.

> Here we were able to procure such things as were really necessary to make us comfortable:...an abundance of substantial food... To see houses, farms, mills, storehouses, shops; to hear the busy hum of industry; the noise of the workman's hammer; the sound of the woodman's axe; the crash of the falling pines; and to enjoy the warm welcome of countrymen and friends.

> Our arrival [because of the large number of immigrants] had a great effect upon the country. The people were beginning to feel lonesome, and to fear that it would be long before these far distant wilds of Western America would be settled. Property was of doubtful value, and their once high anticipations were fading away. . . . [After the immigrants' arrival] instantly every thing revived; improvements went rapidly on, and the expectations of the people were again excited. We found at the Falls, a small village of about one hundred inhabitants. Lots were laid out on both sides of the River; those on the East side, by Dr. Mclaughlin, Chief Factor of the Hudson's Bay Company, West of the Mountains, and called Oregon City; those on the West [side of the river], by H. Burns, and called Multnomah.[6]

The winter of 1843-1844 seems to have been one of religious contentment for Chloe. She wrote of feeling much peace of mind and in close communion with God as well as of William and herself being blessed with comfortable health, prosperity, peace and plenty. However, she did experience several bouts of loneliness during January and February. Chloe's "dearest earthly friend" was absent for extended periods of time, serving the vast valley and north coast area as both physician and preacher.

On February 1 she wrote in her diary: "Next month I hope to be with the partner of my joys and sorrows. The time he has been absent seems very long." Also absent from her care were two little girls, an Indian child and a young daughter of David Leslie. Chloe missed each of her "family" members enormously, but she kept her courage and composure by communing frequently with God.

Periodically stories of imminent Indian attacks spread through the valley. Chloe noted in February that several murders had been committed among the Indians and that the lives of a number of white men had been threatened. Then on March 8, 1844, she wrote: ". . . three of our fellow citizens have been wounded by the Indians. Two have since died of their wounds."

Chloe's reference was to the following violent incident:

> The Cockstock affair was the outgrowth of a private dispute between two negro settlers, Winslow Anderson and James D. Saules, and a Wasco Indian named Cockstock, who had been hired by Anderson to perform labor on a land claim, in payment for which he was to have received a horse. Before the completion of the contract Anderson sold the land claim and also the horse to Saules, who refused to deliver the animal to Cockstock. The latter then appropriated the horse; the negroes appealed to Dr. Elijah White and he compelled Cockstock to surrender it. Cockstock threatened all concerned with violence, and White offered a reward of $100 for Cockstock's arrest. March 4, 1844, Cockstock and four Molalla Indians rode into Willamette Falls, armed, and, in an attempt to arrest them, George W. LeBreton, clerk and recorder of the provisional government, a highly esteemed citizen, received a fatal gunshot wound and a man named Rogers was wounded by a poisoned arrow, dying on the following day. Winslow Anderson, going to the rescue of LeBreton, dispatched Cockstock by breaking his skull with the barrel of his rifle.

> The incident created great excitement in the Willamette Valley and resulted in the organization of the mounted rifle company known as the Oregon Rifles...This constituted the first military force authorized in the Oregon Country. The company, however, was never called into action.[7]

On March 9, William served as chairman of the meeting called by the executive committee to organize military forces for defensive measures following the Cockstock affair.

As usual, Chloe did not mention William's civil activities, but her diary does indicate that some personal decisions were confronting them.

March 20, 1844. I have for some time past felt that there were two ways before us. That one of them was the path of duty and of course the path of safety. And the other, though pleasant and profitable so far as it relates to this world, would in the end lead us into difficulty. The way is open for my companion to continue in his business and increase his earthly store and another way is open for him to give up all and devote himself wholly to the work of the ministry. A Preacher is much needed at the Twallaty plains. Mr. Willson has been solicited by the preacher to go and take the oversight of the church there. We are only waiting that we may know the will of God.

March 24, 1844. I have been privileged with hearing the sweet sound of the gospel as it fell from the lips of my companion. He is able to save to the utmost all that come to God by him also... Every circumstance seems to say that the time has fully come for my companion to give up his earthly business and devote himself fully to the work of saving souls.[8]

Oregon City continued to change and grow. By the summer of 1844 there were three saw mills, two grist mills, four dry goods stores, a school, two churches, a public library, law offices, physicians, various shops and craftsmen, and a population of about three hundred.

On May 26, Chloe wrote a letter to Laura Brewer who, with her husband H. B. Brewer, was living at the mission at Wascopan (The Dalles). This letter was misplaced, probably during the Willsons' move from Willamette Falls to The Institute on the Chemeketa Plains (Salem), and was added to later. The conditions and concerns of the missionaries at their various locations is quite poignant. Though lengthy, Chloe's letter offers some unique insights into her world.

Wallamette Falls May 26, 1844

Mrs. Brewer, Very Dear Sister,

Having heard of your difficulties with the Indian I feel it my duty to write and let you know that you have our earnest prayers and sympathies in the midst of your trials. I have thought much of you since Br. Perkins and family left you. I think that you must have been very lonely, alone;

yet not alone, for God was with you. A present help in every time of need. I found him so two years ago when a Molaly Chief raised his knife at Mr. Willson. Though he was not permitted to injure him, he gave us to understand that his heart was not too good to do it.

I know not what is before us in this land. No doubt trials and afflictions await, but shall we through fear leave the field and leave the heritage of our God to the will of his enemies? What would be the state of this country 5 years hence if every Christian should leave it? Fear not them that kill the body and after that have no more that they can do, but fear him who is able to destroy both soul and body. I find it very profitable to meditate upon the works of our dear Redeemer. A point of time, a moments space removes me to yon heavenly place or shuts me up in hell.

Soon, very soon if faithful to God, we shall have done with the trials of earth, and heaven with all its glories will be ours forever. We shall not go there and enjoy the unspeakable bliss of "the eden of love" a few days, or years, and then feel the bitter pang of parting with dearest friends and above all of parting with our adorable Redeemer who hath washed us in his own blood and made us kings and priests unto God. No! no! but we shall be at home, with our own Fathers family forever. No foreigner of a strange spirit will be there to break in upon the lovely, loving circle. O that I were already there!

Were it not for the hope of drinking more fully into the spirit of the heavenly world and of influencing souls to go with me, I should be almost impatient to be gone. I love the spirit of love, it is exceeding lovely. I feel fully to adopt the dying words of Dr. Fisk, "I love to love and never more than now."

The yearly meeting was held here last week. Their decision was that Br. Leslie should remain at the school, Br. Hines at the Falls, Br. Waller to travel and labor among the Indians, Mr. Willson at the Plains. If the Lord will, we shall move to the Plains next week. Pray for us dear sister, for I assure you we shall need your prayers. We shall have hardhearted sinners, luke warm professers and backsliders to deal with, but few, if any, resolved to save their souls alive. I am to have a school there and Mr. Willson is to make it his business to point sinners to the Lamb of God who taketh away the sin of the world. We give up all prospects of worldly gain and go out trusting in him for food and raiment who hath said, "Low I am with you always."

Br. and Sister Parrish were here last week. Sister Parrish finds it quite lonely at Clatsop, but endures it cheerfully, that they may be instrumental of doing good. They both seem to have their work at heart. The Lord bless and prosper them in it.

I have spent the past year very pleasantly in teaching. The Lord has blessed and prospered me in the world.

Oregon Institute October 29, 1844
Dear Sister Brewer

I do most heartily beg your pardon for not sending this before. It was accidentally laid away with some other papers and I supposed it was forwarded to you. I have just been reading Br. B's letter to Br. Campbell. I feel to sympathize with you and Br. Waller's people in your families' sickness. It must be very trying, particularly as you are at so great a distance from a physician. I hope and pray that your dear little ones may recover. My own health and husband's is as usual. I enjoy myself much in my school. I have a good opportunity to be useful. Pray for me that I may have wisdom and grace to discharge every duty in the fear and love of God. Tell Br. and Sister Waller to keep good courage, and labor on confidently expecting the crown [writing obliterated] the end of the race.

Oregon is to be converted, Indians, Catholics, Priests and all. Why not? The Lord's arm is not shortened that it cannot save.

The blessing of the Lord be upon you and yours. Much love to Br. Waller's dear family.

Your Sister in Christ, C. A. Willson[9]

William's experience in the secular world, particularly in his role of treasurer of the provisional government, brought some interesting situations to light. The money the treasurer would handle was to come from voluntary pledges of the populace. The annual payment of the pledge was revokable by paying all arrearages and notifying the treasurer. The first treasurer's report to the June session of the Legislative Committee on June 20, 1844, indicates some of the difficulties encountered in both the collection and the record keeping of the provisional government funds.

To the Honorable, the Legislative Committee of the Territory of Oregon

The time has come when the laws of this Territory require me to report to your Honorable body the state of the Treasury. This report would have been submitted on the opening of the present session of your Honorable body had I not been so unfortunate as to lose my Pocket Book which contained the only copy of the subscription list in my possession. I can, however, state to your Honorable body the amounts of money received and disbursed with the present liabilities of the Treasury

Amount of money received		$81.50
Amount of money paid out		$91.50
Present liabilities		
Due on G. W. LeBreton's Drft		
favor L. H. Judson		$ 9.00
Commission on $81.50 at		
5 Percentum		$ 4.07

The original subscription will be found in the hands of the Executive Committee of last year. I am sorry I can not say how much money remains on subscription. I think it will not, however, exceed the claims against this government which have as yet not been filed in.

Begging your allowance for inaccuracies

I have the Honor to (be) Your most obt. Humble Srvt.

W. H. Willson, Treas. Oregon Ter.[10]

Eventually the funds were forthcoming to balance the treasurer's account but his claim for his commission on handling the public funds was ignored.

At the same meeting, the Legislative Committee acknowledged the failure of the subscription process and decided to try a voluntary tax. It levied 1/8 of one percent on certain items of personal property as well as a fifty cent poll tax on all males over the age of 21 descended from white fathers. Anyone not paying lost his ability to sue in the courts against claim jumpers and debtors, and could not vote.

The Tax Book of 1844 shows W. H. Willson with taxable property values of: $300 town lot; $12 clock; $100 watch; $100 horse; $40 cattle, for a total taxable valuation of $552. His taxes were $1.19 including the poll tax.

As small as this tax bill was, the tax rate did not seem insignificant to a person with no ready cash. Perhaps the financial straits of the people, particularly of those newly arrived, is best illustrated by the following story. Joseph Watt's arrival at Oregon City in 1844 was auspicious.

While walking down the street, Doctor McLoughlin, the greatest figure in Oregon pioneer history, stopped him and after a brief conversation turned to a clerk and said, "Give this man some clothes. Tut! Tut! Tut! What people these Americans are. Wandering vagabonds across a *continent. What are they coming here for? Give him some clothes."* Watt secured work as a carpenter and paid his debt, an obligation many of the Americans never fulfilled.[11]

By 1856, Joseph Watt was a major influence in the construction of the canal to divert water from the Santiam River into Mill Creek and in establishing the Willamette Woolen Manufacturing Company in Salem, acting variously as organizer, financier, and company director. Dr. McLoughlin had helped yet another financially strapped but industrious man.

---

[1] Willson, Chloe, "Diary of Chloe Clark Willson."

[2] Letter to Mary Norton from Chloe Willson, in the possession of Chloe's great-great granddaughter Elizabeth Kate Moore Barker, Lake Oswego, Oregon, 1996.

[3] Willson, Diary.

[4] Hussey, John A., *Champoeg, Place of Transition*, p 178-179.

[5] Ibid., p 151, p 352 footnotes.

[6] "Migration of 1843," by Overton Johnson and Wm. H. Winter, *Oregon Historical Quarterly*, V. 7, p 103-104.

[7] Carey, Charles H., *General History of Oregon*, p 522-523.

[8] Willson, Diary.

[9] Willson, Chloe, Letter to Mrs. H. B. Brewer, May 26, 1844. Original in the Archives of the Oregon-Idaho Conference of the Methodist Church, Willamette University, Salem, Oregon.

[10] "Finances of the Provisional Government," by F. G. Young, *Oregon Historical Quarterly*, V. 7, p 393.

[11] Lomax, Alfred L., *Pioneer Woolen Mills in Oregon, (1811-1875)*, p 60-61.

Part 5: The Mission At Chemeketa and The Oregon Institute

The original mission site near what is now the east landing of the Wheatland Ferry was on low, wet ground which was suspected of contributing to the fevers and other health problems of the missionaries and the Indian children. After Jason Lee's return in 1840, it was decided to move upriver about ten miles to the area known as Chemeketa Plains where the mission had a saw and grist mill under construction, and where it was hoped the higher, drier ground would provide a more healthful environment.

Four members of the mission agreed to claim sections of land that more or less abutted each other on the Chemeketa Plains. These men, L.H. Judson, James Olley, H. B. Brewer and David Leslie, were in reality holding the four sections for the mission's use. After the 1841 relocation the mission consisted of the mills, a few buildings, some fields of wheat, and vegetable gardens scattered across those four sections of land. The mills and Jason Lee's house were located on a stream of water they called Mill Creek, in the northwest corner of the mission claim, near the Willamette River.

A building to house the Indian Manual Labor School was begun about two miles southeast of the mill site, with the intent of keeping the Indian children separated from the river area where it was expected that white settlers would choose to live. The missionaries' desire was to prevent the prejudicial attitudes and rough behavior of some of the whites from influencing the young Indians.

By the autumn of 1842 the Indian school was housed in this $10,000 building and the basic work of the Oregon mission was well under way again.

However, within two years the Indian school would close. The purpose of the Oregon mission would be dramatically altered by decisions of the Board of Missions in New York. There were several reasons for the seemingly abrupt change of direction.

Partly because of the nomadic lifestyle of the Indians, their numbers seemed greater than they actually were. Indian deaths from illnesses were noted by the whites, but when the missionary groups were just getting a foothold in the 1830s, there seemed to be unlimited opportunities for missionary work. It was not until early in the next decade that the reduced native populations became obvious. The mission board, on the east coast, was expecting large numbers of converts in Oregon, but that was not happening. What the board eventually learned was that because of disease the few newly converted Indians were often soon recorded among the dead.

In January of 1842, Jason Lee proposed that an educational institution for the white and half-breed children be founded. The idea met with the approval of both the mission and non mission settlers. They selected the name Oregon Institute and elected a nine member board of trustees who proceeded to choose a site for this new school on Wallace Prairie, about three miles northeast of the mills. (This is about where the State School for the Deaf is located in 1996.)

The initial efforts of funding and building the Oregon Institute were undertaken by all parties as individuals and not as official church representatives. However, by October of 1842 a group from the mission saw a need for firmer committment to the effort and so formally pledged as a branch of the Methodist Episcopal Church in the United States to make every reasonable effort to support the school.

The selected builder was W.H. Gray, a former lay member of the Whitman mission, who erected a partially completed structure valued at $4,000 by November of 1843. But this building on Wallace Prairie was never used as a school. A very unexpected event occurred.

Throughout 1843, the Board of Missions had been finding fault with Lee's fiscal management, record keeping, missionary results, and what they perceived as a lack of information from him. They recalled Jason Lee and sent out the Reverend George Gary as his replacement.

Rev. and Mrs. Gary arrived in June, 1844. Soon after his arrival, George Gary surveyed the mission's holdings, projects, and Indian school, and determined that all of these secular activities should cease. After getting the reluctant agreement of the missionaries, sale of the improvements with possessory rights to the land immediately took place. Those laboriously cleared and planted fields, the original primitive saw and grist mills, the blacksmith shop and mission store, and the Indian Manual Labor School building were sold, mainly to local settlers connected with the mission. The primary objective was to stem the financial drain on the Methodist Episcopal Board of Missions. During the dissolution, the lay people were given the choice of remaining in Oregon or returning to the East. Most stayed. Of the clergy, Leslie, Waller, Hines, and Parrish chose to remain and serve as ministers in the Methodist tradition.

Even though they decided to dissolve the mission, the Board of Missions did desire to retain a Methodist presence on the Pacific frontier. They truly believed that the immigrants moving west should be greeted by the wholesome influences of religious institutions, and most especially their own. To have the majority of their mission workers choose to stay in Oregon was a boon to their cause.

Rev. George Gary, second superintendent of the Oregon Mission.

As to the specifics of the disposition of the mission property, Alanson Beers and Joseph Garrison bought the original mission farm on Mission Bottom. John Force bought the saw and grist mills, then immediately sold them to L. H. Judson and William Willson. The Board of Trustees of the Oregon Institute, with William now a member, purchased the building for $4,000 that had housed the Indian Manual Labor School. They then sold their partially completed building on Wallace Prairie. Oregon Institute was now located at Chemeketa.

As previously noted in Chloe's letter to Mrs. Brewer, by late spring of 1844, Chloe and William had been asked to move from Oregon City to Chemeketa Plains. William was requested to serve the area as an itinerant preacher and Chloe was chosen to open the Oregon Institute. Since the local Methodist ministers held the majority positions on the committees and boards that made such choices, it is reasonable to assume that these appointments were made by essentially the same people though the school at that time definitely was not an official offshoot of the Methodist church.

On July 10, Chloe wrote: "...it is thought best that we should open a boarding school immediately and try to give a proper direction to the minds of the youth of this country..."[1]

On August 13, Chloe opened the Oregon Institute, housed in the three story building that had been the Indian Manual Labor School for the past two years. Chloe enrolled five students on the first day. A month later she had thirteen. The institution that would become Willamette University had begun with devout dedication and many prayers from Chloe Willson. She earnestly desired to discharge her responsibility to the children and the institution by doing God's will and with His blessings. She wrote: "O my Father ...thou seest the desire of my heart for the prosperity of this institution, but without thy blessing it can never prosper."[2]

William was called upon to continue his medical profession. The twin practices of preacher and physician kept him busy and away from home a great deal. Distances and the difficult methods and conditions of travel were always major considerations. A lonely Chloe wrote in her diary in late September:

...My husband left yesterday and unless he can find a Physician who will go in his stead he must go to Clatsop and be gone several weeks. This is a trial to me as he has been obliged to be absent so much lately. He had just returned from the Falls and I fondly hoped he would not be called away again so soon.

Hendricks quoted Chloe and explained:

"October 30, 1844...The constant care of my scholars in school and out keeps me very busy." In fact hers was largely a boarding school, at first. She was president, dean and faculty, registrar, solicitor and all the other functionaries that make up a college force — and besides this she was foster mother to her boarding students and thus looked out for their proper diet and their correct conduct generally.[3]

Early in December of that year, Mrs. L. H. Judson died. She had suffered from illness for three years. Chloe spoke highly of her, of her Christian patience and of her submission to the will of God. Two years after Mrs. Judson's death, her second oldest daughter went to reside in William and Chloe's home. She lived with them until the summer of 1849.

The Oregon Institute, originally the Indian Manual Labor School.

---

[1] "Bits For Breakfast," by Hendricks, R. J., *The Oregon Statesman* 5/29/35.
[2] Ibid.
[3] Ibid.

Part 6: The Willsons In Salem • 1844-1847

The yearly influx of new settlers caused rapid growth and change in the valley. Though by no means densely populated, still the area took on a new feel. The pulse of activity began to quicken. Destinies began to change.

James Olley had been holding one of the four sections of land across which the relocated mission spread its mills, school, houses and farm lands. Olley was drowned in a log rafting accident on the Willamette. Mrs. Olley held the land claim until her marriage in January 1844 to widower David Leslie. The Olley claim was then assigned to W. H. Willson to hold for the mission, thereby joining him with Leslie, Brewer, and Judson in that endeavor.

As a member of the Board of Trustees of the Oregon Institute since 1843, William was involved with the plans and construction on Wallace Prairie, with the sale of the Wallace Prairie site, and with the purchase of the Indian Manual Labor School building and a large tract of land for the Oregon Institute. At this time all land was being held essentially by squatter's rights augmented by the recognition of the provisional government. The Oregon Institute could not receive a charter from the provisional government, so it did not legally exist as a corporation. And that meant it could not hold land. The large number of settlers arriving by wagon train in 1843 and 1844 caused the trustees to fear the Institute's claim would be jumped.

On May 25, 1845, the trustees made several decisions that would support and protect their school. They would survey and lay out a city on the school's tract of land. They would sell the town lots to raise money to support the school. In order to protect the land, the trustees arranged with Rev. David Leslie, L. H. Judson, Henry B. Brewer, and William H. Willson to extend the lines of their adjacent claims to cover the Institute's tract. The four men all being members of the mission group, and with at least three of them serving on the Institute's board, agreement was reached and Judson provided 320 acres, Leslie 200 acres,

Brewer 80 acres and Willson 40 acres by reducing their own claims by these amounts. The bonded agreement was that the four men would hold the land as a partnership claim until the board could incorporate and receive back the property. William filed the city plat for an area thirteen blocks by five blocks, bounded by the Willamette River, Mission Street on the south, Church Street on the east, and Division Street on the north. The Institute settlement contained about fifteen families.

Chloe noted that Doctor Whitman came to visit in June, and that William preached at a camp meeting held near David Leslie's home in early July. Then in late summer, William and Chloe took several weeks for traveling and camping along the coast. Chloe came home with improved health and enthusiastically returned to her teaching duties.

The school continued to grow. Midway through the second year an enrollment of forty children of various ages required an additional teacher. Alanson Hinman, a young man of twenty-two, had recently come into the area. He was hired to conduct the male department and was soon held in high esteem. Chloe was relieved of some of her original heavy responsibilities and continued her valued work, conducting the female department and overseeing the health and well-being of the boarding students.

In fact, the settlement around the school drew a number of new residents in 1845, so Oregon Institute, Champoeg County was made an official postal destination by February of 1846.

The Trustees of Oregon Institute saw the advantage of selling town lots, or of even giving some lots to encourage specific tradesmen and churchmen to build in their settlement. Both the income from the land sales and the additional settlers with their goods and services would enhance the prospects of the school. Toward this end, the trustees made a new arrangement with the landholding partners.

Rev. David Leslie

In March, 1846, it was arranged by the Board, in connection with the partnership, that W. H. Wilson, one of the partners, should as agent of the concern, take personal charge of the premises for safe keeping. On the twenty-sixth of May, Mr. Wilson, by unanimous vote

of the Board, was confirmed in the agency, and empowered to transact the business of the Oregon Institute, and he was authorized to sell lots and receive pay for the same, and as a compensation for such service he was to receive seven per centum of all sales effected. It should be distinctly understood that at this time the institute land which was held by the partnership arrangement embraced the whole of the present site of the city of Salem. The city is indebted entirely to the Board for the magnificent plan upon which the plat was surveyed, a plan that will ultimately make Salem of Oregon one of the most beautiful cities upon the continent of America. The liberality of the Board appeared not only in respect to the town survey, but also in the encouragement given to mechanics and others to settle and improve within the city limits. Instruction was given the agent, W. H. Wilson, to make a donation to worthy individuals of one lot to each, to the number of twenty lots, according to his discretion. This was designed both to encourage individuals, and to give a start to the embryo town. [1]

Two highlights for Chloe during the summer of 1846 were the camp meetings she was privileged to attend. In June the Methodists and their friends met on the Tualatin Plains and in early July the group met near the institute. By the end of July the fourth school term was underway and afterward Chloe wrote in her diary that she had never spent a happier week.

In a letter to the editor, announcing the new school term, David Leslie wrote:

I feel a pleasure in announcing the names of our former teachers, Mr. Alanson Hinman and Mrs. Willson, each of whom are entitled to high confidence, as persons well qualified for their work, and happily adapted to the duties of their respective departments.

The boarding department is in charge of Mr. James Force and his excellent lady, and we have every assurance that all reasonable satisfaction will be given to both pupils and patrons, and that the comfort and health of the scholars will be amply provided for. [2]

The number of students had become so large that Chloe could no longer provide the room and board for them along with her teaching responsibilities. With Mr. and Mrs. James Force providing the living accomodations for the students, they apparently became the resident managers of the institute and the Willsons would need to live elsewhere.

In the late fall of 1846, William built their first family home on the river front. (The present 1996 Boise Cascade property at Front and Ferry-Trade streets.)

A Lt. Howison made a brief visit to the Willamette Valley in 1846, and seeing the growth and development from a nonresident's eyes, made this disdainful observation in his report:

> *A sixth spot dignified with the name of town is Salem, high up the Wilhammette, of which too little exists to be worthy of an attempt at description.*[3]

Opinions like Lt. Howison's notwithstanding, efforts to promote the settlement and expansion of Salem continued. An announcement that William, as agent for the trustees, put in *The Oregon Spectator* in August of 1846, read:

> *Notice. The Subscriber will sell Lots in the town of Salem, at public auction, on Thursday, the 10th of Sept. next. Terms — One third in twenty days — the balance, on six and twelve months. The sale will open at 12 o'clock. M. W. H. Willson, agent. Salem August 14, 1846.*[4]

William's public service and professional activities went on apace. When he held the offices of Judge of Probate and President of the Bench for Champoeg County he handled some interesting legal matters. On October 1, 1845, it was he who received all the papers and documents related to the unfinished business of the estates of Joel Turnham, who had been killed in a personal dispute, and of Ewing Young, the wealthy man of several enterprises whose death, intestate, set in motion the movement toward the provisional government. A reminiscence of F. X. Matthieu, who had served as a justice of the peace in Champoeg County, describes some of the work that judges encountered in that era, as well as the experience he and William had in one situation.

> *He had some trouble with distillers, who sometimes set up little stills in out of the way places, and made liquor to intoxicate the Indians. He recalls one case in which he and Doctor Willson, the judge, traced a distiller out into the woods, back of French Prairie, at DePot's, and found him over a teakettle, which he used as his still, manufacturing what was*

called "blue ruin"—a liquor made out of Sandwich Island molasses, and was an article so destructive as to almost relieve the authorities of the necessity of estopping the manufacture—the juice being the executioner of its producer.[5]

Then in October, 1846, at a camp meeting held on the Yamhill River, William was doubly busy, as doctor and as preacher.

> *October 2, 1846,...Last night a little after midnight, Mrs. (Francis) Fletcher gave birth to a fine boy in a tent on the ground; I suppose there was not time enough for her to be taken to her house about a mile and a half off; so the camp ground became the place of this child's nativity. Well that Doct. Willson was on the ground...2 p.m., W. H. Willson preached a good sermon for him....*[6]

As he so frequently did, William joined with several other civic minded men, this time in an attempt to establish a local newspaper. They saw the need for more widespread communication and they knew of an available press. Alanson Hinman went to Lapwai to contact Reverend Spaulding about obtaining the old press from the American Mission. It was willingly sent to The Dalles, but Spaulding wanted too much control over the paper. The Salemites refused to accept his conditions and the press eventually wound up in Hillsboro. William did not become a newspaperman and the Salem area would not have a regular newspaper for several more years.

Early in 1847, the news of the resolution to the boundary dispute with England had reached the Oregon settlers. Their concerns now turned to retaining their informal legal agreements and most particularly they wanted a guarantee that their land claim boundaries would be accepted. The uncertainty about the allowable claim size and boundaries went on for months. Hundreds of new families arrived in the Oregon country to find that the limited amount of "best land" had already been taken. Few people cheerfully settle for second best, and these new Oregonians were no exception.

The Oregon Institute claim had continued to be held by the four partners, in addition to each man retaining his individual claim of less than a section, adjacent to the Oregon Institute claim. A change in arrangement was to occur. Of the partners, only the circumstances of Leslie and Willson remained little changed. Henry Brewer had returned to the states, and Lewis Judson relinquished his claim to his son-in-law J. B. McClane.

In July, 1847, the original partners consulted

with J. Quinn Thornton, an attorney in Oregon City, to determine the best method to safely hold the property for the Institute and yet release the partners from their responsibility.

William was willing to continue to represent the Board of Trustees of the Oregon Institute as he had been doing since May 26, 1846.

Under the new agreement, the four members of the holding partnership were released and Willson assumed the Institute claim under definite conditions and obligations to the Institute. He was to assume the obligation to the Missionary society covering the original purchase price of the Institute and accrued interest on the same. He also assumed other Institute obligations of a specified total ($1,562.75). He was to "use all due and proper diligence to perfect a title to said claim...If when the said title is perfected he shall convey to the first annual Conference of the Methodist Episcopal Church which may be established in the Oregon Territory by the General Conference of the Methodist Episcopal Church in the United States or to the lawfully authorized agents of the said Conference such titles as he may himself obtain to the sixty acre tract in the said body of land known as the Institute Reserve [description of land claim]: In trust that the same shall forever be used and employed as an institution of learning and religion, and under such regulations and laws as may be adopted from time to time by said Conference or its lawfully authorized agents." Until such time as this legal title could be given, the named trustees and their successors were assured of "having the entire control and possession of the same."

After the debts assumed by Willson for the Institute had been paid from proceeds from the sale of lots and land, one thousand dollars was to be paid on finishing the Institute building. After these obligations had been satisfied, the proceeds from sales were to be divided, "two-thirds of the amount for which they are so sold (taking no account of such lots as the said William H. Willson may deem necessary to give away in view to the advancement of the said town of Salem) for the use of the said institution of learning. . . ."

Discharge from the terms of the bond was to be granted when Willson had perfected title to the lands, and paid the specified sums, and turned over the amounts due the Institute, and by conveying to the school "by such title as he may obtain two-thirds in value of the said lands and lots remaining unsold."[7]

William was to receive in return one-third of the land sales proceeds and one-third of the unsold lots and land. To comply with the terms of the new agreement, William sold his land claim for $1,000. It eventually became part of the J.L. Parrish claim extending from present day Capitol and D streets eastward to about Park Avenue.

William remained busy with his various interests and professional roles. In at least one instance he was called upon to give medical testimony to settle a dispute. It happened that about mid-year of 1847 a disagreement between two settlers, Bosworth and Popham, erupted into a fight. Popham died. Bosworth was arrested. Then:

The body was disinterred, and Dr. J. W. Boyle, assisted by Dr. W. H. Willson, opened the body of Popham ...but on his [Boswell's] trial was acquitted by the jury on the testimony of the physicians...[8]

Two new men of influence arrived in Salem on June 27, 1847. James H. Wilbur and his wife traveled to Oregon aboard the same ship that brought the Reverend and Mrs. William Roberts to his new appointment. Reverend Roberts was the man selected to replace Reverend George Gary as Superintendent of the Oregon Mission of the Methodist Church. During the voyage Roberts and Wilbur had become close friends and remained so ever after.

Rev. James H. Wilbur

Rev. William Roberts, third superintendent of the Oregon Mission.

These two newly arrived families found lodging at Oregon City and traveled out from there to get acquainted with the Methodist settlers and with the lay of the land. The Willsons were among those families who welcomed the travelers into their home.

James Wilbur noted in his diary:

July 20, 1847, we go to Br Leslies. am pleased with the Location and general appearance. At 2 Oclock Br R preached at the Institute a verry good time. Stayed with Br Wilson Sister Wilson professes to enjoy the blessing of holiness.

August 14, 1847, Br and Sister Wilson Br Clark & Br Garget called on us enjoyed a good season of prayer this evening: felt the Lord was near to hear and answer prayer. Some seem to be anxious about their souls. I trust God is about to work here.[9]

The Wilburs decided to move from Oregon City to Salem. Mrs. Wilbur and their daughter were escorted by land while Rev. Wilbur and a crew of Kanakas (Hawaiian) men moved their goods by boat. Wilbur and his men spent five arduous days in and on the Willamette River from Bute (Butteville) to the Institute (Salem). For example:

Aug 25, 1847, Today we started with our goods to move to the Institute, arrived at the Bute a little after dark stayed all night with Mr. Hall.

Aug 26 Put my wife and daughter in care of Brs Hoxies & McLane to go by land. Started with the Boat & goods at about nine o clock: found the Walamet very rapid: the night overtook us when we had crossed the Yam Hill River where we struck up a fire and encamped I had prepared myself with a Bare Skin, and a couple of Blankets on which I camped, while the clouds gathered over our heads and some refreshing drops came down upon our unsheltered heads. The skin on which I reposed reminded me that wild Beasts were in the country and as soon as the darkness of night had settled down upon, or around us: the howling of the Wolves, and the Screaming of other unknown wild beasts, assured me that the Skins on which I slept, or on which I was reclining was but a skin representation of the hundreds around me that were walking in darkness seeking prey: Here I spent the night but with little sleep.

Aug 27…breakfast made of bread and Beef and a prayer of thanksgiving from the heart offered to the Lord and we started again for
our destined place…Wading in the water from neck to the depth of my hips more than half of the day the rain is falling plentifully from the clouds…rest well. No wild Beast to disturb the night.

Aug 28 Saturday. I had calculated to get through to day but find we cannot. the day is fine but the river rapid. Wading most of the day in water succeed in getting Boat up the River today about ten miles Camp again for the night and for Sabbath. Some Rain: have had nothing today that I could eat my food today has consisted of a bit of Bread as big as the palm of my hand have a restless night…

Aug 29, Sabbath …Nothing that I can Eat Beef is spoiled and the bread is a pill to swallow. Eat nothing but a small piece of Bread…

Aug 30 Monday Start from our camp at five Oclock eat no breakfast think we shall get through to day. Stream verry rapid have to wade in the water more than half of the time. Feel weak and faint nothing I can eat At 2 Oclock we arrived at the Institute Landing having been from Wednesday morning until Monday 2 Oclock Succeed in getting an ox team and getting my goods from the Boat to the Parsonage at ten Oclock at night. Stay with Br Parrish. I should have said that I took supper with Sister Wilson and never do I remember to have eaten a meal that relished as well.

Sept 4 We have goods arranged and every thing seems much like home. Feel quite lame I think in consequence of wading in the water.[10]

When, three months later, on November 29, 1847, the Indians attacked the Whitman mission, it was a severe blow to the settlers of the Willamette Valley for a variety of reasons. Foremost was the friendship between the Whitmans and the families of the Oregon Mission. Both Marcus and Narcissa had been guests in the homes of the Methodists, including the Willsons, and the deaths of the Whitmans was cause for personal grief. Also, the valley settlers saw this Indian uprising as the prelude to a united Indian attack throughout the Oregon country, and the settlers had no organized defense.

Word of the Whitman Massacre was received in Oregon City on December 8, 1847. The legislature of the provisional government was meeting at the time, and they quickly agreed to send fifty mounted men to effect a rescue of the hostages, and to organize several hundred men into an army to pursue the Indians and capture the killers. The provisional government had no money to fund these activities, so a commission was set up to solicit funds and loans from the local population and from Fort Vancouver. The settlers had little actual money, consequently they pledged crops and orders on the stores. James Douglas, Chief Factor at Fort Vancouver, was not allowed to make loans. It seemed as if no cash could be found for provisioning the local army.

However, the situation was so serious that James Douglas accepted securities from Governor Abernethy and commissioners Applegate and Lovejoy, and in return advanced about $1000 worth of equipment which allowed the first company of Oregon riflemen to take the field.

The original commissioners continued to seek funds, but by mid December they had only $3600 secured, a much too insufficient amount to finance an army of 500 men traveling in winter through areas where construction of wagon roads would be required. The first commission resigned, and the legislature appointed A. L. Lovejoy, Hugh Burns and W. H. Willson to mount a new effort. These commissioners had to settle for taking orders on the stores in Oregon City, frequently being obliged to discount the subscriptions by twenty-five percent in order to get cash. The cash then was used at Fort Vancouver and elsewhere to purchase the hand tools for road building. The citizens and the volunteers doing the work provided much of the equipment, accepting a receipt from the provisional government for any large amount of personal property used in the war effort.

An example of the cost of goods in Oregon City comes from a letter dated December 20, 1847, written by Reverend Wm. Roberts.

Flour $4/hundred, Sugar 12 cents, Butter 25 cents per lb, Tea $1.50, Coffee 25 cents, Nails 20 cents per lb, fir wood $3, oak and ash $4.... it is by no means certain that any horse can be had for love or money.[11]

One aftereffect of the Whitman Massacre touched the lives of families in Salem and on the Tualatin Plains for several years. Among the survivors were four Sager sisters. They and their two older brothers and a younger sister had been orphaned in 1844 when their parents died on the Oregon Trail. With the help of other families in the train, the seven children made it to the Whitman mission. The Whitmans provided a home for the Sager children and eventually adopted them. The two teenage boys, John and Francis, were killed in the massacre. Their next youngest sister died from complications of the measles a few days later. The four remaining girls

were part of the group held hostage by the Cayuse Indians until Peter Skene Ogden of the Hudson Bay Company effected their release.

Upon their arrival at Oregon City, Catherine, age 12, and Henrietta, age 3, were taken in by Rev. and Mrs. William Roberts. Soon after, Henrietta was given to another family. Catherine remained with the Robertses until she married.

Elizabeth, age 10, spent two years with the Robb family. When they left for California in 1849, Elizabeth went to live with William and Chloe. Elizabeth later wrote:

... Mrs. Robb got Mrs. W. H. Willson, for whose husband Willson Square in Salem is named, to take me. J. K. Gill married one of Mrs. Willson's daughters.

I worked for the Willsons for a year. During that time I attended the Oregon Institute... After staying for a year with the Willsons I went to work at the home of J. L. Parrish. Mrs. Parrish at that time was slightly deranged, but most of the time she was very good to me. Later she lost her mind entirely.[12]

Matilda, age 8, lived with Reverend and Mrs. Henry Spaulding for four months. She was then sent to live with a young couple, Mr. and Mrs. Geiger, on the Tualatin Plains.

The older Sager girls and many other survivors of the Whitman Massacre joined the various valley settlements and became part of the fabric that made those small communities strong. And strength was needed. Fears of Indian uprisings continued for years and several occurred. Also, people of strong wills and strong opinions collided in true frontier fashion as the settlements grew.

William and Reverend Roberts undoubtedly had some disagreements regarding management of the Institute claim. Roberts wrote in his December 20, 1847, letter to the mission board:

A few remarks on the Oregon Institute and I have done, the claim on which the building is located is now held by Wm. H. Wilson in trust for a Board of Managers and excepting the Buildings and a reserve of 60 acres he is to have one third of all the claim for holding it etc. The arrangement was concocted before I came and consummated in the presence of Mr. Gary a day or two before he left. [Reverend Roberts was in Oregon and was a member of the group which met with the lawyer, J.Q. Thornton. It was to this group that Willson pledged $100,000 in bonds on July 11, 1847]. If Bro. Wilson were a thorough going business man it might be a tolerable plan but as it is I dislike *it exceedingly, and am trying to persuade him to give it into other hands. It is possible I may succeed. Bro. Wilbur could hold it just as well and it would cost nothing and he would transact the business in due form and order. …Oregon City seems to be the proper place*

for me to reside, at least for the present and is the key to the whole territory.[13]

Reverend Roberts remained in Oregon City and William and Chloe continued to reside in Salem, but this would not be the last disparaging opinion expressed by Roberts regarding William.

[1] Gatke, Robert M., *Chronicles of Willamette,* p 89.
[2] Ibid., p 93.
[3] "Report on Oregon, 1846," by Lieutenant Neil M. Howison, *Oregon Historical Quarterly,* V. 14, p 44.
[4] Gatke, p 90.
[5] "Reminiscences of F. X. Matthieu," by H. S. Lyman, *Oregon Historical Quarterly,* V. 1, p 95.
[6] "Diary of Reverend George Gary—III (Continued)," Notes by Charles Henry Carey, *Oregon Historical Quarterly,* V. 24, p 326.
[7] Gatke, p 189-191.
[8] *Salem Directory 1871,* p 45 & 47.
[9] Wilbur, J. H., *Travels of J. H. Wilbur,* p 88 & 91.
[10] Gatke, p 98 & 99.
[11] "Roberts, Reverend William, Third Superintendent of the Oregon Mission, The Letters of," Edited by Robert Moulton Gatke, *Oregon Historical Quarterly,* V. 21, p 41-43.
[12] Helm, Mike, Editor, *Conversations With Pioneer Women* ; The Lockley Files by Fred Lockley, p 62.
[13] "Roberts, Reverend William, Third Superintendent of the Oregon Mission, The Letters of," Edited by Robert Moulton Gatke, *Oregon Historical Quarterly,* V. 21, p 41-43.

Part 7: The Willsons In Salem •1848-1849

As 1848 opened, an army of 400 men, including both soldiers and teamsters, under the command of Colonel Gilliam, was on its way to the Whitman mission site. The men would have a constant need for equipment to clear roads, for wagons and teams, for harness and feed, and for food and clothing to name only some of the many supplies that had to come from the settlements. William Willson would continue as a commissary agent throughout the Cayuse War.

Though the settlers were generous with orders on the stores and with their volunteer labor, the shortage of money in the settlements really hampered the commissary efforts. A letter written by Rachel Fisher Mills on March 13, 1848, provides glimpses into several aspects of the daily life in the settlements.

Oregon City appears to be quite A flourishing little town there is something of A spirit of reform existing there, there is A temperance meeting A licium two common day schools, and two diferent religious meeting up there. he situation of the place seems to me to be rougher than any place that I ever seen in Iowa. the bluff coming up to within a stonethrow of the river, leaves A small space for A city, but its advantages of mill privileges can not be exceled in any place the falls of willamet being just at the upper edge of town.

There is a great call for machanics of different kind, (vis) Cabinet, Chair Sadling, coopering, shoemaking, fanmaking, thrashing, tanner brickmaking and laying, hatting wheelmaking housejoiner and millright these are all in good demand and perhaps others that I do not think of.

Women work is from one to three dollars per

week. wheat is $7 per bu. pork 6-10 cents per lb, bacon from 16 to 20 salt 50 cents per bushel masured at that, Sugar from 5 to 12 cents per lb, coffee from 3 to 5 lbs to the dollar, factory (made cloth, usually cotton) from 10 to 20 cents per yd, beef from 2 1/2 to 3 cents per lb.

Fruits of some kind grow in abundance such as strawberries, gooseberries, raspberries, blackberries, hucleberries, cranberries, dewberries, sallal berries sarvis berries, etc there is not much fruit that grows in trees unless it is planted. The growth of timber is pine, fur, cedar, hemlock, white oak, alder, ash, cottonwood, dogwood, cherry, maple and hazle the main growth of which is Evergreen. They make brooms, barrel hoops and wriths of hazle they also use cherry for brooms etc.…there is salmon and trout fish here plenty and there is deer, bear, tigar elk panther and wolves plenty there is chickens turkeys and ducks that is tame and wild fouls about as they were there [Iowa] except wild turkeys there is none of them here. [1]

In the previous year William Roberts had chosen to locate in Oregon City and thereby made it the headquarters for the Oregon mission which he supervised. From June of 1844 the Methodists' mission was to supply itinerant preachers for the widely scattered settlers of the Oregon Country, with the majority of the preachers travelling the Willamette Valley and between the Umpqua settlements of southern Oregon. This is a new definition of "mission" as contrasted to their use of the word when Jason Lee was establishing a group of "mission" settlements for the purpose of teaching the Indians about Christianity.

Reverend Roberts wrote with regard to financial considerations of the work he superintended:

Oregon City, March 18th, 1848...I now present the fiscal state of the mission,...there is due to the mission for property sold by Bro. Gary as follows...Judson and Wilson $5122.20 do. of $500...Judson and Willsons Notes are for the Mills and property near the institute payment in currency. The installment for Sep. 1847 and interest is behind except 237. and some lumber for a barn. Wilson is dissatisfied with his responsibility and wishes to get his name off the notes. He thinks Bro. Gary favors his claim on this property as per letter he (Wilson) has written to the board and represents him (Br. Gary) as saying if the '47 instalment was met those for '48 and '49 would perhaps be remitted by the board and certainly not be crowded. If I were to say a word here it would be this that I have not a particle of belief that the board ever ought or ever will remit a farthing for any such plea as is put in his letter. But then all this answers to baffle me in any attempts to collect the notes. ...Wilson, Leslie, Beers, and Abernethy's bond for $4437.83 for the Institute payable in July 1851, etc etc....The amount of property held by the mission is about as follows,...Parsonage at the Institute with 200 acres $1380.08. [2]

Another aspect of his work that provided numerous difficulties for Reverend Roberts was that of ministering to the Oregon settlers.

What I refer to chiefly, is peculiar to newly settled countries, such as "The Scattered State of The Population." It was estimated that there was a population of eight thousand in the country previous to the arrival of the last emigration, which itself amounted to from three to five thousand. But the difficulty is to find them. The arrangement of our provisional government, by which a person, under certain conditions, can secure a mile square of land, tends directly to distribute the people all over the country, and operates most prejudicially against gathering of any considerable congregations in any one place. Our only recourse is to go from one cabin to another, through prairie and forest, which is a slow process, requiring more time and men, and, I may add, grace, than we have at present: add to this the most "impassable state of the roads during the rainy season." We have as yet but very few bridges, and the crossing of many of the streams is perilous and often impossible. Some of the sloughs are as miry as that of Despond, into which if Bunyon's Pliable ever gets, he is likely, after a desparate struggle or two, to get out of the mire on that side which is next to his own house. [3]

During the spring of 1848, Roberts calculated that the whole population of settlers may have numbered from 8000 to 13,000 people scattered across the valley and into the coast range. Of these, nearly 2000 lived in bustling Oregon City where 185 houses, one Methodist church and one Catholic church, two flour mills and two sawmills had been built. Down river about 12 miles Portland was just beginning, that location being acknowledged as the head of ship navigation. Reverend Roberts had no population figures for Portland but he knew of a considerable population on the Tualatin Plains 25 miles west of Oregon City. He saw French Prairie, stretching between Oregon City and Salem, as primarily a group of French speaking Canadians belonging to the Catholic Church and obviously not a promising area of influence for the Methodists.

As more settlers came into the country it was not surprising that claim jumping and other land disputes continued. William, as agent for the Board of Trustees for the Oregon Institute, had at least one incident to deal with.

Early in 1848 one Joseph Caples made an effort to establish a claim to a portion of the land so recorded, but was brought before the court, and a decision rendered against him, and he was ejected by the Sheriff, and the cabin he had built was delivered to W. H. Willson, agent of the Institute, who speedily demolished the same. [4]

In July, 1848, Reverend George H. Atkinson, a Congregationalist minister, made diary entries which fill in more details about the Willsons in Salem and the activities of the Methodists, as he observed them from his "outside" position.

Dr. Wilson has a young babe. He now lives in the Institute Building. It is a large and noble structure for an academy at the side of a prairie. A town is laid out. Several good houses are already erected. Several of the brethren own the claims around. Bro. Paris (Parrish), Bro. Waller, etc. Four of the ministers and one licentiate live at that place. They go out to different points to preach on the Sabbath. Their system is fully in operation in the upper country. Their ministers go regularly to different places to preach. They have the largest number of members and a great number of preachers compared with our number. They are of the same grade as in the states except that two or three or four are more educated, having come out as missionaries. [5]

William was one of those employed to preach in the Tualatin Plains and Portland areas but he soon discovered that the gold fever had greatly reduced the number of people to be served. During the summer of 1848 news about California's gold caused such excitement in Oregon that nearly every man and teenage boy who could possibly do so outfitted himself and left for the gold fields. The Willsons continued to reside in Salem.

Some major changes were occurring, though often so slowly or unheralded as to remain unnoticed until much later. For one thing, the federal government finally acknowledged that the U.S. citizens in the Oregon Country should be officially recognized. It extended the status and protection they requested by establishing the Territory of Oregon on August 18, 1848. This was in part another aftereffect of the Whitman Massacre. News of the territorial status would take some time to reach Oregon.

Also, Indian threats, both real and rumored, to attack the Willamette settlements continued to stir anxiety in the people. Chloe wrote:

> *Sept. 14, 1848, The Lord has been with me since my last date in six troubles and in the seventh he did not forsake me. During all the difficulties with the Indians my trust has been with the living God and my mind staid upon Him.*

> *Birth of Frances Willson. Thank the Lord O my soul for his goodness to thee. My heavenly Father has increased my responsibilities by committing to my charge a lovely daughter. I feel that the trust (is) one of very great importance and that my influence upon her will be felt through all eternity. My constant prayer is that I receive grace and wisdom from God to discharge my whole duty to the child. Grant O my Father that she may be an eminently devoted Christian on earth and a glorified spirit in heaven and to thy name shall be the endless praise.* [6]

(There is some question as to the year of Frances Willson's birth in the Earle Howell information quoted by Seiber. However, George Atkinson's quote that "Dr. Willson has a young babe" in mid July 1848, seems to imply that Frances was then but a few weeks old at most. Also, J. K. Gill's family Bible shows Frances' birth date as July 13, 1848, and that Frances was baptised by Reverend David Leslie on August 28, 1848.)

The evolving business community in Salem got a real boost during the summer. Barter was the accepted method of exchange though a few coins were available. When Thomas Cox arrived in 1847 he had a small stock of dry goods in his wagons for which he found a ready market. In the summer of 1848 he built a two story house on the northeast corner of Commercial and Ferry streets, opening the lower floor as a store. This was the first store building in Salem and the first structure built after Salem was surveyed. There were perhaps six houses in Salem at the time.

However, during the autumn and winter, business in Salem was nearly at a standstill. Even that year's immigration was reduced by people turning south at Fort Hall to join the chase for gold, so there were few able-bodied males available to hire for farming, carpentering, or timber cutting and hauling. Generally it was the women and children who kept the young settlements and homesteads going.

In December of 1848 the legislative session failed for lack of a quorum. Several of the legislators had joined the mass exodus to the California gold mines. A special election was held, and on February 5, 1849, a special session of the legislature met to deal with the expenses of the Cayuse War and to provide for coinage.

Superimposed on the trade in wheat, pelts or orders on the stores was the advent of gold dust and nuggets. Inconsistent measurement made dust inconvenient and impractical. Then the Hudson's Bay Company dropped the price of gold from 16 dollars the troy ounce to 12, 11, then 7 dollars. Trade nearly halted, ships sold their cargo elsewhere for lack of a stable medium. Even with Oregon's territorial status, no provision was made for providing coinage. Desparate, the people demanded the provisional government mint some coins.

The provisional legislature determined to establish a mint, and selected William to be the melter and coiner. But before the work got under way, Governor Joseph Lane arrived, the Territorial Government began, and minting of coins was declared illegal. Determined to do something to improve the situation, eight community leaders agreed to form the Oregon Exchange Company, and operate as a private mint. Federal laws notwithstanding, coins were minted in five and ten dollar denominations. As these Beaver coins began to circulate, the price of gold steadied at 16 dollars the troy ounce. The Beaver money was of such purity that each coin contained more gold than those minted by the federal government. Oregon Exchange Company lasted only a few months but it was a sincere attempt to help solve the perennial problem of a standardized medium of exchange for the early Oregon settlers.

Among the eight men who made up the private mint were Theophilus Magruder who had been both recorder and auditor, W.H. Rector who was a member of the legislature, George Abernethy who had been the Oregon Mission steward and the governor, and William H. Willson who had been the first treasurer—all officials of the provisional government.

The change from provisional to territorial government seems to have occurred with very little fanfare. The various historical descriptions imply that Governor Abernethy handed to Governor Lane the records kept during the provisional period, Lane accepted them, declared the Territorial Government in operation and everyone went on about their business undisturbed and unimpressed.

Chloe's diary offers a few final insights into what the Willsons were doing domestically.

May 21…My dear Frances is beginning to require correction and wholesome discipline. I feel my insufficiencey. I look to thee for help, O my Father, in training her for the skies.

We have held another annual meeting of our Juvenile Temperance Society. It was very interesting and profitable to the children. The Lord has heard and answered my prayers for this infant society. The little band which I was permitted to organize six years ago has come to be quite a cold water army. May the blessing of the Lord still rest upon the juvenile band.

My dear companion is away on an errand of Mercy for his Master. O that the Lord may bless and direct him in all things.

Time is hurrying me on to eternity. Thirty-one years of my life have already past, it is my hearts desire that what remains may be devoted to God.

June 24, My dear companion has gone to Fort George to see what can be done for the souls of the people. He has been absent several weeks, and writes me that he has been greatly blessed in his own soul. I trust his efforts to preach will be crowned with success. O my father attend thy word with thine own spirit's powers. I think my devotion to God and his cause is becoming more consistant. O that I may hence forward walk before the Lord with a perfect heart. Life is made up of little things. I fear that I have not always been so careful of the happiness of others in small matters as I should have been. I would bear in mind, that "nothing is a trifle which is displeasing to a friend, and that nothing is insignificant which gives pleasure to a friend." [7]

For several years, a board of nine Oregon residents had been the trustees who managed the Oregon Institute. The Methodist Episcopal Church Board of Missions in New York continued to select many of the teachers and pay their way to Oregon even though the Board of Missions had no direct control nor legal connection with the Oregon Institute. In September 1849 the Methodist ministers on the west coast organized the Oregon and California Conference of the Methodist Church. At the first session, which was held in the Oregon Institute, the men reaffirmed the action taken in 1842 that as a branch of the M-E Church, they would make every reasonable effort to sustain the Oregon Institute. The group also formed the Oregon and California Missionary Society and William was elected to the Board of Managers and served with the Reverends Roberts, Leslie, Waller, Wilbur, Parrish and McKinney.

In his new capacity as president of the Oregon and California Missionary Society, William Roberts reported to the Board of Missions:

Connected with the [Oregon Institute] building is a reserve of 60 acres forming the South East corner, nearly, of the entire claim of 640 acres. The entire claim is held by Wm. H. Willson for which he is to receive one undivided third but on this reserve he has no claim for 1 third as he has per agreement July 11, 1847 on the other part for holding the claim and getting title from the United States.

No doubt need be entertained for a moment as to the safety of the Money [owed on] the Institute, none whatever, for it will be payed unquestionably. The property is valuable and increasing in value every day, "The Location is admirable", the land good for the purposes for which it is needed, and in the "absence of blunders and mismanagement" both here and with the Board may with God's blessing be made available for the most valuable purposes. [8]

As 1849 rolled into 1850, trade between Oregon and California increased rapidly. Food, lumber and other raw materials flowed to the California miners and gold dust flowed to Oregon farmers and mill owners. Speculation in Oregon land and businesses was frequently excessive, so bankruptcy was all too common when a market change occurred. This exuberance for speculation continued well into the next decade.

---

[1] Holmes, Kenneth L., *Covered Wagon Women 1840-1849*, V. 1, p 105-107.

[2] "Roberts, Reverend William, The Third Superintendent of the Oregon Mission, The Letters of, Second Installment," Edited by Robert Moulton Gatke, *Oregon Historical Quarterly*, V. 22, p 226.

[3] Gatke, Robert M., *Chronicles of Willamette*, p 72-73.

[4] *Salem Directory 1871*, p 21.

[5] "Diary of Rev. George H. Atkinson 1847-1858," Edited by E. Ruth Rockwood (Part IV), *Oregon Historical Quarterly*, V. 40, p 355.

[6] Seiber, Richard, Editor: *The Journals of Brewer and Clarke*, p 130.

[7] Ibid., p 132.

[8] "Letters of the Reverend William M. Roberts, Third Superintendent of the Oregon Mission, Third Installment," Edited by Robert Moulton Gatke, *Oregon Historical Quarterly*, V. 23, p 166.

Two additional plats were recorded in 1850, extending Salem's boundaries and considerably enlarging the Salem townsite. In February, L. H. Judson and J. B. McClane platted North Salem and in March, William Willson officially recorded the portion stretching east from Church Street to Capitol Street and north from State Street to Division Street, the approximate southern boundary of North Salem.

Also in March, various settlers recorded seeing eruptions of both Mount St. Helens and Mount Baker. Though widely observed, they caused some comment but apparently no concern.

The Donation Land Law passed by Congress in 1850 secured to settlers already present on the land as much as 640 acres for a husband and wife, each to own half of the total acreage. The white population in the entire territory was only 13, 297 and the widely scattered homesteads lamented by Reverend Roberts in 1848 continued to develop. The Donation Land Claim provision encouraged people to settle rather far apart. This made road building impractical. Oregon's rainy winters kept the swales, sloughs, creeks and rivers full, and made traveling across land very slow, difficult and dangerous. Drownings of people and their horses were all too common and being mired in mud was always possible.

The *Oregon Statesman* on January 8, 1853, published the following dramatic description of the difficulties of travel which were typical throughout the early settlement years.

> *Learning of the arrival of the steamer, we dispatched a messenger to Portland for papers, but after repeated fruitless efforts to ride, walk or row, he was obliged to give up and return. But on Wednesday morning we were agreeably surprised by the appearance of Mr. A. B. Stuart, Adams and Co.'s messenger, with our usual package of papers and letters. He had made the trip on foot, swimming where he couldn't WADE, and surmounting barriers the less resolute would have pronounced insurmountable...[1]*

Canoes, bateaux, and keel boats continued to be the main conveyances for people and cargo on the only good transportation route, the Willamette River. In the autumn of 1850, the first steamboat provided service on the Columbia River and lower Willamette River. It was another year before steamboats ran on the upper Willamette.

Over the years of white immigration and settlement of the Willamette Valley, public meetings centered most often in Oregon City and the early legislative groups usually met there. However, in mid January 1851, the legislative assembly of the territorial government moved the capital from Oregon City to Salem. Considerable controversy arose but eventually the capital city issue was settled, and the legislative assembly met in the Oregon Institute for the 1851-1852 session. During this legislative session, William was elected a territorial auditor.

Meanwhile, at home, Chloe and William welcomed a second daughter. Laurabelle was born July 9, 1851. She was baptized by Reverend Alvan Waller.

On the national political scene, Oregon's first delegate to Congress, Samuel Thurston, died in 1851. His death left an opening in the most sought after position of territorial government. The territorial delegate to Congress could build his political reputation both locally and nationally while awaiting the day when statehood would be granted and he could act with full official authority. Up to this time, national political parties had little or no bearing on local politics in Oregon. With this election, that situation changed. Joseph Lane, first territorial governor of Oregon, entered the election as a Democrat. Some time later, William became a candidate for the same position. Joseph Lane was a well known politician and popular from the start. The editors of the *Oregon Statesman*, *Milwaukee Star*, *Oregonian*, and *Spectator* supported Lane, who was elected by a vote of 1911 to 426. Among William's political burdens was his association with the missionary group which had supported Samuel Thurston, who had angered many Oregon settlers by his manipulation of the land laws against the claims of Dr. John McLoughlin.

Over the next several years William would serve locally in various capacities and continue to be a very active civic leader. As a member of the newly established Odd Fellows chapter, it was he who suggested it be named Chemeketa. In 1852 he was asked by the legislature to serve on the committee to provide for the reinterment of Samuel Thurston's remains in Oregon soil. Also, William assisted LaFayette Grover who in 1853 assembled and edited an official publication for the legislature titled *The Oregon Archives*, *including the Journals, Governor's Messages and Public Papers of Oregon.* William was on the reception committee for the new Governor of Oregon, John W. Davis, in 1853, and he continued to serve as territorial auditor and county commissioner that year. In February when Alanson Beers died, William and Reverend Thomas Pearne were named as guardians for Beers' four minor children.

William's church and school committments continued,too. No doubt Chloe and William were both pleased when, on January 12, 1853, Willamette University was granted a charter by the territorial legislature. William was one of the new university's original trustees and was elected the board's first secretary. Early in the spring William was elected to the Board of Trustees of the Methodist Episcopal Church in Salem.

The year 1853 was a busy one for the Willsons. Chloe had the care of her home and family. Frances would have her fifth birthday and Laurabelle her second. Chloe would be thirty-five and William, forty-eight. During the summer, William began the construction of an Elizabethan style cottage on the northeast corner of Court and Capitol streets, not far from the site where the first capitol building was being erected.

An interesting new family came to Salem and soon became acquainted with the Willsons. The Reverend Obed and Charlotte Dickinson were sent by the Congregational Church. They traveled 17,000 miles by way of Cape Horn during the winter of 1852 and arrived at the Portland waterfront March 3, 1853.

Portland in 1854.

Their itemized account of moving their household goods from Portland to Salem is a fascinating description of the times. They had their personal baggage and simple household furnishings such as a stove, table, chairs and bedding to handle.

The move took the Dickinsons eighteen days and cost them one hundred and ninety-four dollars. First a drayman to move their baggage to the Oregon City boat—$6.00. Freight to Oregon City—$46.00. A drayman to move the belongings above the falls to the boat dock — $10.00. Board at Oregon City while waiting for the boat to leave—$35.00. Freight charges to Salem—$85.00. Passenger fare for the two of them—$12.00. That trip placed them on the river front in Salem where there would be more drayage charges and board costs.[2]

In his March 25 letter to the American Home Missionary Society, Dickinson described the Methodists' influence in Salem, their successes and failures in promoting the interests of religion. And until he met William, he had had some concern about being welcome.

The proprietor of the town, Dr. Willson, a leading Methodist, is anxious that we should occupy that field. He has given two town lots, valued at five or six hundred dollars, as a site for a meeting house. I do not fear that the influence of the Methodist Church, then, will be turned against us.[3]

The two town lots given to the Congregationalists for a church site were on the southwest corner of Liberty and Center streets.

In 1852, William and a partner had opened a general merchandise store near the steamboat landing. In 1853, William established the first drug store in Salem, locating it one block west of Commercial, near South Mill Creek. In this location he combined his services as a provider of medical advice and of medicine. William was also the agent for A. Myers and Company Nursery. The following year William had a new partner in the general merchandise business. As evidenced by William's business ventures, Salem seemed a village filled with hope and prosperity during the spring and summer of 1853. The settlement of five hundred people provided plenty of business for ten dry goods stores, the flouring mill and two sawmills. Numerous craftsmen, lawyers, physicians and general laborers all found employment.

In June, Obed Dickinson offered this description of what he saw.

...the whole surrounding country [of Salem] is a farming region of singular beauty and fertility. From my short experience, I should judge that the future prospects of the steady growth of this place are quite flattering. It is the present capitol of the territory. A state

house is in process of erection which will probably decide the question of whether it shall be the future capital of the state; and furthermore the prospects of acquiring wealth by agriculture and the fact that it will be the home of most of the State officers when their housing will be expanded have induced a large number engaged in the mercantile business to settle here. Many young men are already here. Perhaps the largest number of inhabitants are of that class.

Money was in a measure plenty—businessmen felt full of hope—the future looked bright for the town of Salem. The seat of Government has just been located here—fifty thousand dollars were to be expended during the summer in building the State House and the County House. Packers from the gold mines were bringing in their gold and every sort of eatable produce was bringing the highest prices. Farmers felt encouraged...[4]

By late summer the high hopes and bright prospects seemed to fade. Prices were high and ready cash became less available. For example, funds for constructing the courthouse were so restricted that the promoters resorted to public subscription. The University, through William as its agent, contributed four lots for the promoters to sell and then apply the proceeds to the building.

About the same time, William's responsibility as agent for the Board of Trustees of the University came to a close. Controversy arose.

Willson proved his claim for the land he had been holding under the bond, making his final proof July 28, 1853. A most unexpected contest developed over the fulfillment of the contract with Willson...Under the land law of 1850, half of the claim was given to the wife. To the confusion of the Board, it faced the fact that the bond it held legally bound Willson and not his wife. No one had cause to anticipate any such new provision in a land law. When the claim was established, one half was vested in Mrs. Willson's name; and, despite long negotiations with her, she refused to allow the bond to impair her legal rights. For a time, the trustees were in great fear that the part of the claim on which the Institute building stood would be made her part, and the Board might lose control of its building and campus; however, when the line was drawn, it followed the State street line, leaving the University campus on Willson's half. After many meetings and much working of committees and personal conferences between leaders of the

Board and Willson, the essential terms of his bond were carried out as they affected his half of the total claim. This compromise, which gave the University nothing from the north half of its lands, was accepted as the only one that could be worked out. It was only natural that members of the Board felt bitterly disappointed, because they had built great hopes on endowing the school from the sale of its land.[5]

The trustees of Willamette University appointed committees to reach an agreement with the Willsons about the land in dispute. Alvan Waller was one of the committee members. Apparently some accord was reached during 1854 because no further mention is made by contemporary chroniclers concerning this issue. Notwithstanding this controversy, both Chloe and William were asked to continue serving the University in various capacities. William remained on the board of trustees until his death. Chloe was asked by the University in the 1860s to fill a position similar to Dean of Women, and she continued her association with the University for a number of years. As several researchers have noted, there were definitely two sides to the issue and after the resolution, lacking evidence to the contrary, life apparently went on with no reproach and with what appear to be representations of respect and trust by all parties.

An *Oregon Statesman* item dated January 3, 1854, noted that Dr. and Mrs. Willson had donated the block of land on which the capitol building was being constructed. This block was on the northern half of the land in dispute.

In the spring of 1854, William was busy with the Temperance Association. At an April meeting he was elected to procure a lecturer, in May at the Marion County Temperance convention he declined nomination for the county council, and in June he was appointed treasurer for the Oregon Temperance Society at their Takenah (Albany) meeting.

The Methodists in Oregon City and Salem planned to hold their annual conference further up the valley, where a number of the Belknap families had settled. Ketturah Belknap wrote:

...we had a Beautiful Early Spring and the weather was all that could be desired, no rain the roads were quite good the ground nice and dry...[6]

A bishop from the Methodist Church headquarters in the East traditionally attended and conducted each annual conference. That year Bishop Matthew Simpson came from New York, across the Isthmus of Panama and up the Pacific coast to attend the Oregon Conference of the Methodist Church. The conference site was Belknap (in the general vicinity of present day Bellfountain), a settlement twenty miles from Corvallis. The description of the bishop's travel experiences clearly illustrates what the local conditions were. To briefly describe the bishop's trip and his appearance at the Belknap Conference site after travelling from Salem in mid March, Ketturah Belknap put it best.

> ...the stranger who had traveled all night over Corduroy Roads and stump Roots, and mud of uncertain and varying depths, who had changed from Wagon to Saddle, and had the last of his long and most trying Journey on Horse back and badly spattered with mud ... advanced to the front, amid shouts and Hallelujahs from all sides...[7]

The bishop's subsequent travel in Oregon was equally arduous. He wrote the following account of his Oregon experiences to his wife.

> I reached my Conference on the Sabbath of its session, after having travelled all Saturday night, my guide missing his way in the woods, conference closed on Tuesday afternoon; that evening I rode twenty miles on horseback to Corvallis; spent there three days waiting for a steamboat, but it was sunk on its passage up, and I started on horseback for Salem, some thirty-two miles distant; but my horse gave out, and I was compelled to walk part of my journey. There I spent Sabbath, preaching twice... left on a steamer for Oregon City... arrived Portland; left by steamer to the Dalles. ...There the steamer above the Cascades was broken, and, after having waited for a sail-boat until Monday, I was obliged to hire an Indian canoe, and with Brother Pearne, who accompanied me, to row up the river. About ten o'clock at night we reached the Indian camp, where, as it rained, we were compelled to lodge in a miserable Indian hut...The next evening we reached the Dalles. There spent Wednesday, Thursday tried to get down the river in a schooner, but, the wind being adverse, after struggling for twenty hours, and being nearly capsized, and escaping by a hands-breadth from being dashed upon the rocks, we left the schooner and took a small boat or skiff. We rowed all night, except three hours, when the crew gave out. Making a fire upon the shore, miles from any house, we threw ourselves upon the ground, and I had a good, sweet sleep. Friday reached the cascades, and Saturday, returned here [Portland]. [8]

As spring turned to summer, the civic leaders of Salem began planning for the annual national celebration. Oregon was still a territory, but national pride was in every settler's heart. William was appointed to the Salem Fourth of July committee which organized the day-long festivities of speeches, music, community picnic dinner, and various races and other entertainment. On the evening of July 4, there was a convivial gathering at the Willson home, where William and Chloe entertained their Willamette University friends. As the newspaper reported:

> It was "a feast of reason and a flow of soul." There was instrumental and vocal music and the board was spread with the bountiful good things of the land. The young ladies and gentlemen of the University were present, and much social zest marked the occasion.[9]

By August, the emotional climate changed again, as was so often the case. Some Rogue River Indians became actively hostile and killed a member of the legislature and a prominent doctor. This uprising caused a new wave of fear to move through the valley. Indeed, from 1853 through 1859 some of the most bitter Indian wars occurred and the fear of attack was never far from the minds of the settlers.

Obed Dickinson wrote of continued Indian war preparations and concerns in mid October.

> Four days ago, a proclamation arrived in this place, calling for an enlistment of eight companies of volunteers, of sixty men each for the war, to rescue Major Holler [Haller] and to save defenseless citizens...now the mounted troops are almost ready to march to the scene of hostilities. It is reported that nearly all the tribes this side the mountains are engaged to stand by each other. If so there are more Indians than whites. What will be the result, God only knows.[10]

Not only did the settlers have the Yakima campaign to wage, but they also had the uprising in southern Oregon to contend with at the same time. The territory was short of arms, and this combined with the need to call out hundreds of men made prolonged campaigns on two fronts quite a challenge.

A final note regarding 1854 is that during the year, Margaret Jewett Smith Bailey, a teacher who had come with Reverend David Leslie's missionary party in 1837, published what has been referred to as Oregon's first confession story, "The Grains, or Passages in the Life of Ruth Rover, with

Occasional Pictures of Oregon, Natural and Moral." This was an unsubtle attempt to denounce various members of the mission group, and William in particular. William and Chloe were probably aware of the slanderous material. No contemporary even hints of there being any truth to Mrs. Bailey's accusations and assertions.

By 1855 Salem had a daily stage connection with Portland which helped the process of settlement. It probably transported some of the Methodists to their meeting to organize the Marion County Bible Society, an auxilliary to the OregonTerritorial Bible Society. The main speaker was Obed Dickinson of the Congregational Church, who subsequently was elected president. William, along with Linnas Brooks and Gustavus Hines among others, was elected to the executive committee of the new group.

Kate Augusta Lee, the third daughter and last child, was born to Chloe and William on October 25, 1855. This infant was baptized by Reverend David Leslie.

Late in the fall of 1855, the legislature moved into the nearly completed capitol building, located on the same site as the present capitol, though the earlier building faced west. Because the territorial library had been set up and made available there, various legislators had begun frequenting the building throughout the day and evening hours to use the law books and other materials in preparing plans and legislation. Early in the morning of December 30, 1855, the new building was consumed by a fire which was strongly suspected but never proven to have been arson caused. A joint committee on the burning of the capitol called witnesses whose testimony was then put in writing.

There were several eye witnesses to the fire, only one will be cited here.

Wm. H. Willson: I reside in Salem near where the State House stood. My residence is about sixty rods from the ruins of the building, in a north-easterly direction.

At about half past one o'clock, Sunday morning, December 30, 1855, I was alarmed by the appearance of a strange light, which shown into my bed chamber window, from the outside, in the direction of the State House. I sprang to the window and discovered the State House on fire. I noted the time by my clock, then went the second time to the window to see how the fire appeared before going out; it was half past one. The fire was perceivable only at the two windows on the north side, near the

east end. The fire had evidently been at work for a short time on the out side when I saw it, as the boards nailed up to close the unglazed windows had not yet been charred; the flames which were bursting out of these windows were not more than two or three feet long when I first saw them. The color of the flames was yellow, like that caused by the burning of turpentine. After noting the appearance of the fire, I then ran to the door and cried —FIRE! FIRE! as loud as I could. At that time I saw no appearance of fire at any other of the windows on the north side nor on the east end; the two windows of the library room, on the north side, were dark. I went and dressed and ran toward the burning building. As I was stepping through my gate, I saw that the fire was breaking out through the frieze over the two windows, then it made its way rapidly through the roof of the north-east corner— thence rapidly over the roof to the south. The night was still, but what air there was stirring, was from the north-east, and the fire spread to the south-west. When I arrived at the building, I passed round to the south side; there the building was generally in flames. While I stood there the windows in the Council chamber, which were darkened by smoke, began to redden and the glass began to drop out, and soon the whole was in flames. From the time I discovered the fire, it was about one hour when the whole building was in ruins; not a stick standing.

The north-east corner was entirely burnt out to the naked frame, before the other portion of the building mentioned had been demolished by the flames. There were two windows of the Hall of Representatives, on the north side of the building and in sight of my house; at the time of the breaking out of the fire, these windows were also dark. All the rooms finished and occupied by the Legislative Assembly were on the west end of the building and lighted partly by side windows on the north and south.

Mr. Earle, the door-keeper of the Council, boarded at my house. He came in about half past five, P.M., and said he was not going back to the State House that night; said all the gentlemen who usually stayed there to write had gone away and would not return that night. He stayed at my fire side until bed time and retired to his lodgings. After the building had been burnt, I went to his room and found him still asleep in his bed.[11]

First Oregon State Capitol building.

James F. Earle resided near Corvallis but, as doorkeeper of the Council, stayed in Salem during the territorial legislative session. Mr. Earle had charge of the building most of the time during the Assembly's recess. Part of his testimony was:

I boarded at Dr. Willson's, near the State House. Did not know of the State House being burnt until about half past 2 o'clock, the next morning, when Dr. Willson waked me up and informed me of the fact and asked me if any person had been sleeping in the State House; he said it had burnt down, except fragments of the posts. [12]

While the territorial legislature pursued its inquiry into the burning of the capitol building, it also searched out meeting space for all governmental purposes, and the business of government went on. It would be nearly two decades before another capitol building would be constructed in Oregon.

A deed dated March 6, 1856, indicates that William and Chloe Willson conveyed title to the west half of lots 7 and 8, block 71 to the trustees of the Methodist Episcopal Church, the land on which the present First Methodist Church stands in Salem.

In the early spring William sold lots 1 and 2 in block 32 to Alvan Waller. Waller sold the lots (at 285 Liberty Street NE) in 1861. They were residential properties for decades.

Also in the spring of 1856, William sold to Dr. W. K. Smith the drug store he had established three years earlier. William retained headquarters space for his professional practice.

Unexpectedly, on April 17, William H. Willson died. Lewis H. Judson offered the following account.

...Dr. Wm. H. Willson, proprietor of the University section of land upon which the town of Salem is located, died very suddenly. He had been suffering more or less for some months, but not so much as to confine him to his house, and on the morning of the day of his death, walked from his residence on Capital street opposite the old University building, down into the business part of town. His health was no worse that morning than it had been for some months, and he appeared lively and full of mirth as usual, and while sitting in a chair in W. K. Smith's store, on Ferry street, nearly opposite the Salem Flouring Mills, he suddenly became lifeless, and was soon carried to his home.

Dr. Willson was 51 years of age at the time of his death. He had been raised in Northern New York, near Lake Champlain, reared up to steady industry, was a cooper by trade in the Atlantic States, and had been on one voyage on a whaleship as a cooper, in the Pacific ocean, before he embarked at New York in 1836 for Oregon. He left the Atlantic coast in the employ of the Oregon Mission of the M.E. Church, in company with Dr. Elijah White, physician to the Mission, and Alanson Beers, blacksmith to the Mission, with their families, he [Willson] being unmarried, and after some months delay at the Sandwich Islands, arrived in Oregon in June or July, 1837. He was married in the summer of 1840 to Miss Chloe A. Clark, one of the four single ladies who came to Oregon in the Missionary company just before.

Dr. Willson was a man of a genial and lively turn of mind, a practical man full of life, a man of strong social feelings, a man of sterling integrity, one whom the public looked upon as utterly incapable of a mean action, a man of strong resolution, as evinced by one incident particularly in the latter years of his life: The Doctor had been for many years in the habitual use of tobacco, both smoking and chewing, even immoderately. He at length, about twelve years before his death became thoroughly convinced that the use of the narcotic was an injury to his health. He made up his mind to quit the use of it at once and forever, and he took the following method of conquering the long indulged appetite for the weed which had been continued from boyhood. He put a piece of the best tobacco in his vest pocket, and every time he thought "tobacco" he would take it out and look at it, smell of it, praise it as being first rate tobacco, but said to it in reference to getting into his mouth, 'you can't come in here,' and after carrying this first rate specimen of his old and long indulged solace in his pocket about six weeks, found himself entirely cured of the desire of it, and never returned again to its use. The above narration the writer hereof had from the Doctor's own lips. Dr. Willson was an accredited member in good standing in the M. E. Church, from the town he left in New York, in 1837 [1836], till his death; and a few years before his death, held the position of local preacher. As a man and a Christian, he had in all respects as few faults or failings and as many excellencies as are often found among fallible mortals. We trust he "rests from his labors, and his works follow him," and he has already entered upon his everlasting reward.[13]

Reverend Gustavus Hines offered this tribute:

No persons in the country showed a more lively interest in the welfare of the school [Oregon Institute/Willamette University], and none were more liberal in the use of time and money in its support, than were Mr. and Mrs. Willson. Dr. Willson himself was one of the early secretaries of the Board, and officiated in that capacity for some years. He was also for years the efficient agent of the Board, and contributed much by his counsel as well as means to carry forward the enterprise toward ultimate success...True to the interests of the Church, and faithful in the observance of all religious duties, from his geniality and kindness, and the vein of good feeling that always seemed to be running through his entire nature, he was remarkably popular in all the associations of life.[14]

William's burial was near the family residence on Court and Capitol streets. A few years later his remains were removed to the I.O.O.F. Cemetery (Pioneer Cemetery) where a marble monument marks the gravesite he shares with Chloe.

Sometime after William's death, Chloe took the three little girls and returned to the East near her relatives.

The Marion County assessment roll of 1856 listed Mrs. C.A. Willson, widow, as having 20 acres of real estate valued at $3000, eighteen lots valued at $3000, and personal property valued at $150 for a total taxable property value of $6150.

Changes continued apace in town and at Willamette University. For example, in 1861 the University board granted the new Willamette Woolen Manufacturing Company the right to construct a mill race across University property, where it still runs today, and a building site was donated for the company's mill. Conversely, travel conditions in the interior and the lot of the ministers changed very little.

The physical circumstances surrounding the work of the frontier minister in those years were forbidding in pressure and magnitude. When William Alfred Tenney came to Oregon as a Congregational missionary minister...he walked forty miles getting from Salem to his Eugene charge, walked in mud and November rain, wading through rain-swollen streams, wet through, with blistered feet—and then had to walk back again to get his wife and belongings. It took Tenney five days through overflowing creeks in the flooding upper Willamette Valley riding on ox carts or lumber wagons to get his wife and belongings from Salem to Eugene. It would take a stubborn courage for him then to stand before a few hardy and half-interested people at Skinner's Butte and attempt to preach the gospel of a loving, caring God.[15]

---

[1] Gatke, Robert M., *Chronicles of Willamette*, p 126.
[2] Oliver, Egbert, Editor, *Obed Dickenson's War Against Sin In Salem*, Intro. p. iii.
[3] Ibid., p 3.
[4] Ibid., p 5 & 9.
[5] Gatke, p 190-191.
[6] Ibid., p 127.
[7] Ibid., p 128.
[8] Crooks, George, *Life of Matthew Simpson*, p 322-323.
[9] *Oregon Statesman* July 1, 1854.
[10] Oliver, p 54.
[11] *Ladd and Bush Annual 1931*, p 20.
[12] Ibid., p 15.
[13] "Sketches of Salem," by Lewis H. Judson, *Salem Directory 1871*, p 37.
[14] Hines, Gustavus, *Oregon and Its Institutions*, p 173-174.
[15] Oliver, p 188.

Though Chloe and the girls left Oregon for a few years, they were destined to return. In the meantime, Salem and the other settlements in the territory continued to change and grow, if sometimes slowly and with difficulty.

For example, the development of public schools barely continued because the men of wealth bitterly opposed the taxation proposals. Or, when adopting a state constitution, the majority voted to oppose slavery and to exclude both free Negroes and mulattoes from residence in the state, to prevent newly arriving Chinese from holding or operating any mining claim, and to disqualify Negroes, mulattoes, and Chinese from voting. On the other hand, those same men did vote to protect a married woman's property or pecuniary rights from the debts or contract obligations of her husband.

Obed Dickinson described the psychological state of the people around him in Salem during the summer of 1857.

Although our Indian troubles have been at an end for more than a year, we have not, till this summer, settled back into the quiet of peaceful improvement. Now, things in our town are going ahead as if people expected to make Oregon their home. That excitable, feverish do-nothing state of mind, which many of the people of this territory have been in for the last two years, is giving way to more rational feelings. The excuse for doing nothing for body or soul...the "I don't expect to stay here" excuse so often heard by ministers...is heard less than it was a year ago. The people of this town are beginning to make improvements more as if they expected to make Oregon their home for life. Good substantial dwellings are being erected. A school house . . . is going up as if the people expected to stay here for the next twenty years and educate their children in it. A woollen factory, also. . .is henceforth to exert its influence in Salem. . . All these things we regard as civilized and Christianizers of the people.[1]

In 1858, Chloe deeded two lots to Archbishop Blanchet for $100. The deed stipulates that those lots are to be used *forever* as a Roman Catholic church site.

A financial depression hit Salem early in 1859 when sales to the California gold seekers dramatically slowed. Then, the federal auditors reduced by 55 percent the Indian war expenditures claimed by Oregon and Washington territories. This was a huge loss for the sparsely settled areas to sustain, and many business failures resulted.

During the year, Willamette University urgently needed a piano and somehow in this time of scarcity, found $250 to buy an instrument from Chloe.

The people of Salem received the news of statehood from a messsenger on horseback who rode up from Oregon City. He and the news were received with little enthusiasm. Persistent hard times had reduced the hopeful outlook of many, and the prospect of additional taxes to pay for a state government loomed ominously when they considered their pinched means. At the time, the benefits of statehood seemed heavily outweighed by the disadvantages.

In the spring, according to Ben Maxwell, Rhoda White started a ferry service between Salem and Polk County, using William's old landing at the foot of Ferry Street. The charge was 75 cents for a wagon and team crossing to Polk County, and just 40 cents for the return trip. At the same time, food prices included potatoes at 75 cents a bushel, cheese was 25 cents a pound, eggs were 25 cents a dozen, and wheat $1.00 a bushel.[2]

A large number of immigrants arrived by wagon in the fall, swelling the population of the settlements and causing business to pick up when serving their needs. As would be the custom for several more decades, there was no commercial exploitation of the Christmas season. A primarily commercial yuletide gift exchange had not developed, and if there were special church services, they received little public notice. The new year came with little fanfare, but with very frigid weather which clogged the Columbia River with ice and closed it from Vancouver to The Dalles.

The census for 1860 showed that Portland had more than doubled Salem in population, 2917 to 1068, and that Oregon City was barely holding its own with 428 inhabitants.

During this same time, Chloe and the girls were living on the east coast. Chloe opened her home to students for room and board. In 1861, one of these students was Joseph Gill who, at age 13, had emigrated with his family from England in 1854. Chloe found him to be a very satisfactory young man and allowed him to become acquainted with her oldest daughter, Frances. In the spring of 1862 Joseph Gill and Frances Willson became engaged.

"Important business made it necessary for Mrs. Willson to return to Oregon in 1863 taking her family with her," wrote Joseph K. Gill in his recollections. He joined the Willsons in Salem later.

Robert Gatke described Chloe's continuing association with Willamette University:

In 1864 Mrs. Chloe Clark Willson, who had been the first teacher of the Oregon Institute, "was appointed Governess of the Ladies Department of the University." Into her lovely home young women of the school were taken as boarders, and her supervision and care made it, not a boarding house, but a responsible university home. Part of her work, which continued until Lucy Anna Lee was appointed preceptress, was to give lectures to the girls. We find her lecture for November 29, 1864, on "The Sphere of Women" revealing of the position she took, one which, because of her social prestige and character, must have made a marked impression upon the young women who heard her counsels.

"Do you ask what is the sphere of women?" she phrased the question to answer it:

"Surely not the halls of Legislation, the Bar or the Pulpit—but the sweet Paradise of home—the refined social circle. Do you inquire of her mission? It is to mold character. The instrument with which she is to accomplish this great work—the affections. Love is the power with which she is to melt and mold the character. Gentleness, loveliness, sweetness and purity are the elements of her power. . . . The training which you here receive is not to elevate you above your sphere, or to remove you from it, but to qualify you to move in it with ease, grace, and dignity."[3]

The young ladies living in Chloe's home could receive lessons in music and painting in addition to board and room for $4.00 a week.

Chloe continued as Governess, or Dean of Women, through 1865. In July of that year, her daughter Frances was one of five people in the graduating class of Willamette University. The era of the early mission period overlapped with the post mission period when the university's faculty for the 1865-66 school year included Chloe, her daughter Frances, Jason Lee's daughter Lucy Anna, and University President Reverend J. H. Wythe. Reverend Wythe, a truly exceptional man

in his own right, was destined to become the father-in-law of William and Chloe's daughter Laurabelle, and to make a home and provide for Laurabelle and the children after his son died in early adulthood.

Chloe was active in at least one church organization during those years. She presided over the Ladies Centenary Association of the M E Church in Salem, a group whose goal was to help in every possible way to furnish and equip the new University Building (Waller Hall).

J. K. Gill wrote this description of Chloe's later years in his recollections:

The latter part of June returned to Salem, Oregon, [he had been here in 1864] and was married to Miss Willson by Rev. J. H. Wythe, August 17, 1866.

Mrs. Willson decided that if we returned to Massachusetts, she would also return with her two younger daughters. It seemed better for me to remain in Oregon, where Mrs. Willson's life had been spent. This course was agreed upon and I have never regretted it.

On our wedding trip we went up to look at a school at Jefferson, or Lebanon, which was offered to us, but as it did not seem attractive, we declined the offer.

Mrs. Willson owned a half interest in a store at Salem - one side stocked with drugs, the other with books and stationery. She wished me to take charge of her half of this store, which had not been profitable thus far.

I entered upon the work, giving my entire attention to the book and stationery side. The holidays soon followed and meantime I was getting acquainted with teachers and the public, and the business soon began to increase.

In the following spring Mrs. Willson exchanged her half of the drugs for the half of the book stock, and I purchased from her that half of the stock, giving my note for the amount—about $1800, as I now remember.

We all lived together and shared our family expenses. The business grew steadily. I began to order my stock from the East, as far as possible, although the larger part was from San Francisco.

In 1868 I purchased from Mrs. Willson ground adjacent to our store for a new and larger building. This was a two story brick building, which is now standing [1922] and which although very plain and modest, was a very nice store [356 State Street] and a very great improvement over the old one.[4]

Eighteen sixty-nine marked the closing of the pioneer era. As Ben Maxwell noted, Salem was still a frontier village, but there was a new feeling of progress despite the fact that no Salem home had either running water or inside plumbing. Early in the year epidemics of both smallpox and measles ran their course with such severity that the city council appointed a health committee to care for the ill.

Ladd and Bush Bankers opened for business with about $51,000 in assets, and loans were made at 12%. There were several businesses providing employment including Willamette Woolen Manufacturing Co., Kinney and Co. Flour Mill, Capital Lumber's sawmill, Drake Iron Works, and Pioneer Oil Co. which made linseed oil.

Steamboats still plied the Willamette between Portland and Salem, and stage coaches stopped overnight on their five day run between San Francisco and Portland. A new steam ferry crossed the Willamette at Salem.

There were seven hundred private homes and good rental houses were scarce. The five schools had seating for five hundred although there were more than 1100 children of school age. Teachers were paid on average $45.00 per month in gold or silver coin. Salem was home to eight churches. Maple trees were planted on Willson Avenue to enhance the landscape from that of an open field, and those intriguing velocipedes arrived in town. On streets deep carpeted with dust and lined with ruts, the velocipede riders caused considerable havoc among men and horses while gaining some desired attention from the young women and children.[5]

The census of 1870 shows Salem's population totaling 1139, of whom 13 were Negro and 17 were Chinese. There was a water plant, a gas works, and in September a train from Portland brought mail and passengers to the State Fair. There was considerable debate between those townsfolk who preferred to cling to the past and those who through civic pride and/or business benefits promoted a head long rush into the future. That year there were thirteen saloons, three drug stores that sold liquor and two breweries. Although Indian reservations had been established years before, there was still an Indian camp on the edge of town near the mouth of South Mill Creek.

The Willson era in Salem was closing. By 1871, Chloe and J. K. and Frances Gill were living on State Street between Cottage and Winter streets. J. K. was serving as Superintendent of the Sabbath School for the M E Church, and the Presbyterian Church held its services on the second floor of J.K.'s business building. Sometime during the year, Chloe and the Gills moved to Portland where J.K. established the business he would carry on into the twentieth century.

In December 1872 the old Oregon Institute building on the Willamette campus was destroyed by fire.

Chloe Clark Willson continued to live in the home of her daughter and son-in-law until her death at age 56 on June 2, 1874, in Portland.

Robert Gatke said of Chloe:

Teaching was to her a great work of love. Into this labor she entered with the confident trust that God would bless her efforts to influence Christian lives. She was never happier than in the schoolroom unless when within her own home, which was to her the shrine where womanhood was permitted to serve God fully. To both, she brought fully consecrated talents and great love.[6]

William and Chloe Willson each filled a special sphere of influence in the development of Salem as well as in the establishment of religious, educational, and governmental institutions in the area. Typical of the time, they functioned independently of each other in their public lives. Privately, they formed a loving family, a hospitable home, and exemplified the successful pioneer family of the western frontier.

The Willsons and their colleagues, the earliest of the permanent white inhabitants in the Willamette Valley, were a remarkable group of people about whom there is still so much to be learned.

[1] Oliver, Egbert, Editor. *Obed Dickenson's War Against Sin In Salem*, p 82-83.

[2] "Salem In 1859," by Ben Maxwell, *Marion County HISTORY*, V. 5, p 12.

[3] Gatke, Robert M., *Chronicles of Willamette*, p 249-250.

[4] "Record of the Business of the J. K. Gill Co.," by Joseph K. Gill, in the possession of his great granddaughter, Elizabeth Kate Moore Barker, Lake Oswego, Oregon, 1996.

[5] "Salem in 1869: A Year of Transition...," by Ben Maxwell, *Marion County HISTORY*, V. 3, p 25-30.

[6] Gatke, p 97.

A. N. Bush Photographs

Panorama History
By David Weiss

These photographs not only give a glimpse into Marion County history, but are unusual as to the camera equipment used to produce the image. Asahel Nesmith Bush, an ardent photographer, toured in his automobile, driven by his chauffeur, photographing scenes that now have a tremendous historical value. The value of his work increases because he made extensive notes as to what he was photographing. He did his work in Salem and the surrounding countryside.

A.N. used a panorama camera to capture these wide-angle images. The unique thing about the camera was that on making the exposure, the lens rotated from one side to the other, capturing a broad expanse on a curved strip of film.

The A. N. Bush collection of about four hundred negative images, from which these photographs were obtained, is in the possession of the Oregon State Library.

Successful panoramas, using curved daguerreotype plates, were produced as early as 1845 with this principle remaining in use for many years. George Eastman, in about 1900, improved panorama photography by introducing mechanical improvements, economical production methods, improved lenses, and the much more rapid roll film. Kodak last produced panorama cameras in 1928; however, panorama cameras are still available for the popular thirty-five millimeter film. *Photos continue on pages 56 and 80...*

Rosedale
Prune dryer on left. South Salem was the prune center of the valley. June 18, 1911.

Aspinwall Bros.
Loganberry dryer at Brooks, Oregon. August 14, 1913.

Durbin Livery Stable

By Jordis Schick
Previously published February 1993, Vol.31, No.1

This photo shows the original Durbin Livery Stable on the northeast corner of State and Commercial Streets in Salem.

According to the January 20, 1862, *Oregon Statesman*, the Willamette River had frozen over and on Friday "appeared ...16 horses, all in one team, two abreast. They drew three sleighs, fastened together, and were driven by a man sitting on the seat. They went around a square and turned with much facility. The sight was photographed."

The *Centennial History of Oregon* says, "In1862, when there were six weeks of sleighing here, he (Solomon Durbin) had a sixteen-horse team which was the largest sleighing team in this state, there being a rivalry at the time in owning and driving the largest sleighing team."

Incidentally, the stable pictured was destroyed by fire on November 27, 1862, but new stables were built and a Cotillion Party was held (the tickets cost $4 including supper) on March 16, 1863. Solomon Durbin and his brother Isaac, who for some time owned the stable together, were the sons of John and Sarah Durbin who came to Oregon in 1845, driving overland 100 head of cattle and bringing a large family. Their original donation land claims were near Mission Bottom, north of Salem.

Of special interest to MCHS members involved in the Wilson-Durbin house restoration would be the fact that Joseph Gardner Wilson, who built the Wilson-Durbin house in 1861, sold it to Isaac Durbin and his wife in 1863.

In 1866, Isaac's parents acquired the cottage. For the next 50 years it was owned and occupied by a succession of family members.

Durbin Family Oregon Trail Saga

By Jordis Schick
Previously published February 1993, Vol.31, No.1

 The story of the Durbin's overland crossing is also interesting. According to *The Centennial History of Oregon, 1811-1911, Volume II,* "they made arrangements to remove to the northwest in the spring of 1845. They left St. Joseph, Missouri, for Oregon on the 10th of May, traveling with ox teams in a train of 65 wagons.

However, on reaching the Platte river there was a division made of the train and again at Independence Rock. About 12 or 14 wagons came through with the Durbins and Solomon Durbin, then a boy of 16 years, drove one of the wagons. They came by way of Meek's Cut-Off, struck the dessert (sic) and could not get water. They therefore made for The Dalles and when they arrived there built rafts with logs. On those they put the wagons,

and Indians took the women of the party in canoes down to the Cascades, while the cattle were driven down to the river and made to swim across at Snow's Island.

They cut a road around the falls for about seven miles, after which the Hudson Bay boats took the families and supplies down to the mouth of the Willamette River. The Durbin family made their way to Washington County and soon afterward rented a place in Yamhill County where they remained for about three months. At the end of that time they purchased a place ten miles north of Salem. There the parents of Solomon Durbin resided for over 30 years, after which they took up their abode in the capital city, where the father died at the remarkable old age of 102 years, while his wife reached the age of about 91 years.

Weaving the Way to the Oregon Trail

By Al Jones
Previously published February 1993, Vol.31, No.1

Much was written and said about the Oregon Trail in the 1993 celebration of the 150th anniversary of the "beginning of that tortuous track through 2,200 miles of wilderness."

Those who traveled the trail were "emigrants" from the homes they left, but "immigrants" to the Northwest in the greatest mass migration in U.S. history.

One fresh way of viewing the Northwest's history is to liken it to a colorful fabric into which are woven the threads that make up the pattern we know today.

Here, in approximate order, are the threads as one led to another:

❖ The Indians had been here as long as 50,000 years, probably traveling originally over the Bering Strait from northeastern Asia and then continuing their migration over North America. An estimated 30,000 were in the Oregon Territory in 1830 but, by the time Jason Lee arrived in 1834, white man's diseases had proved fatal to about 75 percent of the Willamette Valley's Kalapuyans.

❖ Then, after Captain James Cook's 1778 visit and Captain Robert Gray's 1792 landing, came the explorers—British, Spanish, French, and Russian—competing for influence in the Northwest and finding it a rich source of furs.

❖ President Jefferson's Louisiana Purchase in 1803 led to sending Lewis and Clark to see what was out there beyond the Rockies. That 1804-06 expedition reported favorably and, in 1811, John Jacob Astor established the Pacific Fur Company. In 1813 his partners sold it to the Northwest Company, which merged with the Hudson's Bay Company. Hudson's Bay abandoned the Astoria property (Fort George) to establish Fort Vancouver under John McLoughlin in 1824-25. Dr. McLoughlin

remained there for 22 years, and was hospitable to both missionaries and colonists.

❖ Fur trading and agriculture expanded at Vancouver and from there down into "French Prairie" where Hudson's Bay employees retired, spurred by Etienne Lucier. By 1829, some fifty families were living on French Prairie. In late 1834, Ewing Young and Hall Jackson Kelley (who had extolled Oregon long before he saw it) arrived from California. Young returned to California with William Slacum and came back to Oregon with 600 head of cattle in 1837.

❖ Back east of the Rockies, interest in the Oregon Territory grew with the reports of trappers and fur traders, the writings of Hall J. Kelley, and the findings of explorers like Nathaniel Wyeth, William Sublette and Captain Bonneville. Congress and the president paid little attention until 1835, when President Jackson sent W.A. Slacum to visit the settlers and Indians to learn their views on whether the U.S. or the British should control the region and how far south British control should extend. Slacum insisted that the U.S. hold out for the 49th parallel rather than the Columbia River. U.S. Senator Lewis Linn of Missouri in 1838 also fought for U.S. control.

Grandpa Gobin, a French Canadian builder and trapper for the Hudson's Bay Company, retired to a claim on French Prairie. The doughty old father had 11 or 12 children by three wives and one unnamed "savage woman." He outlived all wives and all but three children, or so he claimed.

COURTESY JOE MCKAY, ST. PAUL MISSION HISTORICAL SOCIETY

❖ A financial depression back east, plus a growing scarcity of good farmland, increased the urge to go west for the free land and wealth of the Oregon country. In 1841, Lt. Charles Wilkes visited and reported favorably on the region, but thought there weren't enough settlers to form a provisional government. Many of the settlers were here just because they wanted to get away from the slavery controversy in the South.

❖ The arrival of the missionaries in the 1830s did much to link the needs of the settlers, Indians, and government. Methodist Jason Lee and four others came with Wyeth in 1834 as a result of a trek by four Nez Perce Indians to St. Louis to seek either "The Book of Heaven" or to ask for priests. The Presbyterians sent Dr. Samuel Parker, Marcus Whitman, and H.H. Spalding and their wives, and W.H. Gray in 1835-37. The Catholics established a mission at St. Paul in 1839, and the Congregationalists came in the late 1830s. They all found the Indians devastated by diseases—rapidly dying off and beyond the reach of aid.

❖ The first year of the Oregon Trail was actually 1840, when the Thomas Farnham "Peoria Party" left to tackle the long, strange route. They had heard Jason Lee's challenge in 1838 on the first of his two trips east for "reinforcements" and to try to get Congress more interested in the Northwest. About 13 persons were in that 1840 overland emigration. About 24 traveled the trail to Oregon in 1841 and another 34 separated to go to California. Other estimates of pre-Gold Rush emigrations to Oregon:

YEAR	EMIGRANTS	YEAR	EMIGRANTS
1842	125	1846	1200
1843	875	1847	4000
1844	1475	1848	1300
1845	2500	1849	450

As you can see, when the "Oregon Fever" turned to "Gold Fever" in 1849, only 450 emigrants came to Oregon. Another 25,000 turned to California. In 1850, the number was 6000 for Oregon while 44,000 headed for the Golden Bear state. Historians estimate that, in the two decades after 1840, there were 65,000 going to Oregon and 203,000 to California.

❖ After the Donation Land Law in 1850 (when Congress granted 320 acres in the Oregon Territory for men who had resided on the land for four years and 320 acres more for the wife if intentions were declared before December 1, 1850), overland emigration increased to an even greater extent.

❖ When population grows, the need for industry, transportation and government also grows. This led to a meeting of the Willamette Valley settlers on February 7, 1841, at Champoeg (to find a way to get rid of predatory animals) where they also heard Jason Lee's advice on drafting a code of laws for government.

That's the longterm result of the brave-hearted emigrants who survived physical and mental hardships, disease, injury, and death on foot or in the hard seats of their rumbling, jarring wagons.

Terence O'Donnell in his *1985-86 Oregon Blue Book History* says, "A distinction is sometimes made between the kinds of people who went to Oregon and those who favored California. And some say the distinction is valid. From the beginning California tended to attract the single adventurer, particularly with the advent of the Gold Rush. Oregon, on the other hand, from the beginning often attracted sober and respectable individuals."

Oregon Trail In Keizer?

By Ann Lossner
Previously published May 1993, Vol.31, No.2

When Mary Schneider came to the Keizer area in 1906 as the bride of Albert Petzel, he pointed out to her how North River Road had been relocated. In the early days it had no official name and was sometimes called Champoeg Road and sometimes St. Paul Road. He showed her how the original road, called the Oregon Trail by the early residents, meandered through the Beckner, Diems, Petzel, Zieber and Claggett farms. The original houses were built close to this narrow dirt road.

The *Illustrated Atlas Map of 1878* shows the new road and the homes of the above mentioned families, which then sat some distance east. The still-existing Petzel home is two thirds of a mile from the present River Road. According to Erma Keefer Bunnell and Grace Petzel Lindquist, the trail was located west of the Petzel and Diems homes, east of the Zieber house, and then passed just west of the Claggett house.

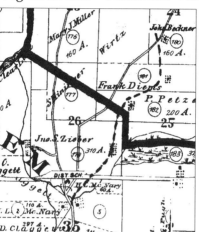

The map shows the Diems, Petzel, Claggett, Zieber and Beckner homes and the trail as described by Nolan, Schaefer and Lindquist.

Al Nolan, a descendant of John Eliza Sloan Zieber, still lives on a portion of the Zieber claim. He was also aware of the early designation. He told of how his great grandfather used to walk down the trail to the Claggett house. From the old Nolan wheatfield, now the Country Glen subdivision, it was possible to look north toward the Zieber homesite (towards County Glen between Village Place NE and Ridge Top Drive NE) at an opening which may have been the road over one hundred years ago. Al points out landmarks of the road which lead into a farm road on his own property. This can logically be followed south to the old Claggett homestead. Al notes that with all the recent building in the area it is difficult to get one's bearings.

The big Claggett house had a room on the north side of the front door with only an outside entrance, used by travelers coming down the old trail. A bed was always ready for them so they could come and go without disturbing the family.

The room had not been used for some time when the D.S. Keefers purchased the house and farm in 1904, so Keefer closed off the outside entrance and cut a doorway into the main house so the large family could use it as an additional bedroom. When it was determined that the foundation timbers (which were placed on large rocks) had rotted out, Keefer built a new house in 1917 with the help of his son Hal.

The younger Petzel children, Elsie Gardner, Grace Lindquist and Carl, born in the teens and the 20s, were well aware of the old one-lane trail connecting the early homes, but never heard it designated as the Old Oregon Trail.

However, Frances Schaefer, a granddaughter of the Keefers, heard the road referred to as the Oregon Trail when she was a small girl visiting the Keefers. She says that in those days—when there was no TV, radio or movies—adults conversed in the evening and told stories of the "olden days," which the youngsters absorbed.

But it is Frances' opinion that while it may well have been the end of the Oregon Trail for many of those settling in the Keizer area, the official trail ended at Oregon City, and Keizer's Oregon Trail was merely one of the many trails leading to small settlements.

On Al and Dorothy Nolan's property (part of the original Zieber land claim) looking toward the northeast where the Oregon Trail goes down the slope, left to right, through the center of the photo.   AL JONES PHOTO

Lute Savage at the Waconda crossroads, ten miles north of Salem. September 14, 1913.

PUBLISHED WITH PERMISSION OF THE OREGON STATE LIBRARY

Looking south on High Street from State Street in Salem. Cherry City Hotel is opposite Oregon Electric depot in the Oregon Building. Circa1914 PUBLISHED WITH PERMISSION OF THE OREGON STATE LIBRARY

Looking west down street car tracks on State Street in Salem. Large buildings along High Street are the Masonic, I.O.O.F. with a bell tower later lost in a storm, and the old county court house. Note the winter supply of wood used for heat. September 11, 1912.

PUBLISHED WITH PERMISSION OF THE OREGON STATE LIBRARY

E.D. Baker

By Al Jones

The eloquent speaker at Salem's Fourth of July celebration in 1860 had crossed paths with an impressive number of famous friends and enemies.

He was Edward Dickinson Baker, a friend of Abraham Lincoln, nationally known as a soldier, statesman, criminal lawyer and orator. Salem was said to have felt lucky to have Baker speak following the parade led by the Salem brass band, the Alert Hook and Ladder Company, and a "Liberty Wagon" of 36 young girls representing the 36 states.

The program was in an oak grove on Court Street, on the north side just west of Liberty Street. Baker led the crowd in three cheers, prompted by the growing tension between the North and the South over slavery and secession. Baker, known also as Colonel and the "Grey Eagle," then spoke for an hour.

Edward Dickinson Baker, a Representative from Illinois and a Senator from Oregon, was born in London, England, February 24, 1811, and immigrated to the United States in 1815 with his parents who settled in Philadelphia. He studied law, was admitted to the bar in 1830, and commenced practice in Springfield. He served in the Illinois Legislature, then was elected as a Whig to the U.S. House of Representatives. He resigned, to be commissioned a colonel of the Fourth Regiment, Illinois Volunteer Infantry, on July 4, 1846, and participated in the siege of Vera Cruz. He later again served as a Republican in the Thirty-first Congress from Illinois. He moved to San Francisco, California, in 1851 and resumed the practice of law.

Baker moved from California to Salem in January 1860 on invitation from Republicans wanting to seat their candidates in the U.S. Senate in the 1860 elections. In those days, the legislature elected U.S. Senators, and the Oregon body chose Republican E. D. Baker for the short term and abolitionist Democrat James Nesmith for the longer term.

Nesmith became the only Democratic senator to vote for the Abolition Amendment to the Constitution, as did Baker.

That was the year that Lincoln was opposed by Democrat John Breckinridge, whose choice as running mate was Joseph Lane. Lane was a pro-South sympathizer from Oregon whose path had crossed Baker's often. Lane had been appointed as Oregon's first governor of the Territory in 1849, serving until June of 1850 when he was elected delegate (Democrat) to Congress.

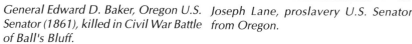

General Edward D. Baker, Oregon U.S. Senator (1861), killed in Civil War Battle of Ball's Bluff.

Joseph Lane, proslavery U.S. Senator from Oregon.

Baker, newly elected as Oregon's U.S. Senator, hurried to Washington, stopping in Springfield, Illinois to visit his mother. That was where Baker had practiced law with Abe Lincoln, J. D. Stuart and Stephen T. Logan after serving in the Black Hawk War.

Lincoln had told Baker, "I'd rather have you elected Senator than any man alive." Their friendship hadn't been damaged earlier by Baker's victory over Lincoln in the Whig primary, when Baker was elected to Congress in 1844 from Illinois.

Senator Baker had the privilege of introducing Lincoln at the Presidential Inauguration in 1861, which happened to be twelve years after Lincoln turned down President Zachary Taylor's appointment as Oregon territorial governor in 1849. In the U.S. Senate, Baker was Republican party whip and handled patronage.

The political malady called "secessionitis" was growing and by March of 1861 only 27 of 33 states remained in the Union. Baker's political oratory stirred him to seek military rank and glory in the Union's struggles, so he left his Senate seat and recruited the California Regiment in Philadelphia.

Baker previously had served in the Black Hawk and Mexican Wars and was given the rank of colonel. On September 21 he was appointed Major General of Volunteers.

Already, Federal forces had made three thrusts into Virginia, losing the largest battle of 1861 at Manassas in July under Gen. Irvin McDowell to Gen. "Stonewall" Jackson. On October 21 the North suffered another costly setback at Ball's Bluff, about thirty miles from Washington, on the Potomac River.

Union General Charles Stone ordered Baker to lead three regiments in crossing the swollen Potomac and on up the bluff. It was all in vain, for the Confederates were reinforced, concentrated their fire on Baker and cut him down with a hail of lead.

The Union defense crumbled, but managed to keep the Southern soldiers from taking Baker's body. A Confederate newspaper later said, "The loss the Yankee cause suffers from his death is as great as could be inflicted by the death of almost any man of their side."

In the Ball's Bluff battle the North lost 200 killed and 200 wounded, including the son of jurist Oliver Wendell Holmes.

Upon hearing of Baker's death, President Lincoln wept, and his eight-year-old son, Willie, wrote a memorial poem and sent it to the National Republican editor:

> There was no patriot like Baker
> So noble and so true;
> He fell as a soldier in the field,
> his face to the sky of blue.

Lincoln had Baker's body brought to Washington, and Congress placed a statue of him in the Congressional Hall of Fame. The body was taken to San Francisco in December 1861, to the Laurel Hill Cemetery, and buried with full military honors.

In the late 1940s the body was moved to the Presidio when the old cemetery was cleared for commercial uses. But in 1979 the tombstone from Baker's grave was found in a barn in nearby Colma, California.

The discoverer noted that the inscription said that Baker had been a U.S. Senator from Oregon, and called Oregon's Senate historian, Cecil Edwards.

Edwards called Senator Debbs Potts of Grants Pass, in the Capitol at the time, and Potts agreed to pay the $200 and to drive his old pickup to San Francisco. There he was met by some who objected to its being taken to Oregon. But they helped load the one thousand pound, 4 by 10-foot tombstone. It eventually wound up in Baker City, named for the colorful U.S. Senator.

M

Winifred Byrd

America's wonder pianist

By Al Jones
Previously published February 1995, Vol.33, No.1

 Salem-born Winifred Byrd was a small young lady, but when her fingers flew over the 88 keys to energize the music of Chopin, Beethoven, Schumann, or Liszt, it seemed as though sparks came from them.

Take the word of music critics and symphony conductors of her day in the 1920s, after her debut in New York in 1918.

Her "fleet and accurate fingers" showed a "mixture of fire, delicacy, energy, impetuosity of youth, excellent left hand and singing tone," wrote Chicago reporters.

In San Francisco the Salem product was "one of the most brilliant to come out to the coast, displaying a piano technic [sic] that fairly carried her audience off their feet."

From New York came such praise as her being "the little devil of the keyboard." And as she was repeatedly called to the footlights to play encores, Winifred was described as being "among the great ones of her profession."

With New York's Symphony Orchestra conducted by the legendary Walter Damrosch, she was said to be "the feature of the concert, not easily to be forgotten."

"She seemed a fairy figure, clothed in a unique shade of blue, with an air and profile delightfully childlike, but an intensity and remarkable fire and passion to her playing."

In Boston, Winifred displayed "a high order of musicianship, excellent tone, nice phrasing and nuancing, sprightliness, impishness."

And where did her talent come from? What served to inspire her in Salem, then a small town of 17,679?

Winifred's mother, Teresa Holderness Byrd, received a music degree from Willamette University in 1873 and taught piano in Salem until her death in 1886. Winifred was only two when she lost her mother. She was then placed under the influence of her aunt, Bertha Byrd McMahan of Fairfield, north of Salem.

Winifred's father was Dr. William H. Byrd, who was a Salem doctor for 48 years. He was the

Left: Winifred Byrd.

Above: Dr. William H. Byrd, Winifred Byrd's father.

COURTESY MARTHA BLAU

dean of the Willamette University College of Medicine from 1900 to 1913, when it was moved to Portland. He remained in practice in Salem until his death in 1929. His son, Roy, later was superintendent of Oregon Fairview Home.

With her inherited talent, Winifred attended Salem schools and Willamette University for a year. She then went to the New England Conservatory of Music in Boston, and still later traveled to Europe for graduate study.

Did Winifred ever perform in her hometown? On December 19, 1933, she was soloist in the Capitol Theatre in Salem with the Portland Symphony, conducted by William van Hoogstratten. Tickets were 50 cents, $1.00 and $1.50 and a Steinway piano was used.

Winifred lived in Los Angeles in the 1930s, then moved to the San Fernando Valley, where she died in 1970 at the age of 86.

Martha Byrd Blau of Salem, a niece of Winifred's, said that Winifred would play for her and Sandy Blau, Martha's late husband, when they visited in California. Winifred also visited Elizabeth Lord, pianist Dorothy Pearce, and Alice Crary Brown in Salem.

On November 23, 1923, a *Portland Journal* newsman summed up her Oregon appearances:

"Miss Byrd had a wonderful house in Portland, the big audience being composed of many of the music lovers and leading families of the metropolis. By her own genius and power she is entitled to approval in her own home state among her own home people."

WINIFRED BYRD

AMERICA'S WONDER PIANIST

Huneker, N. Y. Times: "She blazes with temperament."
Chicago Tribune: "One of the most interesting personalities in the field."
San Francisco Daily News: "Displayed a piano technic that fairly carried her audience off their feet."

Management: HAENSEL & JONES, Aeolian Hall, New York
STEINWAY PIANO USED

COURTESY MARTHA BLAU

Salem's First Postmistress

By Al Jones
Previously published February 1994, Vol.32, No.1

The official records of the U.S. Postal Service don't recognize the facts, but Salem at one time had a female postmaster (or postmistress) and her name was Helen Dearborn.

She was the widow of Richard H. Dearborn, who had been appointed by President Grover Cleveland just four days before Benjamin Harrison, a Republican, became president. Dearborn had been a Democrat.

Dearborn died at age 57 on August 29, 1889, after a long affliction of "dropsical nature," (fluids in pleural regions). He had come to Oregon from Indiana in 1853 and married Helen A. Funt in 1859 in Roseburg. When he moved to Salem, he became involved in many community and state activities. The newspaper said Dearborn was "true hearted, faithful, manly, honest without an enemy."

The widow, mother of five, was appointed postmaster by seven "bondsmen" who happened to be Republicans. It was "a graceful act, to which there is not a doubt the people will say 'well done,'" the newspaper wrote.

It was not until December 20, 1889, that President Harrison appointed Andrew N. Gilbert as Salem's postmaster. That meant Helen A. Dearborn held the position for 113 days.

But her picture is not among those on display now with all postmasters at the main office on 25th Street SE.

This close-up of Richard and Helen Dearborn is taken from an 1889 photo of the post office staff at that time. She became postmaster after his August 29, 1889 death.

State Archive Site Revisited

By Adele Egan
Previously published February 1993, Vol.31, No.1

In 1913, D Street was the northern edge of town. In that year my grandfather, Frank G. Deckebach, acquired and finished a Craftsman style home at the address of 940 D Street. It was the family home from 1914 to 1944.

Mr. Deckebach loved gardening and soon added lots along D Street, gradually increasing his garden until the entire area from D Street to Parrish Street and between the two alleys was fully landscaped into formal gardens—some featuring roses, some with peonies or iris, with both fruit trees and ornamentals. There was a large fish pond, rose and grape arbors, stone benches, and places to sit and enjoy the views. There were many fond memories connected with those gardens for the grandchildren and the neighborhood children.

As the gardens expanded, Parrish Junior High School was built across Capitol Street and more homes were added in the block and across Parrish St. After Mr. Deckebach died in 1937, all but the house and lot were sold and 12 little cottages were built on the site of the gardens. Margaret Cooley (Maulding) and I used to play in them after the workers left in the afternoon. About the second such group of homes in Salem, they were popular and more soon followed around town. These were within walking distance of the Capitol and Willamette University, they were on the bus line, and a neighborhood store was in the same block.

In 1944 my grandmother, Adele Deckebach, sold her home. (I lived with my grandmother at the time, attending Willamette University.) Eventually the home and the cottages were acquired by the State as part of the Mall expansion program and they were State rentals. Then one year there was a fire in the kitchen and the State decided to raze this lovely home with its bird's eye maple floors rather than remodel it.

We had understood for years that the Mall was intended to go as far north as D Street. When it came time to clear the area for the Archives building there was much concern about losing so much good housing. I was very pleased with the efforts made to save and move these nice little homes to their new location on Williams Street. Even the lovely Cooley home was saved and sits regally on Chemeketa Street.

In retrospect, I find the new Archives building and its serene landscaping a fitting and lovely replacement for the home, gardens and neighborhood I remember so fondly.

COURTESY ADELE EGAN

These Gunnell Garden Studies photographs are dated 1925. The top photo is Mr. Deckebach's beautiful garden. Below is another view of the gardens with Parrish Junior High School in the background across Capitol Street.

COURTESY ADELE EGAN

Hooked On History

400 years of Eoffs

By Jordis Schick

Previously published August 1994, Vol.32, No.3

Tracing a family history can lead people down strange paths and byways according to Joy Eoff, wife of Joseph Irwin Eoff of Salem.

When she was given the Eoff Family Bible (which records family births, deaths and marriages from 1812 to 1915) for safekeeping by her late father-in-law Asel Craig Eoff, Joy knew the Eoffs were early Oregon pioneers but little else. Now, with help from distant relatives over all the U.S.—especially William E. Dunn, Jr. of Beaverton, Oregon, who compiled a genealogical chart—she knows where the Eoffs originated; when, how and why they came to the U.S.; much about what happened after their arrival; and many other interesting details—not the least of which is that even the name Eoff is quite accidental and could just as easily be Off, Aff, Offa, Ooff, Offen, Hoff, or whatever.[1] You get the idea.

Back to our "Oregon" Eoffs. Actually, we can let George W., the first Eoff born right here in Marion County in 1848, tell the story in his own words. George was interviewed by Fred Lockley for the June 15, 1923, *Oregon Daily Journal* when he lived at 1804 Ferry Street, near the corner of 17th.

My father, John Leonard Eoff, was born in Pulaski County, Kentucky, July 2, 1812," said Mr. Eoff. "His father, John Eoff, was born in Virginia in 1777. My grandfather, with his folks, went to Kentucky in 1780, where he lived all his life. My father was a good wrestler and could hold his own in the sports of that day. When he was twenty he fell in love with Mary Routen (actually Roughton)[2] and as her people opposed the marriage the young people eloped on two good Kentucky saddle horses, heading north until they reached Indiana. This was in 1833. Neither was of age, but they found someone who would tie the knot; so they were married. They lived for a couple of years in Indiana and then moved in 1835 to Illinois, and in the spring of 1841 they moved to Davis county and in 1847 they pulled out across the plains for Oregon.

George Eoff (George W.'s uncle) married Nancy English in 1841. In 1845 Captain

English,[3] her uncle, had moved to Oregon, settling on Howell Prairie, near Salem. It was the good reports he sent back to his relatives that caused my father to come to Oregon. My father took up a section of land on Howell Prairie and I still own half of our old home place.[4] I was born on that old place September 12, 1848. I am the only one of a big family of children now living. In 1871 I trailed a band of sheep across the mountains to Morrow county. In 1873 I took another band to Rhea Creek, not far from Heppner. I stayed there four years.

Joseph I., an eleventh generation Eoff.

I was married in 1867 to Nannie Robinson. Two of my boys are still on deck and I have five grandchildren and four great-grandchildren. Four generations of Eoffs have been born on the old home place on Howell Prairie. My oldest sister, Cynthia Ann, married Herman Geer, son of Joseph C. Geer, who had ten children. When Herman was ten years old they moved from Ohio farther West, settling near Galesburg, Illinois. Seven years later the family came across the plains to Oregon. This was 1847. Herman and my sister had four children; only two of whom grew up. My nephew, Theodore Geer, became governor of Oregon, the first native son of Oregon to be elected governor. His sister Theodosia married Joe Janes. She lives in California. When I was a baby, back in 1849, father used to do his trading at Oregon

*City. But within a few years a settlement sprang
up here at Salem, so he traded here. In the last
75 years I have seen Salem get to be a tolerably
good town, and it is growing all the time.*

George died at age 74 on December 25, 1923,
six months after this interview. John Leonard Eoff
and Mary Ann (Polly) Roughton actually had ten
children, only three of whom lived to maturity.

According to the Eoff Family Bible, Cynthia
Ann was born in Illinois in 1833, Sarah Jane was
born in 1835 and died at eleven months, and
Minerva was born in 1837 and died on Christmas
Eve at one and a half years.

As if that wasn't heartbreaking enough, the
Eoff's next two daughters, who must have
successfully crossed the plains to Oregon, died soon
after they arrived—Mary Emily, born in 1841, died
at age six on October 31, and Nancy Elizabeth, born
in 1843, died five days after Mary Emily, on
November 5 at age four.

A son, James Fleming (1845-1889)[5] was also one
of the four children who traveled with his family
in the covered wagon. As previously noted, our
beginning narrator, George W., was the first Eoff
born in Oregon in 1848. His two sisters and brother
all died in childhood.

Three generations of Eoffs: Asa Irving Eoff, Asel Craig Eoff
and Joseph Irwin Eoff.   COURTESY JOSEPH I. EOFF

What sad and silent witness this small plot
bears to the devastating pain pioneer parents
endured, trying to raise families in the days before
911 and wonder drugs.

Oscar and Asa Irving are the two children
George W. tells us are still on deck in 1923. Asa
(1875-1954) is the present Joe Eoff's grandfather
and, during his lifetime, he became quite renowned
as an Oregon sheepbreeder. His name appears on
a bronze breeder plaque at the State Fairgrounds.

At the same time in 1949, Asa was named
"the Statesman Farmer of the Week." Lillie L.
Madsen reported that Ace,
as he is known to Marion
County, was born in a sheep
camp in eastern Oregon
when his parents went to
the other side of the
mountains to look after
their flocks.

*His grandfather, John
L. Eoff, homesteaded on the
edge of Howell Prairie
between Macleay and
Pratum in 1847. His father
was born there and Ace
still owns 300 acres of the
original land.*

*In 1910 he started
raising Hampshire sheep and now runs some
400 head not only on the old place but on the
additional 200 acres he owns.*

*He has spent much of his time this week
watching the sheep results in the State Fair
judging rings.*

Eoff's success with Hampshire sheep was
written up in both the *Oregon Magazine* and *The
Sacramento Bee* circa 1949. Joe Eoff tells us his
grandfather also raised Suffolk sheep and the
family still has the branding irons Asa used.

Asa Irving Eoff (far left) at Oregon State Fair in 1940.   COURTESY JOSEPH I. EOFF

All five children who died in Oregon are buried
in the Eoff Cemetery on the original Eoff land east
on State Street, about a quarter mile past Howell
Prairie Road.[6]

Others buried in the same small grove of trees
include the pioneer John Leonard Eoff, his wife
Mary Ann, and two of their children, John
Leonard Jr. and Louisiana. The first George Eoff
and his wife Nancy also rest together. Fleming
Eoff (1818-1891), a third brother who came west
at a later date, joins the family at rest.[7]

Ace and his wife, Grace Craig, were the parents of Asel Craig Eoff, born on March 5, 1901, in Salem. Asel married Mary Jane Albert on October 21, 1925. Mary Jane, who died in 1992, was the daughter of Joseph H. Albert— a real pillar of the Salem community who was a partner with R.W. Wallace in the Capital National Bank and numerous other business ventures including Salem's first water district and the land in West Salem that he and Wallace jointly donated to the City for Wallace Park at a later date.

According to an article in *The Salem World* on February 13, 1928, Asel C. Eoff, after college and a few years stock farming, "went into the electrical business as a member of the firm Halik & Eoff. That firm has since become the Eoff Electric Incorporated and Ellis Von Eschen is now a partner."

Asel achieved much success with Eoff Electric and, after turning it over to his son Joe, "retired" to California and immersed himself in yet another successful business venture—raising dates and marketing them under his own Redi-Date label in Thermal, California. Asel died November 6, 1980. One of the interesting tidbits he told Joy Eoff before he died was that he remembered Clark Gable picking strawberries out on the Eoff farm where Gable, as a young man, lived for a short time in one of the shacks.

Asel and Mary Jane's son, Joseph Irwin Eoff, was born on September 20, 1929, and is still going strong although he celebrates his 65th birthday very soon. Since his father's retirement, Joe has steered Eoff Electric to its present position as one of Oregon's top, privately owned businesses, with eight locations in Oregon and Washington, according to *Oregon Business* magazine.

Today Joe serves as the company's chairman of the board, and leaves day-to-day operations in the capable hands of his stepson, Hutch Johnson, another electrical engineer who is the current Eoff Electric president.

Since both of Joe's children are girls, Deborah Ann (born 1956) and Mary Katherine (born in 1961), there will probably be no further Eoffs to carry on the family name in this particular branch.

But there must be thousands of Eoffs in other areas because information Joy Eoff has obtained documents a family saga that began 400 years ago in Germany—200 years before John Leonard's forebears crossed the Atlantic.

It is probably similar to that of many other families who made transition from the old world to the new—maybe even your own. The information that follows has been taken largely from a family history written and documented by Roberta Grahame.[1]

Grahame calls the first Jacob Off "The Patriarch." He was born about 1590 in Krummhardt (now part of Stuttgart) Germany, a village in the Duchy of Wurtemberg. Prior to this some evidence indicates that Offs may have originally come from Austria to this area of Germany.

We don't know too much about Jacob I, except that he married a Catharina mnu* (1606-1667) and lived to the ripe old age of 86 before he died in April 1676—a fact noted in the Parish Burial Register with "on April 8 old Jacob Off of Krummhard fell asleep gently and peacefully in his 86th year."

His son, Jacob Off II (1630-1702), is called "The Missing" because church records only indicate he was married to a Susanna Reutter on June 16, 1664, in Schanbach, Krummhardt, Germany. Their fifth child was Hans Jacob Off III, whom Grahame calls "The Emigrant."

In the Marriage Register of the Evangelical Parish of Grossheppach, Diaconate of Waiblingen, this entry appears:

1702. Monday after the Feast of Pentecost. On the fourteenth of June, in a prayer meeting, after a second proclamation, Hans Jacob Off, son of Jacob Off, deceased, former burgher of Krummhardt, and Maria Magdalena, daughter of Hans Nussbaum, deceased, a former burgher here, and herself a resident here up to this time, were married. A quarter of a year ago the girl, ("Die Dirne") had a child. The authorities made the fellow go through with the marriage. He was still in his apprenticeship as a weaver.

Jacob Off III is the Off who emigrated to America with his family in 1709-1710. And the child who was born three months prior to the marriage was Johann Jacob Off IV, who died in 1780 in Pluckemin, Somerset, New Jersey.

Grahame thinks the "was" in the marriage notation indicates Jacob III had to give up his apprenticeship for his misdeed, which may have been one of the reasons he later chose to emigrate. However, his forced marriage must not have been too unhappy because he and Magdalena Maria had a total of six children, although only three lived to make the trip to the colonies.

Much has been written and published in New York about these Palatine German emigrations to the new world. Evidently the name Palatinate comes from the title of an official, a Palatine, sent by the Roman Caesars to govern the southwestern section of Germany after the conquest of Gaul in the First Century.

The Palatine Families were the people in that area who suffered much because the area was repeatedly and completely devastated by the armies of France from the south and others from the north who continually battled back and forth. When King Louis XIV of France was pursuing his large ambitions to Catholicize Europe in the early 1700s, he boasted that a crow flying over would starve—so completely was the devastation in this land. The area along the Rhine, Main and Necker Rivers was laid in ruins—an area about the size of Massachusetts having a population of 500,000 people. About 1200 towns were destroyed.

Since the Palatines were Protestants, Queen Anne of England considered them allies. She sent representatives to Germany to entice the poor people there to find a better life overseas and populate the colonies. Her main purpose was to have them make tar for the English Navy. Led and encouraged by good Pastor Kochertthal, they embarked for Rotterdam, Holland, and then on to the estuary of the Thames, where they spent two months on boats in the harbor. In the spring of 1710, 3500 people were finally sent to New York on ten small ships. They arrived in New York in the fall and most of them spent several years in virtual serfdom before they migrated to New York State, New Jersey and Pennsylvania to be husbandmen.

All of this information only turned up because someone finally realized the name Eoff must have been something else in the old world. After persistent efforts searching through various Palatine records, even the original subsistence lists at the Public Records Office in London (each family was awarded a small subsistence by the Queen), Grahame finally turned up a Hans Jacob Off and wife and three children who sailed from Rotterdam between June 5 and 10, 1709, in the third sailing of Palatines.

This presented another problem because suddenly Grahame found only a widow named Magdalena and two children listed. Typhoid was known to be a scourge, both on ships carrying the Palatines and also where the families were detained in quarantine, at Nutten Island, Kings, New York, so evidently Magdalena had not only lost her husband in the few short months after arrival, but also one daughter.

Then Magdalena disappears from the subsistence lists (a widow and children were not eligible). Conjecturing that she may have remarried wasn't difficult, but finding out to whom and when was something else. It wasn't until Grahame searched all of the Magdalena's on a list someone made of surviving Palatines in 1716-1717 that a Magdalena Castner appeared with a husband and three children "auf dem Rarendantz," a phrase Grahame finally interpreted to be the Raritan River area in New Jersey. Further delving in the subsistence list finally showed a family that had gained one adult and two children, which eventually led Grahame to a marriage record from the Reformed Dutch Church of New York that showed that a Magdalena Paan (a corruption of Nussbaum), widow of Jacob Hoof, wed a Johann Peter Kassener (later changed to Castner), a widower from the Palatine Electorate, on April 2, 1711. Castner evidently lost his wife in childbirth. He also had a very young child.

So eight-year-old Johann Jacob Eoff IV, the sole progenitor of the Palatine Eoffs in America, ended up in New Jersey instead of making tar, which would have been his fate if he had been two years older when his father died. As it was, Grahame finally found later records indicating Jacob married Marie Magdalena Spanheim, bought 432 acres of land in New Jersey in 1742, established a flourishing inn, and became a leader in the community. When a new church was built in Pluckemin, Somerset County, New Jersey, Jacob made one of the two largest gifts and his signature led all the rest. The new church also stood on his land.

Jacob IV is also the one who probably changed his name to Eoff. Records show that at various times, he spelled it Off and Ooff and even I.of [sic] before finally settling on Eoff.

Jacob IV's son Peter Eoff (1734/35-1787/88) married Elizabeth mnu*. Peter was born in New Jersey, but died at a relatively young age in Kentucky. He evidently took his family there in 1780 and three of his eight children lived out the rest of their lives in Kentucky.

Sometime, however, Peter must have gone to Virginia, because that's where his son, John Eoff, was born in 1777. And this same John Eoff was said to be one of the early pioneers in Kentucky.

John and his Kentucky born wife, Jane Higgins (1783-1820) were the parents of six children, three of whom—John Leonard, George and Fleming Eoff—made the long trek to Oregon.

And that concludes our Off-Eoff saga. Except to mention that the strange spelling of the name is the principal help in tracking family members today.

And Grahame wonders how many of these Eoffs know that one of Jacob IV's grandsons, Garret Eoff, attained eminence as a silversmith and some of his pieces are in the Metropolitan Museum in New York.

Or that a colorful great grandson, Dr. John Eoff, divised home remedies, shipped bass in an early railroad car to stock the Potomac River, put up sizable cement houses, and struggled to synthesize sorghum to make sugar.

Or that yet another great, great grandson, Beverly Eoff, built Eoff's Church (Episcopalian) in Wheeling, Virginia.

Probably not too many. Just as Jacob I and Catharina Off had no idea their descendants bearing the odd family name would number in the thousands today in the new world.

*Maiden name unknown (mnu)

[1] Roberta Margaret Grahame, *The Eoff Family from the Old World to the New*, Amherst, MA: 1980.

[2] Wm. E. Dunn, Jr., "Family Group Records & Documentations," *Pedigree Chart*, June 1994.

[3] Fred Lockley, "Mary Ann Taylor Baker interview," *Oregon Daily Journal*, Sept. 28, 1931. Baker says Capt. Levin Nelson English, "a noted Oregon pioneer, drove to the western slope of the Cascades to meet the immigration of 1847 and piloted his kinsmen to his home on Howell Prairie."

[4] John L. Eoff took up Donation Land Claim No. 396 with 638.13 acres, His brother, George, received Claim No. 105 totaling 639.47 acres.

[5] Tragically, James Fleming Eoff, who had moved to Grant County, committed suicide by shooting himself at age 42 in 1889. *The Dalles Mountaineer* reported he was a "respected resident" and it was "probably due to financial affairs." His wife, Mary Ellen Waterbury, was left with twelve living children.

[6] Elinor Myren, "Who Were They?" *Northwest Magazine*, April 14, 1968. Elinor Myren is a Silverton writer.

[7] Doraleen Phillips Wade, *Marion County, Oregon, Cemetery Records*. Wade verifies these and other burials in the Eoff Cemetery. She also notes that Jerry Miller read this cemetery in 1958 and found evidence of more graves than there were markers for.

Ghosts

Historic Notes by Bonnie Hull
Previously published November 1994, Vol.31, No.4

 It's five p.m., nearly dark; the lights in the old houses on Court Street glow as I head home. The huge sweet gum trees in front of the Crothers' old house (now the Livingstons') are ablaze with pinks and yellows and orange; all the leaves will soon be gone. The holidays are coming and the new owner in the Goodenough's house will probably put wreaths at the windows. Thirteen years ago we moved to Court Street and began our family traditions in the house where Lebolds, McElhinnys and Wallers had spent so many holidays before us. Today when I get home and begin thinking of the holiday season ahead and what we'll do this year and what we've done in previous years, I feel the ghosts around me providing loving warmth and company.

Teresa Ward will soon be leaving the house that she and Connell shared for many years. The lovely Paulsons (Con and Mary) are gone from the

beautiful house on the corner—Mary now alone—a new family putting up trees and celebrating there. Someday another family will be in this house, "our" house, putting up trees, making cookies, the kids sneaking down the curving stair.

And David, David Duniway is gone too. No more questions about this family or that property. No more arguments on whether a thing should be saved or not; no more horrible and funny jokes. I seem to think of something to ask David at least twice a week. But when I think what David and all these friends and neighbors have given me, I am so glad. This beautiful neighborhood with its old houses and tall trees, a sense of Salem's fascinating past and of what it once looked like, a love of Oregon and its history. And from David more than anybody else, these remnants of Salem's architectural past and the sense that any fight to save them is a worthwhile fight, win or lose. This year my stocking is already full—the gifts are under the tree.

Geer Family and Home

Outstanding pioneer example

By Bob Humphreys
Previously published August 1992, Vol.30, No.6

Many of the farm homes of Marion County's early pioneers are no longer standing, victims of fire, decay or modernization. One notable exception is the Geer house, built by Ralph and Mary Geer, pioneers of 1847.

The ten-room home was built in 1851 on a knoll east of present day Salem. It still stands on its original site and foundation with wide porches surrounding the west and most of the north sides. The windows, typical of the period, have many small panes and are in their original 1851 casings.

The farm, which was originally 640 acres, was the second donation land claim in the State of Oregon.

The Geer house is presently owned and occupied by Vesper Geer Rose, a great grand-daughter of the original owners. Vesper, a former MCHS board member, is also active in the Silverton Country Historical Society.

Florinda Geer Davenport, mother of Homer Davenport, world famous cartoonist, was raised in the house, and young Homer spent much time at the old place with his grandparents following his mother's early death.

On the west wall of the house, under the wide porch, Homer drew a picture of himself in a kneeling position with a handkerchief to his eyes with this notation underneath:

Riding Whip Tree
AL JONES PHOTO

"I want to say that from this old porch I see my favorite view of all that the earth affords. It was the favorite of my dear Mother and of my Father, and why shouldn't it be the same for me? It's where my happiest hours have been spent."

The sketch has been enclosed in glass, and is still legible after these many years.

There is another interesting story about the Geer farm. In 1854, Florinda Geer, upon returning from a horseback ride, stuck her switch, cut from a Balm of Gilead cottonwood tree, in the ground between the house and the road. The switch took root and grew, and has been known ever since as the Riding Whip Tree.

In 1935 the DAR placed a plaque dedicated to the tree along the road. However, in 1987 the DAR, the Homer Davenport Foundation, and the Geer family dedicated another plaque placed by the tree. MCHS assisted in the program "To perpetuate the memory of Homer Davenport and his mother Florinda Geer who planted the Riding Whip Tree."

This 1851 house, located five miles south of Silverton, was built by Ralph C. and Mary Geer. It is the home of MCHS member Vesper Geer Rose. AL JONES PHOTO

The tree was one of the first placed on the MCHS register of Historic Trees, and is on the National Registry of Historic Trees. In addition to this tree, there are several fruit trees from the original orchard still producing fruit on the farm.

Another interesting note is that Theodore Thurston Geer, Oregon's first native-born governor (1899-1903), whose home was just a few miles from this house, was a nephew of Ralph and Mary Geer. As a young man, T.T. spent much time at his uncle's farm working in the nursery. Many important meetings were also held at the old house and grounds in regards to problems with Oregon's early statehood.

The Geer house is located in the Waldo Hills area about 12 miles east of Salem on Sunnyview Road, near its intersection with the Cascade Highway.

It is important that the remaining old historic homes in the area be preserved as much as possible. It is one of our MCHS goals to assist however we can in this preservation.

A.C. Gilbert

By Suzanne Stauss
Photos courtesy of Al Jones and A.C. Gilbert's Discovery Village
Previously published Spring 1996, Vol.34, No.1

Most famous for Erector Sets and American Flyer Trains, A.C. Gilbert introduced millions of children to the wonders of science and technology with his sophisticated toys that also included microscopes and chemistry sets.

A true Renaissance Man, Alfred Carlton Gilbert was born in Salem, Oregon, on February 14, 1884. Athlete, magician, medical doctor, businessman and inventor only begin to describe his legacy.

The future success of the A.C. Gilbert Company originated in Salem with A.C.'s childhood hobbies of magic and athletics. Known to entertain everyone with his magic, Gilbert became popular as an accomplished amateur magician at an early age.

In his youth, A.C. pursued athletics to develop his frail body. Before long he had turned his family barn into a gymnasium and was coaching other athletes. Teachers, friends and family encouraged A.C. to consider coaching as a career because of his youthful success as an athlete.

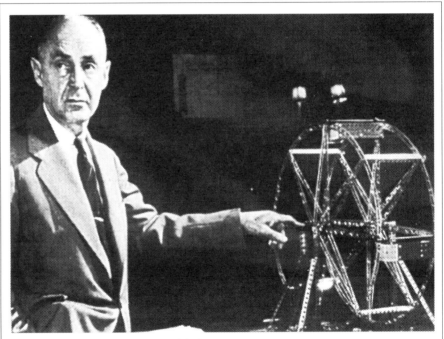

A.C. Gilbert displaying an assembled Erector Set.

At the turn of the century, a diploma for Director of Physical Education was awarded to A.C. after two summers at the School of Physical Education at Chautauqua, New York. While in college, A.C. had entertained the academic community with his magic. He was good enough to join the Society of American Magicians. His audiences frequently included Yale faculty who became his friends. They advised A.C. that the best way to prepare for a coaching career was to obtain a medical degree...from Yale of course.

A.C. carried his magic on to Yale in 1904. It was a time when the world was fascinated by The Great Houdini. Few people were seriously interested in learning the science of magic, but everyone wanted to know a little trick to impress friends at parties.

Soon the idea occurred to A.C. that he could profit from producing a magic kit for these people. In 1907, A.C. became friends with an amateur magician and professional mechanic, John Petrie. John contributed his knowledge to A.C.'s concept and together they developed magic trick boxes for sale. The popularity of the kits put them in business.

Because his available time became limited with his medical studies and new occupation, A.C. focused his athletic career on the sport in which he had participated at home, in Salem. Pole vaulting. He set the world record. He proceeded to win a gold medal for pole vaulting in the 1908 Olympics at London.

When Gilbert returned to Yale from England, he was no longer eligible for athletics and he had few academic requirements to meet before graduation from medical school in1909. John Petrie rejoined him to start The Mysto Manufacturing Company in an abandoned woodshed. They published a mail order catalog that expanded from the original magic kits to feature apparatus for professional magicians.

Back home, A.C.'s father, Frank Gilbert, must not have been discouraged by his son's announcement that he was going to pursue manufacturing, rather than a medical career. Frank Gilbert loaned $5,000 to Mysto Manufacturing. It was a wise investment. The company grossed over $47,000 in two years and $60,000 by 1912.

As Mysto's traveling salesman, A.C. became familiar with his customers' dissatisfaction with the quality of toys for resale. A.C. traveled by train between New York and New Haven on his frequent business trips. He watched the progress of steel girders being erected to support the new General Electric Ignititron Rectifier locomotives that would pull the orange striped passenger cars. He was fascinated by the shapes and construction of the girders as they were installed, piece by piece.

A.C., the young magician.

There it happened. Why not a toy that would give children the opportunity to build objects by putting separate pieces together! It was the inspiration that he introduced at the 1913 Toy Fair in New York as the Erector. (Years later, the General Electric locomotive was the model for the popular S gauge trains that evolved into the American Flyer in 1946).

Mysto Manufacturing became the A.C. Gilbert Company and soon Erector sets became the world's most popular toy. Gilbert profits soared. A.C. set a precedent in the business world for research and development as his company proceeded to introduce the world to new Erector lines. In 1913 A.C. Gilbert Company became the first toy maker to enter the national advertising market, with full page ads in *Popular Mechanics*, *Saturday Evening Post* and *Good Housekeeping*.

The Gilbert Company retooled during World Wars I and II to devote production facilities to war work. War materials included the Colt automatic pistol, Browning machine gun magazine and gas mask parts. War work was a continuation of the engineering and manufacturing quality for which Gilbert Company had become famous. The Army-Navy "E" was awarded to Gilbert Company three different times.

A.C. Gilbert died from a heart ailment in 1960, at the age of 76. His son had become president of the company in 1954. Not long after A.C.'s death,

The Gilbert Company began to sustain financial losses from which they could not recover. In 1965 they called it quits after selling the manufacturing rights of their toy lines to Gabriel Industries in New York. A.C. Gilbert will always be known for his imagination that delighted generations of childen with Erector sets and American Flyer trains.

Salem has a museum honoring A.C.: The Gilbert House Children's Museum [A.C. Gilbert's Discovery Village] located at 116 Marion Street NE.

The Gilbert Family
Source: Gilbert, Frank N,
"The Gilbert Family."

A.C. Gilbert's father was Frank Newton Gilbert, born November 12, 1848, in Kalamazoo County, Michigan. His mother, Charlotte Annie Hovenden, was born November 17, 1860, at Hubbard, Oregon.

In 1869, Frank Gilbert traveled to Oregon by way of the Isthmus of Panama, to join his uncle, who had crossed the plains to Oregon in 1844. When Frank arrived by ship in Portland on April 25, the city's population was 7500.

Frank lived and worked with his aunt and uncle, Mr. and Mrs. Isaac N. Gilbert, on their farm near Salem before becoming employed at the A.I. Nicklen store in the Griswold Building at the southwest corner of Commercial and State Streets. In his biographical sketch, Gilbert talked about drygoods boxes kept on the sidewalk to maintain a prosperous appearance. It made a great rendezvous for town loafers who whittled on the boxes while sharing stories. The proprietor was overheard one day saying that "if time were money, there was more money spent on his store corner than in all Salem."

Frank's brother, Andy, soon joined him from Michigan and the two worked together as bookkeepers at Breyman Brothers. The Werner and Eugene Breyman company was in the Moore Building on Commercial Street between State and Court. The Breymans bought dried apples, butter, eggs and bacon from farmers in Yamhill, Polk and Benton counties. The goods were packed and shipped to San Francisco for resale.

When the Breymans built a new building on the southeast corner of Commercial and Court,

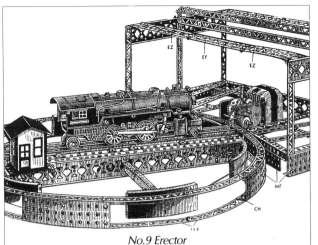

No.9 Erector
"Mechanical Wonders Set with 110 Volt Motor"
Assembled gear box, gears, cams, pulleys, girders, boiler,
etc., for making mechanical movement models…Patented
display and model building tray, digger, scoop, etc…Packed
in red and black high light chest with brass corners.

many people were skeptical about the wisdom of being so far out of the business district, especially since there were no other buildings on that side of Commercial.

In 1880, Frank and Andy established Gilbert Bros. insurance and brokerage office in a small rental space inside the Charles Uzafovage shoe store. Later they moved to the old Farmers Block, near the Chemeketa Hotel, where they continued a prosperous business for years.

In 1880 Frank married Annie Hovenden, the youngest daughter of Alfred Hovenden, an 1849 pioneer. In 1882, the Gilberts built their home on the southwest corner of Cottage and Marion streets where they were living when A.C. Gilbert was born.

At Your Feet

Historic Notes by Bonnie Hull
Previously published February 1993, Vol.31, No.1

 In Salem, Oregon, in the west of the United States, we are lucky to have the history of this land from settlement to the present day. We are not yet so many centuries old that the layers of various cultures blend and erase each other.

This is probably one of the most interesting things for preservationists but also at times a frustrating thing. The signs and signals of the building of our own neighborhoods disappear casually before our eyes. We remember the big losses of our built heritage—the loss of the original state capitol building, the tearing down of the old Salem City Hall, and the razing of the beautiful and stately old neighborhoods, often for undistinguished buildings and parking lots. These are milestones in our memory of loss, but smaller and very telling things are lost without most people even realizing they existed.

My neighborhood, the Court Chemeketa Residential Historic District, was built over a period of years, beginning in the late 1850s and ending in the late 1930s. In 1909 and 1910 my neighborhood was paved and sidewalks were put in, and today we can hardly imagine what a relief that must have been. At virtually every corner is a paver's mark, *D. Korb 1909* or *Veatch 1910*, or maybe *ROWE*. For those of us on foot who pass these marks and read these names daily the loss of these little *notes* to the currently very popular *corner cuts* is sad. So close to a new century we wish that in 2010 a child could pass a mark in the cement from 1910 and wonder.

I have the vantage point of being between those times and can think of the pictures of Ila Spaulding (Griffiths) in her middy blouse on the brand new Court Street sidewalk. Check your own neighborhood corners to learn when your neighborhood was paved and notice even the difference in the cement, and the edges, and the spaces between the squares. Don't *step on a crack and break your mother's back* though! Just do become more aware of the historic texture of your built environment.

What's Really in Gooch Falls' Name?

By Maynard Drawson
Previously published May 1993, Vol.31, No.2

Recently our *Statesman-Journal* newspaper featured Gooch Falls in its "What's in a name" feature. It said "Gooch Falls, on Marion Creek in Linn County, was called Gatch Falls. But the name changed when Nathan Gooch took a squatter's claim near the falls."

That is not just the way it happened because, in fact, it took about 100 years for the name of the waterfalls to be officially changed from Gatch to Gooch, and it went something like this.

One day I drove to Marion Forks with my family to research a story for the Salem *Capital Journal*. At about the same time, the *Oregon Statesman* reported a visit to Willamette University by Admiral Thomas Gatch, the grandson of Professor Gatch. It also mentioned a trek to Gatch Falls later.

Interestingly, Admiral Gatch was the Captain of the famous Battleship X, a "secret weapon" employed during World War II. Actually the ship was the USS South Dakota. But I digress.

Back to my story. At the old Marion Forks Lodge, now a defunct landmark, I inquired as to the way up to Gatch Falls. A perky waitress seemed very interested in the question and asked me to wait while she went to fetch her father who was taking a nap. Moments later I met Scott Young, the patriarch of Marion Forks, whereupon he sternly advised me it was Gooch Falls, not Gatch Falls. Knowing that the falls were named by the John Minto party in 1873 for Professor Gatch of Willamette, I stubbornly challenged the information, surmising it was a misspelling of the proper name.

Thereupon we were led up to the sparkling cataract on Marion Creek by Mr. Young himself and were treated to the whole story. Grandpa Gooch homesteaded the waterfalls area in the 1880s and apparently neither he nor anyone else in the region knew it had been previously named. When we visited, the remnants of Grandpa Gooch's cabin were clearly visible and Scott pointed to the spot where Gooch used to sit overlooking the falls while playing his jew's-harp. Thus, for years, the locals knew the place as Gooch Falls and steadfastly refused to accept any signs posted by authorities proclaiming the falls as Gatch Falls. In fact, they were immediately torn

MCHS member Reid Hanson (left) and Wendell Jones stand atop a knoll at the hard-to-reach Gooch Falls. Jones, a longtime district ranger for the U.S. Forest Service in the Detroit area, was contacted by Maynard Drawson, another MCHS member, to accompany Hanson, himself, and photo editor Al Jones to view the natural wonder.

AL JONES PHOTO

down and replaced with handmade ones proclaiming "Gooch Falls." One such marker was in place at this time.

So, armed with the power of local usage, I petitioned the Oregon Geographic Names Board for a change from Gatch to Gooch. Since Ed Schroeder, Oregon State Forester, was one of the natives of Gooch Country we asked him to present the official petition. After I attended two meetings as a lobbyist along with Earl Gooch, a descendant, the OGNB agreed to change the name. I also suggested moving the name Gatch up the creek to Marion Falls (as there seemed to be a redundancy of Marions—a town, a county, a creek, a lake, and the waterfalls in question).

Thus we now have Gooch Falls but no Gatch Falls. The OGNB has yet to follow through with the other name change.

So today the falls remain in private hands and, over the drum of the falling water, one can imagine the sounds of Grandpa Gooch's jew's-harp faintly carried by the wind.

Hallie Parrish Hinges

The Oregon Nightingale

By Al Jones

Previously published November/December 1995, Vol.33, No.3/4

When President Theodore Roosevelt came to Salem on May 21, 1903, he was impressed by several persons he met, especially the soprano Hallie Parrish Hinges, with her strong, mellow voice.

The President was seated beside Oregon Governor George Chamberlain and dozens of silk-hatted dignitaries on the west steps of the Capitol.

Thousands of people crowded Willson Park. Before Roosevelt gave his speech, the leader of the Cherry City Band signaled Hallie.

She rose to sing the National Anthem, standing tall in her floor-length silk skirt trimmed in sealskin, a brown, sealskin jacket and brown, chenille hat with velvet orange nasturtiums around the crown.

She was 35 years old, granddaughter of Methodist missionary Josiah L. Parrish, and a vocal attraction in Oregon since she was a little girl of six.

She had been called on to sing for President Benjamin Harrison in 1891 and again for William Jennings Bryan in 1900.

The 45-star American Flag rustled in the breeze as her "sweet and powerful" voice began radiating over the throng, and as she turned on her volume in the final stanza, "…O'er the land of the free and the home of the brave!" she was heard by some as far as eleven blocks away on the High Street hill.

President Roosevelt said to Governor Chamberlain, "She has one of the most beautiful voices I ever heard. Have her sing again."

Hallie responded by singing a favorite of the time, "The Flag Without a Stain," and soon the President wiped his eyes, asked for her name and said, "Truly, she is the Oregon Nightingale."

That name stuck to her, a favorite songbird of the Northwest at churches, state fair soloist for thirty years, singer in Reed Opera House and Grand Theater events. And she sang in the first radio concert ever broadcast in Oregon, from the Portland Oregonian tower.

Another testimony to the quality of her voice was what an old Methodist said after Hallie sang at a state Methodist Conference: "What can the choirs of angels in Heaven be like when one woman's voice can be so beautiful on earth."

Hallie would charge nothing for singing at weddings or funerals, for shut-ins or the opening of the Legislature.

Born in Salem January 30, 1868, she died in Salem January 25, 1950, at the age of 82. She is buried in Jason Lee Cemetery, Salem.

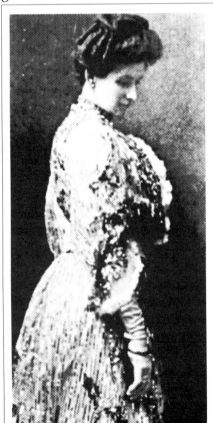

Hallie Parrish Hinges

Photo to right is President Theodore Roosevelt and dignitaries leaving the Capitol after the program in which Hallie Parrish Hinges sang.

The Question Is

Why is a former Missouri governor buried in Salem's Pioneer Cemetery?

By Al Jones
Previously published November 1994, Vol.32, No.4

There it is, the headstone reading: "Hancock Lee Jackson, Born in Madison Co. Ky. May 12, 1796; Died March 19, 1876; May his rest be the rest of the just."

And on the back side it reads: "Ursley D.; Wife of H.L. Jackson; Born in Madison Co. Ky. July 15, 1802; Died March 4, 1880; She rests, sweetly rests."

And why is this tombstone next to those of Zarilda Miller and Gen. John F. Miller? And why are they near the graves of Benjamin Hayden, who happens to have been the grandfather of Ben Maxwell (1898-1967), a leading Oregon historian-photographer who helped found the Marion County Historical Society?

Here are some facts about these persons:

Hancock Lee Jackson had owned slaves in Kentucky and Missouri, where he moved his family in 1821 and then became a sheriff, served in the Mexican War of 1846, in the Missouri Senate, and was elected Lieutenant Governor in 1856. Jackson became governor when Gov. Trusten Polk resigned to go to the U.S. Senate in 1857. He served as governor for eight months; then he was a U.S. Marshal until 1860 when he lost an election to become governor. The story told is that Jackson and his wife left Missouri right after the Civil War "when their property had been all swept away." The Jacksons lived in Salem with Gen. and Mrs. (Zarilda) Miller. Zarilda was their daughter.

Who was her husband, Gen. Miller? A pioneer in southern Oregon after the Mexican War of 1846, he served in the Indian wars in the Rogue River Valley in 1853, was in the Territorial Legislature in 1853-54, was an unsuccessful candidate for governor in 1862 (as a secessionist), and lost a bid for the U.S. Senate in 1864.

Jackson and Miller got to know Ben Hayden of Company G, 1st Oregon Volunteers, Infantry, in the Mexican War of 1846. Hayden married Zeralda Gibson on the Oregon Trail and proved up a donation land claim west of Salem. Their daughter, Medora, married I.N. Maxwell and they became the parents of historian Ben Maxwell in 1898.

Jackson's family tree included Stonewall Jackson on his father's side, and John Hancock on his mother's side (the Declaration of Independence signer with the big handwriting).

Stretching a point, it can be said that Ben Maxwell and David Duniway (1912-1993) were distant relatives, too, with common great-uncle and aunt, Albert Gibson and Mary Duniway.

The left headstone is for Hancock Jackson. The right headstone is for Ursley D. Jackson.

AL JONES PHOTOS

George Putnam

"The newspaper without enemies has no friends"

By Al Jones
Previously published Spring 1996, Vol.34, No.1

 You wouldn't have known by looking at George Putnam at his editor's desk that he was a colorful man who had fought through journalistic fire and brimstone for a community and state that is "decent and honest" and for freedom of the press.

For most of his 88 years, Putnam reported and edited the news and fearlessly took sides with a strong conviction that "the newspaper without enemies has no friends."

His colorful side included the pipe that seemed always to project from the left side of his mouth, underneath the green-visored eye-shade—whether he was busy editing teletype news or writing editorials in pencil with a penmanship that was very difficult to read. He trusted only one Linotype operator to set his editorials in type, and only one proofreader, Wilda Hancock, to proof them by comparing his scribbling with reality and his line of reasoning.

When an office visitor asked to see him, the caller was informed, "If you can't state your case in five minutes, you don't understand it yourself." His lawyer was the only exception to the rule.

Putnam walked to work daily from his home on Fairmount Hill, even up to his final years and in all kinds of weather. Often he would bring flowers he had raised to place on the desk of some woman employee, and he anonymously paid the tuition of a Willamette University student.

An avid reader, he would encourage those around him to read also, especially books sent by publishers who hoped to get free reviews. His home library was voluminous.

Putnam also loved to go fishing, using a barbless hook and artificial flies.

When he received an honorary Doctor of Literature degree from Willamette University in 1945, he graciously agreed to wearing a robe, although he objected.

As a wire news editor, he thought the front page should have at least 19 news stories, unless some startling news required a banner headline that used up space.

George Putnam AL JONES COLLECTION

As to the more serious side of Putnam, which nurtured his nationally known reputation as a crusader, he belonged to the Putnam family that was active in the Revolutionary War after John Putnam settled in Salem, Massachusetts, in 1635. His grandfather was a Methodist minister and abolitionist; his father served in the Civil War.

George himself was born in New Orleans September 10, 1872, and was educated at the University of Nebraska in civil engineering and journalism.

After a few years as an engineer in San Diego, where he worked during winters on the *San Diego Tribune*, newspaper tycoon E.W. Scripps hired Putnam as private secretary (1899-1900) and as Pacific Coast manager of the Scripps-McRae Press Association (1901-1902). Putnam founded the *Spokane Press* for Scripps in 1902, and returned to California in 1904 as editor of the *Eureka Herald*.

Next, Putnam ventured into Oregon to become news editor of the *Oregon Journal* in Portland until he bought the *Medford Tribune* in 1907, the *Medford Mail* in 1910, and created the *Medford Mail Tribune*.

It was then that Putnam showed his instinct as a fighter. Here are a few of his battles:

In 1907, railroad president W.S. Barnum, during an argument, picked up an ax and struck at Mayor J.F. Reddy, in full view of Oswald West, state railroad commissioner (and later Oregon governor). The ax missed its target, but when a grand jury (with some of Barnum's friends serving on it) failed to indict Barnum, Putnam took up the challenge, writing an editorial that read:

"It took them just 15 minutes to indict a friendless horse thief, a poor old woman, and a penniless forger. They spent three days on the Barnum case and then justified the murderous assault…But any man can try to brain a man with an ax and secure immunity from the blind-folded representatives of justice."

Challenging his legal right to criticize a grand jury, the jury indicted Putnam for libel, but the sheriff delayed serving the warrant until Putnam was on a train to Portland for Christmas. Then the sheriff hauled Putnam out of his berth at Roseburg and clapped him into a vermin-infested cell in the jail.

Convicted in the Jackson County Circuit Court, Putnam fought his case through the State Supreme Court, which set aside the conviction, remanding it with strong words on the rights of the press to comment on grand jury proceedings.

When Putnam moved to Salem, where he had purchased the *Capital Journal* in 1919 from Charles E. Fisher, he began to battle the Ku Klux Klan and its secret, hooded bigotry. The Klan had its sights set on political control of city and state.

Putnam, in an editorial dated February 9, 1922, warned the public that the Klan called itself a "federation of patriotic societies," but "such fanatical organizations are unpatriotic to a degree and un-American…an anachronism and a menace to democracy."

At this time, the Klan claimed 40,000 members in Portland and Putnam charged Portland newspapers with "entering into a conspiracy of silence, either intimidated by the 'patriots' or in sympathy with their aims."

Putnam also wrote that a "certain secret society of bigots with 'exalted Cyclops of the Invisible Empire' has the avowed purpose of controlling the coming election and naming the next governor and legislature."

In retaliation, the Klan sent teams out to advertisers and subscribers of the *Capital Journal* in the spring of 1922, endorsing candidates who either openly or secretly appealed to racial or religious prejudice and bigotry. Putnam went to

battle editorially, changing his party registration from Democrat to Republican. That was because State Senator Charles Hall was a candidate for the Republican nomination for governor, calling for abolition of parochial and sectarian schools.

Hall's opponent was Republican governor Ben Olcott, who proclaimed on May 13 that "dangerous forces are insidiously gaining a foothold." Olcott ordered law enforcement officers and courts to see that all "unlawfully disguised men be kept from the streets to prevent further outrages and marauding."

Although Olcott won in the Republican primary, he lost to Democrat Walter M. Pierce in the general election. Putnam fought to the bitter end for Governor Olcott, but Pierce was elected by a large majority in a campaign for "lower taxes," the school bill Pierce favored, which eliminated private schools (later ruled unconstitutional by the Supreme Court), and by being sure not to antagonize the Ku Kluxers.

Putnam's editorial after the election included:

"*The Capital Journal* has no apologies to make—it has fought for the right as it was given to see the right and while majorities can legalize a wrong, they cannot make wrong right."

Putnam's next challenge was to take on "goons and racketeers" in organized labor in the 1920s.

More than 250 acts of violence were recorded in Oregon in 1937 and Governor Martin stepped up law enforcement "to expose and punish the guilty regardless of their affiliations." There were 76 convictions of assault and arson, often involving CIO and AFL workers.

It came to a head when Public Utilities Commissioner N.B. Wallace ordered two truckers to deliver to a Salem restaurant through a picket line. The union business agent declared, "Union trucks are not going through the picket lines."

Governor Martin and Putnam agreed on the question of "Who is running the state?" Is it government authority of all of the people, or is it a "handful of union leaders enforced by violence and lawlessness?"

Climaxing a long series of violent acts was the burning of the Salem Box Factory plant in West Salem on November 29, 1937, causing heavy damage to the nearby Copeland planing mill.

Implicated was an ex-secretary of the teamsters' union district, who confessed that the fire was set because the owner wouldn't accept a union operation. Three hirelings and a former AFL secretary were also indicted.

Putnam sold the *Capital Journal* in February, 1953, to Bernard Mainwaring of Nampa, Idaho, a man of high principles who always wanted to return to Oregon as owner of the *Capital Journal*.

Putnam, in his farewell editorial, cited his crusade against gambling, resulting in the ban against slot machines in Oregon, as helping to make enemies, "But as I have frequently remarked, the newspaper without enemies has no friends."

He remained an editor emeritus, and wrote editorials in his hard-to-read penmanship until an early morning fire destroyed his home on Fairmount Hill on August 18, 1961. He died in that blaze, although his 86-year-old sister, Miss Elizabeth Putnam, escaped and was hospitalized.

Putnam's will left half of his wealth to his sister and half to Willamette University, which later became principal beneficiary. The Putnam University Center was dedicated to his memory.

M

Gist Family Tragedy Remembered

By Al Jones
Previously published August 1993, Vol.31, No.3

 The gray, weather-worn tombstone atop the Stayton Pioneer Cemetery (known also as the Grier Cemetery) is cold and silent but its inscription can tell of a tragedy that struck the Gist family in 1885.

On three sides, the dispiriting lettering reveals that the demon typhoid fever was fatal to three of the four children of James and Elizabeth Gist within 15 days in December, 1885.

It was an epidemic disease common in Marion and Benton Counties in 1880, according to Dr. Olof Larsell, author of *The Doctor in Oregon* (1947), which reached serious proportions in 1889 in Portland.

The cemetery had been established in 1876 northeast of Stayton, a settlement platted in 1872, and about seven miles north of Mehama, which merited a post office in 1877. The Gist family lived closer to Mehama in a modest farm home isolated by the heavy snows of that winter.

But the germs of typhus found the Gists and proved fatal to 12-year-old William on December 16, 20-year-old Christopher on December 27, and 18-year-old Mary on December 31.

The father, 52, and son George, 23, also were ill but survived. The father lived to be 83 and his wife Mary lived to be 68. George lived to 1910, age 48.

But there was more despair for the parents when their three children died. Because of

snowdrifts they couldn't get to the cemetery, so Mrs. Gist wrapped the bodies one by one in blankets and placed them in the woodshed.

When roads were clear, Mr. Gist was able to ride to Stayton to get caskets made, and the parents then dressed the bodies in their best clothes and put them in the caskets, which were placed on a wagon for the cemetery trip.

A wheel hit a rut and the caskets fell to the ground. The parents knelt and their tears came in torrents, but then they arranged the bodies and went on to the cemetery.

The *Oregon Statesman* had three brief news items on December 23, 29, and January 5. The last concluded, "Surely the family is bereaved beyond endurance. The heartfelt sympathies of a host of friends goes out to them in their heavy affliction."

Gist family headstone,
Stayton Pioneer Cemetery
AL JONES PHOTO

M

Grandma Reinhart

By Annabell Prantl

 Grandma Reinhart, as she is affectionately called, now at age 86, has possibly resided longer in the Silverton hills than any other living resident. She came to the hills when she was but five years old in 1915, the eldest daughter of Charles and Etta Alexander who farmed for a living when the land offered little else but forests and pastures. Growing up in the hills in those times was harsh and often cruel.

Driving through the Silverton hills today, one cannot help but notice the variety of crops such as the many Christmas tree plantations, the tree seedling nurseries, the strawberry fields and the fields of grass that provide the finest disease free seed in the world. Testimony to the wealth that these crops have generated are the beautiful, opulent homes, and pleasure horses grazing in the pastures. But this was

Grandma Reinhart   COURTESY ANNABELL PRANTL

not always the case. Although the Silverton Hill country was at the turn of the century covered by some of the world's finest timber, its residents were living in the poorest conditions to be found anywhere in the Willamette watershed. Most tried to clear land and farm. The red soil was thin. There was no water for irrigation. Commercial fertilizers were not yet created. Timber prices were so low that they could not harvest the timber at a profit. Family after family lost their farms to back taxes.

In the early part of the century, the Silver Falls Timber Company was formed. They bought up many of the farms high up in the hills in an area known as the basin, for back taxes. Some felt it was like stealing. They constructed a rail line from Silverton to their logging camp. The logs were then shipped by rail to the mill in Silverton and

sawed into lumber. Some of the displaced families moved to the logging camp where the men found work falling and loading trees. The work was hazardous and fraught with accidents.

Cedelia Grace Alexander, (later Reinhart) was born in Lost Point, Mississippi, a small town on the Gulf of Mexico in 1910. The family moved to Idaho Falls, Idaho, for a short time. Then in 1915 her father moved the family, which now included a sister named Lois, to the Silverton hills. He shipped his machinery, three work horses and other stock by rail and settled on a tract of land 160 acres in size on Powers Creek Loop road. One hundred thirty acres was in timber and brush and thirty acres was in pasture which had previously been logged. Many of the stumps still remained and Grace's father farmed around them. His only crop was hay which was fed to the cows and the horses. The family's only source of steady income was from the sale of cream that went to the Mt. Angel Creamery. He also hired out at times with his team to work on the roads which were in deplorable condition. He provided for his family from the land: a large vegetable garden, with hogs providing the meat and chickens providing eggs. All the water was pumped by hand from a well. There was no electricity or indoor plumbing.

Although Grace has no memory of it, there was a very old shack of a house on the place where they lived when they arrived. Her father eventually built a simple new house.

Her mother had three more children, Fern, Ruth and Bruce. Since Grace was the oldest, she was her mother's right hand helper. She especially remembers what seemed an endless task of hanging the diapers on the clothes line and then taking them down and folding them. That chore lasted for most of her childhood. There was little time to play. There were no toys. The children had to create their own fun. Sometimes the girls made mud pies and in the evenings joined the boys in a game of hide and seek.

Her father worked at clearing and burning the brush on his land. Oftentimes when an unexpected wind came up, sparks flew and set fires in the timber. Her father had made trails through the woods, and Grace was given the job of patrolling a certain section to watch and put out fires. This was a dead serious business. There were also fires started by lightning strikes. Her father sold plots of timber and eventually the whole place was logged.

During strawberry season, the family went out and picked berries to supplement their income.

All in all, the family lived much to themselves. Once a year her father hitched up the horses and wagon and they went into the town of Silverton to buy shoes and yard goods for dresses and shirts. They shopped at Diggerness' general store. He carried everything, groceries, dry goods and hardware. He oftentimes gave credit to the farmers, who would then come in after harvest and settle up. A trip into Salem was considered too far away.

Seldom did the family visit the beautiful falls that were not too far away. The roads were very bad. However, Grace remembers going there once or twice on a Sunday school picnic.

Grace and her brother and sisters attended the Mountain View School which was but a half mile from their home. Grace's father served on the school board as he was a strong believer in education. He served as chairman for many years.

When Grace graduated from grade school, her parents sent her into Silverton to live and attend high school, but shortly after school began, her mother became ill, and she was forced to return home and take over her mother's duties. Gone were any dreams of furthering her education.

By the time Grace reached the age of 16, most of the farm was logged off.

John Reinhart also lived in the hills. Grace had known him for as long as she could remember. He was fifteen years her senior. He was a logger and dated one of her teachers from the Mountain View School for a long time. She didn't think too much about him until she was in her late teens. By then there were dances held in the hills at the community hall. Both attended every Saturday night. Their romance blossomed slowly but gradually they fell in love and decided to get married. They went together for some time. Grace was 21 when she and John married in 1931. Her mother died shortly before the wedding.

John owned a small farm on the Silver Falls highway not far from where Powers Creek Loop road and Grade road intersect with the highway, known as Drakes Crossing. (Grade road follows the old railway bed). After they were married, Grace moved to John's farm, and they lived in an old house that was on the place. Their family grew rapidly and Grace was once again washing and folding diapers. In fact she remembers having three children in diapers at the same time. Her oldest, Charles, was one, the twins, Donald and Dorothy were two. Fortunately her next daughter, Barbara, was not born for another three and one half years. Another daughter, Catherine, was born, rounding out the family to five.

John worked and lived in the Silver Falls Timber camp during the week. Grace was alone with the children until he arrived home on Saturday night, then he was forced to leave late Sunday afternoon to catch the train and return to the camp. She counted the days until his return and cherished the brief time he spent at home.

The great depression was in full swing and John's employment was sometimes sporadic. They tried raising turkeys at one time. They also raised strawberries. The price was a cent and three quarters a pound. They paid a cent and a half for picking so that left little for profit. However, what the family was able to pick brought in a little money.

After World War II began, the price of farm crops went up. Berry prices were above thirty cents and John's wages went up. He and Grace made money. They were afraid to spend very much of it for fear hard times would come again. It was about this time that there were great changes taking place in the logging industry in the hills. The railroad was no longer practical. The coming of the heavy duty logging trucks made areas accessible that were not before. The Silver Falls Timber Company no longer maintained a camp. Soon the railroad was taken up. This also meant that areas such as the canyons that were impossible to reach and log before were now being cut. This was very dangerous work. John went to work for Willard Benz logging in the canyons.

John was seriously injured in 1950 when a log rolled down hill over him which resulted in the loss of a leg. He was never well after that. He had several strokes, lived for another five years and died in 1955. The children were not out of school when John died and Grace was alone.

Long before John passed on, Grace had faced the fact that she might be widowed. She kept an eye out for something she might do. At that time, the small schools in the hills had consolidated into one which now bore the name of Silver Crest School. Grace became the school cook. She prepared lunch for the children at noon. The school received government commodities and most of the menu was prepared to take advantage of the free supplies. The mothers' club also helped by freezing blackberries and applesauce. They also canned green beans. She was the only employee so all the dish washing and etc. was up to her. She worked at the school until she was sixty-five.

Grace now lives comfortably in a double wide mobile home on the place she came to as a bride. This is her second mobile home. The first was destroyed in the Columbus Day storm of 1962.

However, this story does not end here. Grace's daughter, Barbara, married Delbert Hupp who also was a logger. They bought a house with some land at Drakes Crossing which is at the junction of the Silver Falls Highway and Powers Creek Loop road. Delbert was also injured and unable to work for some time. In order to generate some funds, Barbara went to work for Ralph Jack packaging seedling trees. She brought home the culls and planted them. She also procured some tree seeds and tried her hand at raising some seedlings of her own. From these humble beginnings, Barbara and Delbert are now the owners of Drakes Crossing Nursery and are known far and wide for their fine seedling trees. Their Christmas tree plantations cover well over a thousand acres.

A special smile comes over Grace's face when she speaks of Barbara and Delbert's son, Jan. He had purchased a part of his great grandfather Alexander's old farm which has once again grown up to timber. At the mention of it, her childhood memories come flooding back remembering those harsh times when she was her mother's right hand and her father put her in charge of a section of a path through their forest where she watched for fires. To see her grandson on the old place taking care of his timber where she left so many memories seems to make her hardships all worth while.

St. Louis Circa1912
The church, former rectory and graveyard still exist. The Oregon Electric Station was east.

PUBLISHED WITH PERMISSION OF THE OREGON STATE LIBRARY

St. Paul
Main Street looking south from the four corners. August 20, 1911.

PUBLISHED WITH PERMISSION OF THE OREGON STATE LIBRARY

William H. Egan Farm
North River Road, north of Hopmere. September 14, 1913.

PUBLISHED WITH PERMISSION OF THE OREGON STATE LIBRARY

Aurora

Oregon's utopian colony

By Ted Dethlefs

Previously published August 1993, Vol.31, No.3

Fancy a community wherein all are close friends; everyone has a job he likes; the children are all in school; all material needs can be obtained at local shops at no cost; food is unsurpassed; children, handicapped, and the elderly are all provided for; there is literally no crime; everyone sings; recreational needs are met with an excellent park and the best bands anywhere; and most other needs are furnished!

Is this possible, you say? Apparently this was the picture in Aurora during its heyday in the late 1800s. The basic rule was "from every man according to his capacity, to every man according to his needs."

Dr. William Keil

It began with Dr. William Keil (Kile), a German immigrant who appeared in 1837 at George Rapp's Old Harmony Colony in western Pennsylvania as a young man with some knowledge of medicine. He quickly entered into the life of the community, soon had a following of his own, and started a settlement at Phillipsburg.

Things got too crowded, so in 1843 they moved to Shelby County, Missouri, creating the town of Bethel, which became very successful. After a few years Dr. Keil and others began to dream of setting up a new town in the Oregon Territory. He sent a group of eight men and one woman to scout the area and they selected a site at Willapa on Shoalwater Bay in Washington, now near Raymond, Washington.

A covered wagon train of 250 people led by Dr. Keil started for their new home in 1855. Dr. Keil's son, who had been promised the trip, died four days before departure. Because promises must be kept, he was placed in a leadlined casket in a hearse-like wagon, and that wagon led the procession. When they made it safely across the

plains, even though they passed through particularly hostile Indian country, many attributed their safe journey to Indian superstition because the hearse was always in front of the wagon train and the whole group was always singing.

The Willapa site proved to be unsuitable for such a large group. After a careful search they decided on Aurora Mills, just south of Portland, where there was a grist mill, sawmill, forests for wood, and cheap land. The name was shortened to Aurora for one of Dr. Keil's daughters, who in turn was named for the dawn. And another wagon train of 250 people came from Bethel in 1863.

The move out west was made to get away from people, but the new location itself made them become involved. Stage coaches traveling between Portland and points south stopped for lodging and food. The colonists took care of all who came and Aurora soon acquired a well-deserved reputation for the best food obtainable anywhere.

The Colony Hotel was a favorite stopping point for travelers between Portland and San Francisco. Soon a restaurant was established, serving food to all comers. A beautiful park was built, lined with flowers, and equipped with a bandstand and speaker's platform. Aurora became "the place" to go for holidays and vacations. The Colony also had a well-attended restaurant at the State Fair in Salem where literally the whole town would help out each year.

In the meantime, two more groups of Keil's followers came from Bethel. Altogether the Bethel-Aurora community eventually grew to about 1,000 persons, with three-fourths of them at Aurora. They also had about 23,500 acres, with 18,000 at Aurora.

Residents were assigned work that best suited their abilities, and most all needs were met. Everything went into the common pot and everyone could draw from the stores and other areas as they wished. No one was to live lavishly, but neither was anyone to suffer.

The people had achieved a veritable utopia for themselves, with Dr. Keil making all major decisions, even though there was a board of trustees. This proved to be their undoing. An agreement had been drawn up for continuance after Keil's death, but it had never been voted upon and signed.

Dr. Keil died rather suddenly in December, 1877. When no one else was able to generate the extreme trust he had been accorded, the colony decided to disband. Everything was divided equitably among the membership, and the Bethel-Aurora Colony was officially disbanded in 1883 with many of the residents staying where they were.

In 1993 Aurora is celebrating its 100th Anniversary (at the same time the Oregon Trail celebrates its 150th) with the theme *"Aurora, Oregon—A Unique Beginning."*

The celebration began on February 20, Aurora's founding day, and later events have included a Spinning Wheel Showcase, Oregon Trail Quilt Show, and the August Aurora Colony Days. An Aurora-sponsored Oregon Trail Wagon Train is to arrive in October, with Aurora businessman Earl Leggett driving an authentic restored and painted wagon taken from the Aurora Museum for the occasion. It is reputedly the only wagon on the Oregon Trail this summer actually in use in pioneer times. Starting in Independence, it will cover all six states of the Trail.

Aurora today is a community of 614 residents, many descended from the colony. The town is designated a National Historic District, and the area surrounding it is heavily agricultural, with hazelnuts, English walnuts, hops, and other crops much in evidence.

Walking through the charming town, it is easy to imagine that the old Colony is still in existence.

The Steinbach Log Cabin, built in 1876, is one of the five buildings that make up the Old Aurora Colony Museum. COURTESY OLD AURORA COLONY MUSEUM

Brooks Historical Society

Preserving the past/enriching the future
By Mary Jane Chambers

 It was more than 150 years ago that the great migration over the Old Oregon Trail began, bringing thousands of people west to settle in Oregon and California. One couple who made the difficult journey was Linus and Eliza Brooks, who arrived here in Oregon in October 1850.

Mr. and Mrs. Brooks were undoubtedly just ordinary people of their time, with a dream and the tenacity to see it through. It is unlikely that they envisioned a town, a school and a railroad depot all bearing their name, and yet that is how it turned out.

The donation land claim of Linus and Eliza Brooks was granted in 1851, and claims of other settlers were soon granted as well. Mr. Brooks, who made and sold furniture in addition to farming, soon recognized the need to provide education for the children of the settlers. Classes were first held in a log house in 1852, and taught by Mr. Brooks' daughter, Maria.

As time passed, two school buildings were completed—the first in 1858, the second in 1917. The local population grew, children entered school and graduated, and later their children entered school and graduated.

In 1985, 130 years after the first classes were taught at Brooks School, its 8th grade class undertook a major history project to write and publish a book commemorating the founding and history of their school. Led and advised by their teacher, Robert Ostrom, the class interviewed many Brooks residents and conducted other research.

To help the class identify and contact people to be interviewed, Mr. Ostrom enlisted the help of Lena Beilke Carney, a long time Brooks resident. Mrs. Beilke was able to suggest several persons with stories to tell, and it was through this process that the need to preserve the oral history of Brooks was truly appreciated for the first time. As a result, Brooks Historical Society, Inc. was officially founded and incorporated in March 1986 by Lena S. Beilke, Robert Ostrom and Mary Jane Chambers, who were its first officers. The 8th graders published their book in May of that same year, and it was used as the basis for the very brief synopsis of Brooks history included here.

Mentioned in passing in the class's book is the fact that the Oregon & California Railroad laid tracks across the property of Linus Brooks in 1870, and installed a small depot. The impact this had on Brooks was great; communication in the 19th century pioneer settlements such as this was, at best, slow. This is easy to forget as we drive along today's modern highways or answer the telephone.

In 1887 the O & C Railroad was taken over by Southern Pacific (now Union Pacific) and sometime thereafter several warehouses were added in Brooks. The railroad maintained its dominance for quite some time, and the little depot was a very busy place. Eventually, however, the use of the building was discontinued. The depot was abandoned and moved a few miles south to Keizer in November 1984.

In 1988, Brooks Historical Society was contacted by the owner of the little depot who offered it as a donation if the Society would move it. Arrangements were finalized and a contract signed in April 1989. Four months later, the depot was hitched to a truck and moved to its new home at Western Antique Powerland, back in Brooks, where it has been refurbished and restored.

Brooks Historical Society was founded primarily as a result of the history project undertaken by the 1985-86 8th grade class at Brooks School. These young people understood the need to preserve the history of their school before it became too late. Ironically, the school from which they graduated has since been replaced by a new building.

In addition, the Brooks that we see today has very little in common with the little town at which the old Oregon and California Railroad stopped over one hundred years ago. The town itself seems to have shifted east, away from the railroad tracks and toward Highway 99E, as may towns did, with the coming of the automobile.

How we remember it: Brooks Depot in the 1940s.

COURTESY MARY JANE CHAMBERS

Mt. Angel

A trail from Klamath Indians to Oktoberfest
By Ted Dethlefs
Previously published Spring 1996, Vol.34, No.1

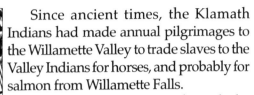

Since ancient times, the Klamath Indians had made annual pilgrimages to the Willamette Valley to trade slaves to the Valley Indians for horses, and probably for salmon from Willamette Falls.

The route crossed west through the Cascades between Three-Fingered Jack and our present Santiam Pass at a point called Minto Pass. When it reached the present Stayton-Sublimity area, it turned north, along what is now our Cascade Highway (Stayton-Silverton). It then crossed Silver Creek about two miles west of present day Silverton.

A second trail, used by the eastern Oregon Indians, came west along Abiqua Creek. The two trails crossed near the butte they called *Tapalamahoh* (the place of communion). They had a small circular shrine on the south side of the hill. In this small space they paused from their travels to sit on benches and meditate about the Great Spirit as they looked out over the beautiful valley.

Benjamin Cleaver came to Oregon in 1848 and settled at the present site of Mt. Angel at the foot of that butte in 1850. Some years later he planned a town site to be named Roy. Apparently it was not built. His adjoining neighbor, George Settlemier, whose son later founded Woodburn, platted a town with the name Frankfort. Cleaver bought the town site in 1882 and changed the name to Roy. A narrow gauge railroad was built through the area in 1880 and a year later a station was established with the name of Fillmore, for James M. Fillmore, an official of the railroad.

Father Adelhelm Odermatt, O.S.B., a native of Switzerland and a member of the 800 year old Benedictine Abbey of Engelberg, came to the U.S. in 1873. He served in a church and abbey in Missouri before arriving in Oregon in 1881. After an extensive search all over western Oregon, he picked the butte for a new abbey. Before he could proceed he had to return to Switzerland and obtain permission from the Abbot and Community of Engelberg to bring recruits to build the new monastery and convent.

When he returned, a temporary monastery was set up in the Catholic church and parsonage in Gervais. The abbey was dedicated in October 1882. A pilgrimage chapel was built in 1883 on the summit known as Lone Butte, Lone Tree Butte or Graves Butte, for John P. Graves. At that time, Father Odermatt renamed both the butte and community Mt. Angel, the English translation of Engelberg.

Sixty acres were donated as a building site at the base of the hill. The monks moved from Gervais to the abbey in 1884. They began a school for boys, which evolved into Mt. Angel Seminary. In 1949 it became a full, four-year college.

St. Scholastica's Academy was founded in Gervais by Benedictine Sisters from the convent in Maria Rickenbach, Switzerland, in 1883. It was an elementary and secondary day and boarding school for girls and boys.

The Sisters moved to Mt. Angel in 1888 to establish the Mt. Angel Academy to prepare secondary students to become teachers. It was accredited as a two-year college, able to grant degrees in 1897. In 1947 it had also become a four-year college. Classes for men were added in 1957, and the name changed from Mt. Angel Women's College to Mt. Angel College.

Mt. Angel college ceased operation in 1971 when it became Cezar Chavez College. This college existed until 1976. The buildings were reacquired by the Benedictine Sisters in 1985 and are now used for home health, physical therapy, homeless shelters and day care.

Both the monastery and college were completely destroyed by fire in 1892 and both were rebuilt. Planned by Mathias Butsch, the original St. Mary's Catholic Church opened in 1881 at the site of the present St. Mary's cemetery on Marquam Road. Because the church soon became too small, the congregation relocated to the monastery chapel at the foot of Abbey Hill. It burned in 1892. A wooden church was built near the present one and dedicated a year later. The present brick church was completed in 1912. Some consider it to be the most beautiful religious edifice in Oregon. [It was seriously damaged by the 1993 earthquake. It was rebuilt and recently was rededicated.]

Selecting the butte as the location for a Benedictine monastery served as a draw for the German Swiss in the 1880s. The resulting German influence was the basis for the annual and successful Mt. Angel Oktoberfest, beginning in 1966.

Mt. Angel

A place of religion for thousands of years

By Ted Dethlefs

Previously published August 1993, Vol.31, No.3

It was the custom of the Klamath Indians to make annual pilgrimages to the Willamette Valley to trade slaves with Valley Indians—for horses and probably for salmon from Willamette Falls. Their route crossed the Cascades near Mt. Jefferson and then turned north through what is now the Stayton-Sublimity area, crossing Silver Creek about two miles west of present-day Silverton. A second trail, used by the eastern Oregon Indians, came westward along Abiqua Creek. The two trails crossed just east of present-day Mt. Angel.

The butte now known as Mt. Angel was known to the Indians as *Tapalamahoh* (the place of communion). They had several small circular shrines on the south side of the hill. In these small spaces they would pause in their travels to sit on benches and meditate as they looked out over the beautiful valley. The butte, therefore, has been used as a sacred place since antiquity.

George Settlemier was the first settler in the area and was quickly followed by others. Soon the clashes between the settlers and the Klamath, Molalla and Cayuse Indians developed into real battles. The Battle of Abiqua just east of Mt. Angel in 1848 was the last, and the Indians migrated southward.

By 1867 there was quite a group of German Catholics living in the area. Robert Zollner and his family were first, settling on a hill just north of Mt. Angel near a creek that now bears his name. A little later Mathias Butsch moved in and was so impressed with the area he advertised its advantages in two midwest German-language newspapers. He became the local leader and is recognized as Mt. Angel's true founder.

The local people had to travel to St. Louis nine miles to the west to attend church, so in 1881, just a year after the railroad came through, they built a church for themselves. Father Adelhelm Odermatt, O.S.B., a native of Switzerland and a member of the 800-year-old Benedictine Abbey of Engelberg, Switzerland came to the U.S. in 1873 and arrived in Oregon in 1881. After an extensive search all over western Oregon, he picked the Mt. Angel butte for a new abbey. The town at the foot of the butte went through a variety of names—

Fillmore (after the U.S. President), Frankfort and Roy among them. But when Father Adelhelm decided to build the monastery there he asked the postmaster to change it to Mount Angel, the anglicized name of his Benedictine headquarters in Switzerland.

Father Odermatt served as pastor in Gervais, Fillmore and Sublimity while the abbey buildings were being built. He preached in English, French and German each week in Gervais, where a temporary monastery had been set up, then in German once a month in Fillmore and Sublimity. Sixty acres were donated as a building site at the base of the hill, and the abbey was formally dedicated in October of 1882. The monks moved from Gervais to the new abbey in 1884.

Saint Mary's Church

COURTESY STATESMAN JOURNAL NEWSPAPER

They began a school for boys which developed into Mt. Angel Seminary, and, in 1949, it became a full four-year college.

St. Scholastica's Academy was founded in Gervais in 1883 by Benedictine sisters from the convent in Maria Rickenbach, Switzerland. It was an elementary and secondary day and boarding school for girls and boys. The Sisters moved to Mt. Angel in 1888 and their school became the Mt. Angel Academy, preparing secondary students as teachers. It was accredited as a two-year college able to grant degrees in 1897, and in 1947 as a four-year college. When classes for men were added and also opened to non-Catholics in 1957, the name was changed from Mt. Angel Women's College to Mt. Angel College.

When the college ceased operation in 1971, the buildings were sold and it became Cesar Chavez College until 1976 when it was reacquired by the Benedictine Sisters. The buildings are now used for a number of purposes including home health, physical therapy, shelter for the homeless, and day care.

Planned by Mathias Butsch and opened in 1881, the original St. Mary's Catholic Church was at the site of the present St. Mary's Cemetery on Marquam Road. It soon became too small for the congregation, so they moved to the monastery chapel at the foot of Abbey Hill.

Both the monastery and college were completely destroyed by fire in 1892 and when both were rebuilt, the monastery was put on top of the hill. A wooden church built near the present one was dedicated a year later and the present brick church was completed in 1912. Some consider it the most beautiful religious edifice in Oregon.

Selecting the butte as the location for a Benedictine monastery served as a considerable draw for German Swiss in the 1880s, resulting in a heavy German influence in the area. This trend has continued and was the basis for the very successful Mt. Angel Oktoberfest which began in 1966.

Mt. Angel itself is today a thriving community of 3,000 with a base of both agriculture and industry. Berries, row, seed and grain crops, and dairying form the farm base; industrial zones adjacent to the Southern Pacific line contain a number of industrial firms. The Benedictine Center for Nursing and Rehabilitation, with 106 beds, is licensed as a convalescent hospital and is Medicare-certified.

On May 23, 1993, an earthquake centering a dozen miles southeast of Mt. Angel caused considerable damage in the community. Some of the worst was to various religious buildings. St. Mary's Catholic Church, built in the shape of a Latin cross, had the roof separate several inches from the walls in the cross portion. Several cracks also appeared in the 200-foot steeple.

Luckily, only one of the elaborate stained-glass windows cracked. A five-foot statue of St. Benedict pivoted 45 degrees, turning from the church to the wall. "It's like," one church leader commented, "he turned his back on everything that was happening."

Of much concern was the possibility of severe aftershocks, but fortunately they did not materialize. Church services moved to the Oktoberfest Beer Hall and finally to the family parish center until sufficient repairs were made.

The Benedictine Abbey on top of the hill lost plaster but apparently had no structural damage. Queen of Angels Benedictine Monastery also suffered some nonstructural damage. While insurance covered some of the damage to these buildings there was still a considerable financial burden to face. Although there was not a lot of residential damage, businesses suffered about a $100,000 loss.

On a lighter note, Mt. Angel participated in its year long Centennial Celebration. Its "Charter Day" was on April 3, 1993—100 years from the day it officially became a city. The program featured a volksmarch and an old-fashioned street parade. A 50-year time capsule was buried in the new Engelberg Centennial Park. The Oktoberfest celebrated "100 years of German hospitality." In December a Kris Kindl Markt, featuring handmade Christmas ornaments, decorations and toys, topped off the year-long festivities.

Men in Octoberfest costumes.
COURTESY OCTOBERFEST

With the earthquake and Centennial events, 1993 will be a year not to be forgotten in Mt. Angel for a long time to come.

SESNA

Historical notes within Southeast Salem Neighborhood Association

By Lloyd Chapman

Southeast Salem, the area roughly between State and McGilchrist Streets and east of 12th Street, was organized as an early neighborhood association in the mid 1970s. However, the Southeast Salem Neighborhood Association (SESNA) encompasses one of Salem's oldest neighborhoods. Much of the important early history of the city took place in the neighborhood and some of the city's greatest treasures remain there.

SESNA and Salem's Founding

Salem was founded in 1840 by Jason Lee and other members of the Methodist Mission. They decided to move the mission from its previous location at a site called Mission Bottom along the Willamette River near the Wheatland Ferry. The new community site (near the current Boons Treasury at High and Liberty) was chosen because of the water power available from Mill Creek. A sawmill and grist mill were soon built at the site.

Central to the mission in Salem was the Indian Mission Manual Labor School. The school, which replaced an earlier one built at the Mission Bottom site, was built on the current site of Willamette University in 1842. It was built apart from the remainder of the mission to try to separate the

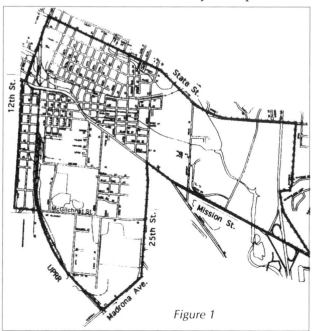

Figure 1

Indian children from the white community and the diseases they carried. Gustavus Hines built a parsonage near its current location at Mission Mill Museum in 1841 to house staff of the school. This was the first building of a non-Native American in SESNA.

The Oregon Institute was organized in 1842 to educate the children of the missionaries. Land on Wallace Prairie near the current Oregon State School for the Deaf was purchased for the school. However, the Methodist Conference, which governed the mission, decided in 1844 to close the Indian School, and the school property (Willamette University site) was then sold to the Oregon Institute. The sale was in two parcels, the bulk of the area to the Institute itself and the eastern portion (12th to Strand Street) to the Methodist Episcopal Society. See Figure 1.

Donation Land Claims

The founders of the Oregon Institute feared that claim jumpers would seek to take over the land around the Institute. This was all the more likely because the school was not incorporated and could not hold land in its own name. Since Oregon was governed by a Provisional Government (Oregon did not become a Territory until August of 1848), the issue of land ownership was not easily resolved. In 1844 the four surrounding landowners, W.H. Willson on the north, H.B. Brewer on the east, David Leslie on the south and L.H. Judson on the west, all enlarged their claims to encompass the school grounds and surrounding property.

In 1847 William H. Willson became the agent of the Institute and the Institute land was transferred to him and his wife. The area surrounding the Institute itself was then divided into small lots and put up for sale by Willson on behalf of the school. This included the area from the Willamette River to Cottage Street and Division Street to Leslie Street. Income from the sale of the lots was to be an endowment for the school. (Title problems arose because Mrs. Willson refused to relinquish her right to the land north of State Street. Sales of lots in this area benefited

Mrs. Willson, not the Institute.) A town plat for the area was filed with Marion County by William Willson in 1850.

In 1850 Brewer sold his claim to land covering much of SESNA to A.F. Waller, who filed a donation land claim on the property in July of 1853. The claim states that he settled the land on April 15, 1848. Waller had returned to Salem in November of 1847 after hurriedly leaving the mission in The Dalles where he was working with Brewer. (After the Whitman Massacre in Walla Walla in November 1847, Cayuse Indians were reported headed for the mission at The Dalles, and whites at the mission fled to the Willamette Valley.) Claims in the SESNA neighborhood include the following: (See Figure 2.)

- William H. Willson—West of 12th Street from State to Mill Streets, east on Mill Street from 12th to Strand, south on Strand to Mission and west on Mission.
- Methodist Mission—12th to Strand, and Mill north to Marion Street. Gustavus Hines' parsonage was on this donation land claim. Hines' house was known as the Parsonage or the Old Parsonage and this claim was often called the Old Parsonage claim.
- Alvan F. Waller—South of Center (diagonal line), south on 25th, east on Lee, south on Airport Rd, west on McGilchrist, north on 24th to Oxford, northeast to 22nd and Hines, west

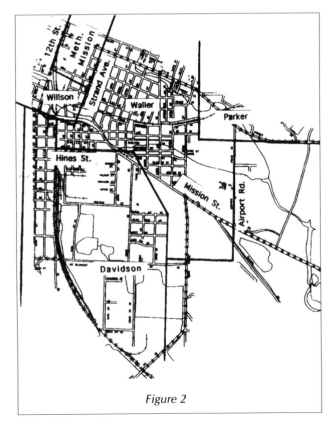

Figure 2

on Hines to the alley between railroad and 14th, north to Mission extension, southwest on Mission extension to extension of Strand, north to Center.
- James Davidson—South from Waller D.L.C. between railroad and 24th.
- F.S. Hoyt—Railroad, Mission, Berry and Hoyt.

SESNA Area, Geography and Streams
Growth of the Town

Most of the men in Salem and the Willamette Valley went to California during the Gold Rush of 1848-50. That made for a very hard year for many remaining families. Some miners brought back gold. More important, the miners demanded all kinds of goods and produce, and prices shot up for Salem's goods. The town grew rapidly. Additional gold strikes in Idaho and Eastern Oregon further contributed to the economic growth of the community.

The flow of water in Mill Creek was increased by the diversion of water from the North Santiam River in 1856. This was done by the Willamette Woolen Manufacturing Company to power their woolen mill near the corner of Liberty and Broadway Streets. Since there was more than enough water in Mill Creek to power the woolen mill, the company had the millrace constructed in 1864 to divert water downtown to the area near Pringle Creek, Commercial and Trade Streets (Boise Cascade's site 1998). In 1865 the woolen mill constructed the Willamette Flouring Mill at that location. Other businesses soon followed on the millrace, including the Pioneer (linseed) Oil Company where the Thomas Kay Woolen Mill later located, a power plant, the Salem Water Company and several canning and fruit drying establishments.

The city was declared to be a "body politic" by the Territorial Legislature in 1857. However, the charter was found to be illegal, and a new one approved in 1860. The city was incorporated in 1862. The boundary generally followed the Willamette River, east along Mill Creek, south on 21st and 22nd, west on Hines, north on Berry and west on Mission back to the Willamette. See Figure 3.

The mainline railroad, called the Oregon Central Railroad Company—East Side Line, (a different company also named the Oregon Central Railroad Company was a competitor on the West Side Line) was begun in Portland in 1868. The line was completed to Salem in 1870, to Roseburg in 1872, Grants Pass in 1883, and Ashland in 1884. The link to California was not finished until 1887. The Geer Line (along Oak Street) was built in 1881

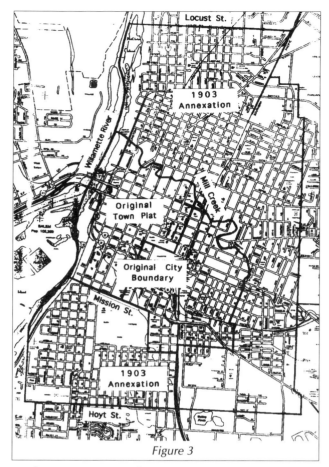

Figure 3

as the extension to the State Penitentiary. It was extended eastward to Geer in 1912.

Annexations

The first major annexation in 1903 more than quadrupled the area of the city and added the remaining developed areas of SESNA. The boundary on the east was slightly east of 25th and the southern city limits were near Hoyt Street.

The Streams of SESNA and Salem

The use of Mill Creek and the digging of the millrace in 1864 have already been mentioned. However, SESNA includes several other interesting waterways. Figure 4 shows existing and historic steams in SESNA.

Railroad Creek

The 1895 Sanborn maps show a stream running through the Depot Addition area south of Mission. A second stream joins Shelton Ditch at Mission Street after paralleling the railroad line. In January 1892 the Council received a petition "that water be turned into natural channels in the University and Depot Additions." In February 1892 the Council ordered that a ditch be cut through blocks 6 and 7 of the Depot Addition and across Turner Road to allow for drainage in Depot Addition.

Mill Street Creek

An early creek originated in the area of 25th and Oak Streets and flowed towards the woolen mill. This creek followed along the millrace, eventually dumping into Shelton Ditch at Church Street. At the northeast corner of 19th and Bellevue, a house was built over the stream.

Shelton Ditch

The 1895 Sanborn maps show a creek in the general vicinity of Shelton Ditch. This stream was often called South Mill Creek.

According to a 1947 Corps of Engineers report, "The ditch was started some 50 years ago by plowing a furrow along a county road to provide relief from overflow from Mill Creek. Continuous erosion entirely destroyed the road and created the present channel... ." In August 1891 the City Council approved a ditch along Turner Road. This was instead of putting a culvert under the road.

The Corps' report of 1947 also stated that "Several years ago the City of Salem inaugurated a program for cleaning and straightening the channel to allow it to take more flood waters from Mill Creek more readily." The control structure at Mill Creek was added in 1938.

Forrest Jones, retired City Street Superintendent, said that the widening/deepening of the channel was done between 1934-37 as a WPA project. This is confirmed in an article on creeks by Ben Maxwell in the Capital Journal.

The Depot Addition Historic Landmark Nomination indicated that the ditch was built on an earlier alignment of Turner Road, which was abandoned in 1931.

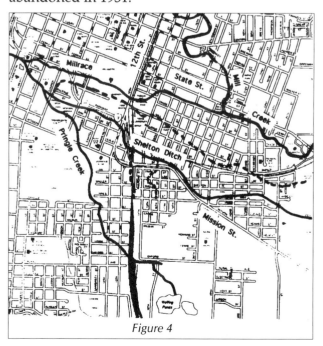

Figure 4

Pringle Creek

Pringle Creek also travels through SESNA. The creek drains the east side of the hills west of the airport, feeds Walling Pond, then flows west along Oxford Street, under the railroad and 12th Street, where it eventually meets up with Clark Creek. The creek then flows through Bush Park, under the hospital and joins Shelton Ditch just west of Church Street.

SESNA Development

The late 1880s and 1890s were a time of rapid growth in Salem. Trolleys, both horse drawn and electric, came to town in 1889-1892. This was also the time of massive subdividing, largely by backers of competing trolley lines. Virtually all of SESNA east of Strand Street was platted (subdivided into lots) in 1889 and 1890. Development in SESNA was particularly rapid because of the construction of the Thomas Kay Woolen Mill in the northwest corner of the neighborhood.

Trolleys

The system began as a horse trolley. Money was raised in November-December 1888, construction began on January 1, and the first car was running on January 16th! City ordinance 183 granted the Salem Street Railway Company a franchise to operate on Center, State, Commercial, 12th and Winter Streets. The State Street terminus was 18th Street. See Figure 5 for a map of the trolley lines. The system was electrified in the fall of 1892. Horse drawn rail lines were being removed in 1898.

Capital City Railway Company was an electrified competitor founded in 1889. It was granted a franchise by the city for Liberty, Chemeketa, State to the Penitentiary, 18th between State and Chemeketa, and on Capitol and Court Streets. The purpose of this line was to bring East Salem into closer contact with downtown.

Capital City built a power house on the south side of State Street near the site of the old oat meal mill at the junction of North Mill Creek. (Shown as the Capital City Railway Dynamo and Car House in 1890 Sanborn maps.) Later a car barn was built nearby. This barn appears as the Salem Light and Traction Company's Car House at the Duck Inn site in the 1895 index to the Sanborn maps. It was located on a half-block along the millrace east of the main channel. Large concrete piers from this building were discovered when

Figure 5

excavating for the Duck Inn. The first line went out Chemeketa to 18th, 18th to State and State to the state penitentiary.

Early in the 20th century the two companies combined. When the system was sold to Portland General Electric in 1906, it included the following lines:

- Straight out State Street to State Penitentiary. Salem Street Railway Company
- From State Street, south on Winter, east on Oak, south on 12th to Hoyt,
- 12th Street, between State and the SP Depot.
- From State Street, north on Liberty, east on Chemeketa, north on 14th, east on Center, to the Asylum. Capital City
- 17th Street north of Center to Madison. Capital City
- North Commercial to where it joins Liberty, north to Hood, east to Fairgrounds Road, northeast to the fairgrounds. Salem Street Railway Company
- South Commercial to Rural Street. Capital City Trolleys were replaced by buses in 1927.

Plats and Subdivisions

Willson's original town plat of March 21, 1850, went from the Willamette River to Mission Street, to 12th Street and diagonally from Union to North Street. One earlier plat, for North Salem, had been filed on February 15, 1850. This plat was north of Division Street between Cottage Street and the river. Boon Island was platted on January 8, 1851, on the area south and west of the mill, near the current location of Boons Treasury.

The next plat was called the University Addition and included the area south of Mission Street and west of High. This area began to develop in the late 1860s. The Sanborn maps of 1884 mapped the area from Center to Trade and from Church to Water streets. (Sanborn maps were created as a basis for fire insurance rates and were updated regularly, showing all structures in the mapped area.) The Sanborn maps of 1888 mapped the area from Mill Street to Marion/Union and from Winter Street to the river. Sanborn maps of 1890 extended out to 14th Street.

The first big expansion of the developed area of the city came in 1889-1892 to the SESNA, NEN, Grant and SCAN neighborhoods. Besides the SESNA plats listed below, the Fairmount Park Addition, Yew Park Addition, Englewood, Pleasant Home (South Salem HS), and Parrish Addition (North Salem HS) were all laid out at this time. These plats were done largely by investors in the trolleys being expanded at the time. See Figure 6.

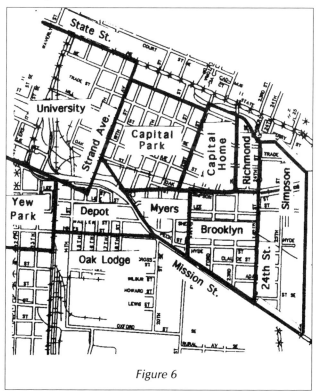

Figure 6

Plats in SESNA include those listed below:

Plat	Developers	Date
University		6/8/1869
Yew Park	J.H. Albert and Vanduyn	3/25/1889
Capital Park	Jessup	1/16/1889
Amended	Blocks 21-22	5/7/1891
	(17th-19th; Bellevue-Oak)	
	Wild and Knight families	
Brooklyn	Johnson/Hyde families	12/7/1890
Capital Home	T.H. Wilson	10/8/1889
Amended		11/19/1890
J. Myers	Jeff Myers	11/20/1889
Simpson	Capital City Railway	5/6/1890
	P.S. Knight, Pres.,	
	David Simpson and the Waltons	
Depot		7/8/1890
Richmond		4/24/1911
Oak Lodge		6/23/1911
New Haven		1950

Services in the City

Water

Water service in Salem began as a service provided by a private company in 1870-72. The Salem Water Co. was granted a franchise to operate on Dec. 30, 1870, by the City Council. The water company was purchased by the city in 1910, following a vote of the people.

According to records of the city, much of SESNA was provided water between 1910 and 1915. The Brooklyn Addition received water in the 1930s and the New Haven addition in the early 1950s when it was platted. However, Mary Eyre, whose family moved to SESNA in 1904 when she was a young child, says that her house had running water in 1904. It is likely that private water service was available, prior to the City purchasing the company.

Many of the early houses had wells that continued to be used for years after city water became available. The well at the Erb house (19th and Oak) was the source of water for the neighborhood whenever the city water went out, into the 1940s.

Fire

Early fire service was provided by up to three volunteer fire departments. These were not fully independent. They often asked for help from the city for a fire station, equipment and water supply. Four cisterns were built in 1871 in the downtown area to provide a supply of water. Each cistern held 15,000 gallons. In 1883 a "City" fire department was established, with links to the volunteer departments. A paid Fire Department was formed to replace the volunteers in 1893. This occurred when volunteers were unable to fight a fire at Waller Hall because they did not have enough steam to pump water. For a brief period of time a fire station was located on Ferry Street between 12th and 14th.

Natural Gas

Gas street lighting in the city was provided by the Salem Gas Plant through a city franchise completed in 1870. Gas was made from coal at a plant on Water Street with one "holder" to handle peak loads. (This is a major source of the hazardous waste currently being dealt with by the City at the Riverfront Park.) The *Illustrated Atlas Map of Marion/Linn Counties, 1878* states that the Salem Gas Lighting Company "has existed for some time past, and supplies light for the streets, and also a fair share of business and private houses of the city." The gas works was included in the sale of the assets of Citizens Light and Traction Company to Portland General Electric in 1906. The deed of that sale mentions gas mains from Front to 14th Streets and Ferry to Union Streets.

Northwest Natural Gas purchased the Salem Gas Plant from Portland General Electric in 1929. In that year they also laid a feeder line down Portland Road to supply the city with gas. Their records show that SESNA was served in 1930-31.

Electricity

The first franchises were granted in 1884 by the City Council. Two systems were franchised, one at the state penitentiary to service state buildings and one to Joseph Holman for downtown. Lights on the Capital grounds were first lit on October 7, 1886. Holman's generating plant operated out of the Ag Works on the millrace and began downtown lighting in the fall of 1886. By January 1, 1887, there were 38 downtown lamps and about an equal number of inside units.

Salem City Council records of the 1890s show many requests for electric street lights, including the following in SESNA:

8/4/1891	12th and Leslie
1/19/1892	12th and State
	17th and Bellevue
9/6/1892	15th and Mission
	by William Wild
11/15/1892	12th and Waller
5/10/1893	Light at the Depot

Mary Eyre reported that her house had electricity in 1904 when her family moved into their house at 21st and Mill.

Telegraph

The first telegraph line was completed from Portland to Corvallis in 1856. However, the lines were on the ground within two years. A second one was built in 1863 with lines completed to Portland in that year. Western Union took it over in 1870.

Telephone Service

Telephone service to Salem began in 1884. Telephone numbers began to show up in advertisements in 1897.

Sewers

An ordinance requiring hook-up to nearby sewers was passed on October 26, 1868. The system really developed in the late 1880s. Lines down Court Street, Ferry Street and from North Salem dumped into the Willamette River and Mill Creek. The state penitentiary and asylum dumped directly into Mill Creek. A 1900 *Oregon Statesman* stated that the city had a "good system of sewers." (By this they meant that it was dumped efficiently into the creeks or Willamette River!)

According to records of the city's public works department, most of SESNA was sewered between 1910 and 1915. The Brooklyn Addition (Claude, Helm, Hyde) was done in the late 20s and 30s.

Mary Eyre said that they had water before they had sewers. There was an outhouse and much runoff from the indoor plumbing went into the yard or a septic tank.

The Council was asked in 1891 to provide sewer to blocks 18 and 19 of the University Addition.

Parks

Lee Park was probably SESNA's first park. It was functioning in 1950. There is no record of the date the park was purchased.

Aldrich Park was set aside for a park in 1950. Its development in the 1970s was made possible by a grant from the Donna W. Aldrich Trust.

Cascade Gateway Park was established on land sold to the State Highway Department by the Salem Chamber of Commerce for use as a gravel borrow pit with the understanding that it would revert to a park for the city. The park once had a Children's Contact Zoo and a formal swimming area. The swimming area was closed for water quality reasons in 1976.

Richmond Park was completed in 1974. It was a joint project between the school district and the city.

Bush Park was willed to the city in 1946 following the death of Sally Bush.

Schools

Park School (in the Yew Park addition) built in 1891 at 13th and Mission, was the first school built in the neighborhood. It was removed after Bush School was built in 1936. Both Richmond and Highland Schools were built in 1912.

The dates of some other early schools in Salem included:

- Garfield School built in 1909 and closed in 1973.
- East School- built at 12th and Center in the 1890s and replaced by Safeway in 1949.
- McKinley in 1915, West Salem in 1911, Swegle in 1923, Salem Heights in 1938, Pringle in 1937.
- Parrish Junior High was built in 1924 and Leslie Junior High in 1927.

Sidewalks

As you walk the neighborhood, you may have noticed street names that were commonly imprinted in the new cement. These names are scattered throughout the neighborhood, including the locations listed below. Occasionally, the name of the contractor and a date are also included. The most commonly seen names are D. Korb and Veatch. Their marks generally date from 1906 to 1916.

Among the examples are the following:

STREET NAMES ONLY	STREET NAMES & CONTRACTOR	
18th and Ferry	23rd and Trade	D. Korb
19th and Ferry	17th and Lee	D. Korb
18th and Trade	18th and Lee	D. Korb
15th and Ferry	21st and Mill	D. Korb
16th and Ferry	16th and Bellevue	D. Korb
	22nd and Lee	D. Korb

STREET NAMES	CONTRACTOR & DATE	
SE Corner 19th & Lee	D. Korb	1906
Alley at 18th between Ferry and Trade	D. Korb	1914
W side 12th between Ferry and Trade	Veatch	1905

Early Residents of SESNA

While a few residences lined State Street and businesses occupied 12th, State and Mission (then Turner) Streets, SESNA was largely rural in the 1870s and 80s. The map of Salem in the *Illustrated Atlas of Marion and Linn Counties, 1878* showed no roads between State and Mission east of Strand Street. The directory of 1889 included fewer than 50 residences in SESNA, virtually all on State Street or west of 15th Street. Residents included contractors, carpenters, brickmakers, clerks, an assessor, stonemason, machinist, teamster, teacher, farmer, laborers, and watchmaker.

By 1893, more than 250 adults were listed in the city directory as living in SESNA. Fourteen were employees of the Thomas Kay Woolen Mill. In several cases members of one family worked in the woolen mill and shared a house in the neighborhood.

The city directory of 1902 included 580 individuals in about 400 separate residences in the neighborhood. (Wives were listed only if they were widowed, "upper" class single women were listed as "Miss," and "lower" class single women were listed only with their first and last names.) By 1902 more than 50 residents of the neighborhood worked in the woolen mill. Other major employers included the Oregon Nursery, located on State Street across from the State Penitentiary (22); the insane asylum (10); the trolley company (10); and the prison (7). More than twenty residents were listed as students at Willamette University. There were also bartenders, farmers, plumbers, a lawyer, painter, canvasser, clerks, teachers, principals, milliner, tailor, and shoemaker living in SESNA in 1902.

It is difficult to identify early leaders of the neighborhood. Certainly P.S. Knight, pastor of the Congregational Church was one. The Bellingers and Rigdons lived at the corner of Mill and 19th Street and were among the early petitioners of the city council for street lights, sidewalks and the like.

The Houses of SESNA

Prior to 1890, there were few homes in SESNA and most were likely rural vernacular farm houses of the period. A number of houses of this style still exist, scattered about the neighborhood.

The rapid growth in SESNA in the 1890s and early 1900s filled the neighborhood with new homes. Many of the early homes were one story with a hipped roof—the Transitional box style, befitting a working class neighborhood. These homes were concentrated in the areas west of 19th Street, primarily in the University, Capital Park and Depot Additions.

Larger houses also were built and houses from the earlier Queen Anne style were popular. Craftsman bungalows can also be found in the neighborhood, especially in the blocks just south of State Street.

A historic inventory of the Depot Addition in 1981 showed the following quantity of styles in homes built between 1890 and 1910:

Traditional box style	18
Queen Anne cottages	10
Craftsman bungalows	11
Colonial revival cottages	6
Rural vernacular farmhouses	7

More than 30 houses in the neighborhood have been identified with patterned shingles, one of the distinctive traits of the Queen Anne style. (See Appendix for a list of these houses.)

Business and Industry in SESNA

Businesses in SESNA initially developed along the millrace, railroads and the major roads of State Street, 12th Street, Oak Street (adjacent to the Geer Line) and Turner Road (now Mission Street).

The Pioneer Oil Mill was one of the earliest businesses in SESNA. It made oil from flax seed at the site that was later to become the Thomas Kay Woolen Mill. Like most industries, the mill used water power furnished by the race from Mill Creek. The company was incorporated on November 1, 1866. The mill was founded in 1867 by Joseph Holman and L.E. Pratt. Both were involved with the Willamette Woolen Mill, which owned the water rights to the millrace.

An irregular supply of flax made the business unsuccessful. The plant appears on the 1888 Sanborn maps, but it is noted that it was not operating at full capacity.

The Oregon State Penitentiary was completed in 1872. As noted earlier, it provided many jobs for the neighborhood.

The *Illustrated Historical Atlas Map of Marion and Linn Counties, 1878* shows a large parcel north of Mission to about Trade between 17th and 19th as owned by the Pacific Threshing Machine Company.

The Thomas Kay Woolen Mill was founded in 1889 on the site "of the old tannery and oil mill property owned by the Gray brothers." (Lomax) Twenty thousand dollars was raised from the community to help Thomas Kay establish the woolen mill. (He had previously operated a mill in Brownsville.) The factory formally opened on March 13, 1890. It burned on November 18, 1895, and was rebuilt in 1896. The mill closed in September 1959.

Plat maps show Edwards Tannery and Taxidermist, located on 12th Street south of Cross, opened in the late 1890s by Arthur and William Edwards and operated until at least 1910. Cecil Edwards, the Oregon Senate historian, was the grandson of one of the founders.

A slaughter house was located on land south of Mission near 22nd in the 1870s. It apparently lasted for many years.

Collins Brickyard is shown on the 1890 Simpson plat map south of 24th and north of the railroad at Bellevue. This business became Burton's Brickyard, which furnished bricks for the new City Hall in 1893.

The Depot Sash and Door Factory was located at the northeast corner of 15th and Oak.

The 1895 Sanborn maps show these SESNA commercial establishments:
- Salem Canning Company at Trade and 12th wye (railroad junction).
- Capital Lumber Co. south of wye, Capital, 12th, Mill.
- Cangora Rug Co. on south Ferry between 13th and 14th.
- Canvas Glove Factory north of Oak between 14th and 15th.
- Falls City Lumber Co. south of Oak and east of 14th.
- Anderson Steel Furnace and Boiler Works at 17th and Mission.—1914 Index
- Standard Oil Co. Warehouse south of Geer Line at 16th.—1914 Index
- Tannery north of Geer Line near Mill Creek around 26th.
- Oregon Nursery west of 12th at Ferry Street.

City directories provide much more information about businesses in the neighborhood. In the early 1900s Charles M. Eppley built a baking powder factory, the C.M. Eppley Perfection Baking Soda Factory, on the south side of State Street across the creek from the Duck Inn. The factory operated until 1917.

Eppley also founded a general store at the southeast corner of 19th and State. The building was built by Jim McGuire to house the Crystal Ice Plant around the turn of the century. Eppley's store remained in operation until 1941. It was torn down in 1949 for a gas station.

Deluxe Ice Cream was founded at its current site early in the 1900s. They have payroll records back to 1911. The presence of the ice factory (mentioned above) was probably the reason for the company to locate here.

The 1927 Sanborn maps show the following businesses in SESNA:
- Bowling Alley at 1340 State Street.
- Fire Station adjacent to church on State Street at 17th Street.
- Dreamland Dance Hall and Skating Rink south of State Street at Mill Creek and 26th Street.
- Tidewater Oil south of the Geer Line between 19th and 20th. Called Associated Oil Company in the 1930s and 40s.
- Anderson Steel became Rosebraugh Foundry and Sheet Metal.

- Market north of Mill at Ford.
- Continental—Dole cannery at 14th and Oxford. This reopened as the Paulus Brothers Cannery in 1947.
- George E. Waters Baseball Park at Post Office site on 25th Street.
- Also a hotel was shown between the railroad depot and South Mill Creek.
- Mill Street went west of 12th with a lumber yard on the northwest corner.

Neighborhood markets were common in the 1930s and 40s. The Chappelles operated one on the south side of Mission Street at 19th from 1936 to 1975. Other neighborhood markets were at 19th and Oak (1930s to 1960s), Bellevue between 17th and 18th and Mill Street at Ford Street.

The northwest corner of 18th and State was the location of an early gas station.

The current site of Tokyo International University was for many years a Del Monte cannery. The site was shown as a hop warehouse in the 1895 Sanborn maps and again in a 1920 Southern Pacific book. The building was originally owned by Southern Pacific. Del Monte took over ownership in the 1930s.

The Schuler Corporation (formerly Westwood) at the corner of 21st and Bellevue, was founded in the early 1950s by Ed Wall. It originally specialized in kiln drying for molding and later went to cabinets.

Curly's Dairy was founded in 1927 at the junction of Portland Road and Silverton Road. In the early 1930s it moved to Fairgrounds Road and Hood Street. The company moved to the current site on Mission in 1960.

Churches

State Street at 18th

This church was built by Rev. P.S. Knight for the Central Congregational Church in1894. A year later the congregation moved to their current site at 19th and Ferry. Christ Evangelical Church was in the building according to the city directories of 1905 and 1909-10. German Evangelical Lutheran Church was listed in the 1895 Sanborn maps; Index of 1908. It showed as the State Street Baptist Church in the 1927 Sanborn maps.

Congregational Church
SW corner of 19th and Ferry

This congregation initially met at the church building at 18th and State (see above), but moved to the Ferry Street site in 1895. A group of local residents met and decided to found a church in East Salem in May 1894. The first Sunday School and service of the Central Congregational Church were held in October 1894. Rev. Plutarch S. Knight was the pastor from 1894 to 1896 and again from 1902 to 1908. Knight had previously been the pastor of the Congregational Church downtown. The Knight family was also involved in platting the Capital Park Addition.

The present site was purchased in 1896 from Mrs. T.D. Jones and a building constructed and occupied that year. The church was a missionary enterprise and received assistance from the Board of Home Missions until 1928. A new sanctuary was constructed in 1926, when the congregation took the name of Knight Memorial Church. The current building was completed in 1966.

Northwest corner of 15th and Mill

This building was first identified in the city directory of 1907 as the Gospel Chapel. It was the Swedish Methodist Episcopal (M.E.) Church in the directory of 1913 and the 1895 Sanborn map; 1914 Index. It became the Trinity Christian Church in 1927. The Wesleyan Church was founded there in 1940 (see below).

Wesleyan Methodist Church

Northwest Corner of 19th and Mill. The congregation was founded in 1940 at the church at the corner of 15th and Mill. It moved to the current location in 1953. (The Rigdon house previously occupied this site.)

Selected References

Sanborn maps; 1884-1926 Fire Insurance Maps for Salem

City Directories for Salem; 1871 through 1950.

Plat maps of Salem, Marion County Courthouse.

Depot Addition Historic Neighborhood Survey, ODOT, 1982

Salem City Council minutes, City Hall.

Illustrated Historical Atlas Map of Marion and Linn Counties, 1878

Appendix
Houses with Patterned Shingles in SESNA

ADDRESS	DESCRIPTION
720? 13th	Near the house on the corner of 14th and Leslie.
320 16th	Cross gable house with unusual concave and convex fish scale pattern shingles.

411 16th	SW Corner 16th & Mill. Varied shingle style. Hipped roof with flared eaves. Gable on hip roof with three gable dormers with pattern shingles (119 16th by old address system).
246 17th	Tall two story structure with cross gables and pattern in the upper gable; shingles include three or four different patterns.
433 17th	Small front bay with curved roof to gable face. Face includes concave and convex shingles. Front door has central glass pane surrounded by smaller colored panes.
475 17th	Gable on hip roof with gable in front. Diamond shingle style.
337 18th	Two story Queen Anne. One of a row of five or six nice houses on 18th from Ferry to Mill. Fish scale shingle style.
395 18th	NW Corner 18th & Mill. Two story cross gable. Set under a beautiful oak tree. Fish scale shingle style.
144 19th	Cross gable in T shape with at least three gable faces (160 19th by old address system). Fish scale shingle style.
306 19th	SE Corner 19th & Trade. Tall two story structure with cross gable. Fish scale shingle style.
344 19th	Another tall two story structure, with cross gable. Alternate Sawtooth shingle style.
573 19th	NW Corner 19th & Oak. Erb house. Queen Anne with cross gables, large porch with decorative columns and small colored window glass. Shingles are a small fish scale pattern.
200 22nd	SE Corner 22nd & Ferry. Two story structure with cross gables. Octagon shingle style.

239 22nd	Fish scale shingle style.
590 22nd	Old farm house looking structure with out buildings at the end of 22nd at the railroad tracks. Fish scale shingle style.
2338 State	Two story, refurbished cross gable house. Fish scale shingle style.
1456 Ferry	Old style with exceptional trim work, some small clear windows and alternate fish scale pattern.
1578 Ferry	Paired with house on SW corner of 16th and Ferry. Only staggered shingle patterns in neighborhood.
1596 Ferry	SW corner 16th & Ferry. Corbel chimney. Staggered shingle style. 560 Ferry by old address system.
1968 Ferry	Hipped roof with large porch gable. Two sawtooth rows of shingles.
1980 Ferry	SW corner 20th & Ferry. Hipped roof with large porch gable. Diamond shingle style. (720 Ferry by old address system).
2040 Ferry	Fish scale style shingle.
1656 Mill	Single row of sawtooth shingles in the front gables.
2047 Mill	Beautiful small Queen Anne with extensive ornamentation, including fish scale pattern shingles. 1902 Directory: David and Ellen McLean.
1441 Oak	Two story, renovated house. 1902 Directory: Rachel Norman Daniels.
1394 Leslie	SW corner 14th & Leslie. Small one story house with fish scale.
1364 Tripp	1902 Directory: Faxon, shingles.
1548 Tripp	Shingles.
1662 Tripp	Shingles.
1715 Lee	Shingles.
1548 Lee	Small Queen Anne, shingles.

Silver Creek Falls Revisited

By Bob Humphreys
Previously published August 1993, Vo.31, No.3

"We had gone fishing and when we got back to camp we found a bunch of hogs had gotten into our tent and really made a mess of everything, including our food." I remember that as one of the stories my father told me about camping and fishing at Silver Creek Falls in the late 1890s and early 1900s.

In those days the area around Silver Creek was known as snag country because of the huge forest fire that had burned over much of the falls area. According to *The Oregonian*, the fire covered 990,000 acres in 1865. It left the falls and most of the surrounding mountains in a forest of dead trees. Early pictures and paintings show the snags all around. I remember grandfather, who was 10 years old in 1865, telling of the smoke from the fire. He said it was weeks before it finally burned itself out.

Fishing in Silver Creek was great in those days. On camping trips, one or two would get out of the wagon a mile or so below the falls and fish up the creek, while the others would drive on to the campsite, generally at the top of South Falls. I recall my grandfather wondering how the fish got above and between all of the falls—did the Indians plant them?—the birds carry them?—an interesting question.

All of the falls and their surrounding area were privately owned for many years. There was a small town just above the South Falls, given the name of Silver Falls City. It consisted of a few houses, a church, dance hall, blacksmith shop, store, and a small hotel. There were several small sawmills close by at different times.

In the 1930s a large dance hall was constructed and it operated for a few years. During this time there was also a Civilian Conservation Corps (CCC) camp close to the falls.

For a time admission was charged to the South Falls (I believe it was about 24 cents per car). In an effort to attract more people the owners hired a man named Al Faussett to go over the falls in a canoe. On July 1, 1928, a huge crowd, estimated at several thousand, gathered to watch the event. The canoe was lined with innertubes to cushion the shock. As the scheduled time arrived and passed, nothing happened. Someone went up above the falls to see what was holding things up and found Mr. Faussett partaking of some liquid refreshment to gather enough courage to make the plunge. He did go over the falls that day and only suffered a couple of broken bones. Lots of bets had been made as to whether or not he would survive.

At a later event a Model T Ford was sent over the falls. For many years a portion of it could be seen at the bottom.

June Drake, a pioneer photographer from Silverton, had long wanted the falls area to be made a national or state park. It was largely due to his efforts (as well as others) that the State Parks Division purchased 40 acres at the North Falls in

South Falls at Silver Creek State Park on May 11, 1993.

AL JONES PHOTO

1931. By 1933 the state owned 1,268 acres, including all of the falls except the Upper North.

On July 23, 1933, over 5,000 people attended the dedication of the park. I remember being somewhat bored by the long-winded speeches of all the dignitaries present, but I do remember one particular statement which declared that hereafter the park would always be free for the enjoyment of the people of Oregon. Times change.

Much of the work of improving the park—the many trails, buildings, tables, etc.—was done by the young men at the CCC camp.

The Park now consists of 8,886 acres, making it the largest state park in Oregon. It attracted almost a half-million visitors last year.

In the late 1930s I worked many Sundays at the Volz property which, although not a part of the park, adjoined it. Leo and Hattie Ceislak had a stand and sold homemade ice cream to park visitors. Then the State acquired that property and the Ceislaks moved the stand to about halfway between the South and Lower South Falls, where their property joined the park. Since it was about 100 feet above the trail, we played a battery radio at top volume to attract people. Leo Ceislak willed his 160-acre farm to the park at his death.

Sometimes we fail to appreciate things because they are so close and we are so familiar with them. But taking people to the falls who have not seen them before and watching their reaction helps us to realize what a natural wonder we have—close enough to enjoy whenever we wish.

Turner's 125th Birthday

By Suzanne Stauss
Previously published Summer 1996, Vo.34, No.2

Marion was the name intended for Turner, Oregon. Lumber was shipped to the site by the Oregon and California Railroad to construct a depot. However, the railroad unloaded the lumber at what is now the town of Marion, seven miles south of its intended destination. When railroad officials realized their mistake, they transported a duplicate shipment to the correct site that was then named Turner, Oregon.

Turner was platted by Henry L. Turner on March 8, 1871. Turner, his wife Judith and their children, Cornelia (14), George (12) and Louis (10), had arrived in Marion County of the Oregon Territory in 1852. They began their rugged trip across the plains from their farm in Scio, Ohio. Scio, Oregon, was also platted by Turner, and named for his hometown. Later, he platted Aumsville.

Turner, his sons and son-in-law Amos M. Davis, built a flour mill on their Turner farm in 1863. Because of his German ancestry, Amos was known as Aumus. He died on December 26, 1863, before the mill was completed. Turner was fond of Amos (Aumus) and named Aumsville in his honor.

Water from Mill Creek was diverted to provide hydraulic power for the grinding stones at the flour and grist mills that Turner soon built. People began calling Turner's farm "Hoggum" because of all the pigs that roamed his property.

Accessibility to the railroad enabled local farmers to transport and market their grains, flax, fruits and dairy products. The town grew to a population of 70 by 1878, and area farm land was selling for $15 to $30 per acre.

Turner was incorporated on February 10, 1905. J.M. Watson was mayor and councilmen were J.W. Ransom, B.B. Herrick, E.L. Martin, I.H. Small and G.F. Robertson. Mrs. Hallie Endicott was Turner's first woman mayor, serving from 1939 until 1941.

Between 1871 and 1910, Turner grew with the construction of the Turner Bank, two general merchandise stores, two blacksmith shops, a grocery, hotel, rooming house (three stories), hardware, implements store, two livery stables, drug store, restaurant, saloon, Turner Memorial Tabernacle and a school house.

Passengers traveled between Turner and Stayton via stage coach. The post office was opened in the railroad depot in 1871. News was collected by telegraphers and made available to the public at the post office delivery window.

Turner began the first rural, free mail delivery in Oregon on October 16, 1897. Fred C. Cunning, George Judd and Philip Pearson were the first rural mail carriers. Cunning delivered Route 1, Box 1, at the homestead of Daniel Delaney, about one mile west of Turner. Daniel Delaney had been murdered on January 9, 1865, by George Beal and George Baker when they attempted to rob him on that Sunday afternoon. Conviction of Beal and Baker resulted in Salem's first hangings.

George Turner signed an agreement with the State of Oregon in 1891 to erect a tabernacle for use by the State Convention of the Disciples of Christ, with the stipulation that the Christian Church Convention would also be held in Turner for 99 years.

Most of the Turner estate was inherited by Cornelia Turner Davis and was the origin of funds for the property and money to build the Turner Memorial Home in 1928 and the Christian Church. The Memorial Home was originally a residence for boys. In 1934, Reverend Ellmore J. Gilstrap and Dr. H.C. Epley cofounded Turner Memorial Home For Retired Christians.

Chief Fred Moore organized the first fire department in 1916, the same year residents voted to allow Turner Telephone Company to erect poles and maintain lines within the city. A local feed mill furnished Turner's first electric power, although there was no power on the day the mill did not operate, Sunday.

Patton picture postcard of early Turner, Oregon.

COURTESY CITY OF TURNER

Weather, Floods & Volcanoes in the Willamette Valley

And how we have always coped

Chronicles of historic conditions researched and compiled by Sybil Westenhouse and Adele Egan
Previously published as "Weather By The Season" in three consecutive issues of *Historic Marion*:
Autumn 1996, Vol. 34, No.3; Winter 1996, Vol. 34, No.4; and Spring 1997, Vol. 35, No.1

The frequently changing weather in the Willamette Valley gets everyone's attention. Farmers, builders, doctors, ministers, shoppers, gardeners, movie goers, and golfers all comment on the weather. People new to the area and people who have spent their lifetimes here find the local weather by turns intriguing and confounding.

While reading and assembling historical data about the local area, the authors were often delighted with the details found on the weather conditions, the sometimes resultant floods, and even the mention of the infrequent volcanic eruptions. These descriptions were marvelous fringe benefits accompanying the topics they were researching. Having thus randomly accumulated an assortment of items and articles which the authors believe other weather watchers and nature lovers will enjoy, they have organized them into the following piece.

Some of the writing was expressed so beautifully and concisely, it is quoted at length that the reader may enjoy the charm of the original.

October 1834

This story of the weather and its effects on the activities of Euro-Americans in the Willamette Valley starts with a specific episode in October 1834, written by Rev. Gustavus Hines. Reverend Jason Lee and his small group of men had recently arrived in the Oregon Country and had just chosen the site for the mission they would establish. They were on the east side of the Willamette River, across the river from present day Wheatland, about seventy miles from Fort Vancouver.

The rainy season was commencing, and as they had no house to shelter either themselves or their goods from the inclemency of the weather, they went immediately to work to prepare logs, etc., to build a house. The rain fell in torrents long before their house was erected, yet they labored constantly during the day, and at night were obliged to lie down together in a small tent, scarcely large enough to contain them, and, wrapped in their wet clothes, seek a few hours' repose to prepare them for the toils and storms of the ensuing day. Their house was 32 feet by 18 feet, and on the 3rd of November they moved their goods into it, though they had put on but ten feet of the roof.[1]

December 1840

On Christmas Day of 1840, Daniel Lee plucked a blossom from a wild strawberry plant, and the mild weather continued for the remainder of that winter.

October 1842

"The weather was exceedingly cold, as it had been for a number of weeks previously,...As there had been but little rain during the fall, the river was not high."[2]

December 1842

On December 7, 1842, Gustavus Hines and five Indian boys had gone from the Salem area to Fort Vancouver to get supplies for the Oregon Mission School. There had been little rain that fall. For several weeks it had been extremely cold. Hines described the trip back to Salem: December 11, 1842, Fort Vancouver.

...having completed my business...we proceeded to our boat and found the Columbia river filled with ice. The weather had been increasingly cold, and the ice came down the river in large fields and threatened to put a stop, for the time being, to the navigation of the stream. However, it had not yet become very hard, and though there was some danger in the attempt, yet we launched forth into the stream, and breaking our way through the ice with our setting poles, we at length succeeded in getting safely into the mouth of the Willamette.

This river being clear from ice, we proceeded up about seven miles, and encamped under a high bluff, which sheltered us from the piercing winds from the northeast. The ground being frozen, the weather exceedingly cold...the mercury is nearly down to zero.[3]

...on the 12th of December, 1842, the Columbia was frozen over, and the ice remained in the river at the Dalles till the middle of March, and the mercury was six degrees below zero in that month, while in the Willamette Valley the cold was severe. On the other hand, in the winter of 1843 there was heavy rainfall, and a disastrous freshet in the Willamette in February.[4]

January 1843

That "disastrous freshet" is more fully described by Hines. On January 16, 1843, Gustavus Hines and L.H. Judson set out from Salem on a trip to Fort Vancouver. In a light canoe, they traveled rapidly down the swollen Willamette, covering forty miles the first day. On January 18, Hines recorded:

At twelve it became quite cold, and began to rain and hail. It continued storming without intermission during the afternoon. This rendered it extremely disagreeable traveling, but there was no alternative; so we continued to ply the paddle, though iced with the falling sleet, until it began to grow dusk. Arriving at a small promontory covered with fir timber, twenty miles below the falls, we landed and commenced making preparations for a stormy night. We were thoroughly drenched with rain, though, as good luck would have it, we had preserved our fire-works from getting wet. The storm beat upon us with violence, but we were twenty miles distant from human habitation, and had no choice; we must prepare to make ourselves as comfortable as possible during the night... . The first thing to be done was to kindle a fire, no desirable task when every thing is as wet as rain can make it. However, selecting a place at the leeward of two large firs, that we might be the more sheltered from the wind and storm, after about half an hour, and when patience had performed "her perfect work," we succeeded in kindling a small blaze, which by extreme care we soon increased to a comfortable fire.

Having prepared our evening's repast, we partook of it with a keen relish, while the large

drops from the spreading branches of the fir-trees, as they were shaken with the wind, fell in showers upon us.

Two days later he wrote:

Thursday, 19th. Left Vancouver in the morning, and after a day of hard toiling in a continued storm of snow and rain, arrived, late in the evening, at the house of Richard McCary, about five miles below the Willamette falls. The night was excessively cold and stormy, and we were pleased to be sheltered beneath a friendly roof.[5]

February 1843

On February 2, 1843, a canoe carrying several whites and Indians was washed over the Willamette Falls. Among those lost in the accident was Cornelius Rogers, a young man who had some personal property at the Falls. Gustavus Hines was appointed to secure and appraise that property. Following is his account of the round trip between Salem and Willamette Falls, and the weather factors encountered.

...I started for that place on the 9th of February, in company with Mr. W. H. Gray. Traveled ten miles, and stopped at Dr. Babcock's, who was the Judge of Probate, to get our instructions, and continued with him during the night. Next morning at daylight, proceeded on horseback toward Champoeg, but as there had been a fall of snow the day previous, and the rain was then falling in torrents, it was almost impossible to make headway.

As we urged our way along, we found the streams and ravines so swollen, that the few bridges that had been made, were either carried away or afloat. However, by fording some of the streams where the water covered the saddles, and swimming others which were not fordable, we succeeded in getting to Champoeg, the distance of sixteen miles, at one o' clock, P.M., thoroughly drenched. As it continued to rain violently during the afternoon, we concluded to stop until morning.

Spent the night in a house or hut occupied by Charles Roe, an American, who was absent with his family from home. ...

Rested as well as we could during the night on a naked plank, rose early in the morning, the rain pouring down with increasing violence. But our commission was one of urgency, so turning horses loose upon the prairie, and borrowing a canoe, we struck out into the dashing current of the Willamette. Already the banks of the river were full, and the rapidly increasing flood was rolling onward with fearful fury towards the Pacific, bearing upon its bosom immense quantities of floodwood ever and anon undermining a large tree upon the shore, which would fall with a tremendous crash into the roaring flood; but keeping our cockle-shell craft in the center of the stream, and carefully avoiding coming in contact with the numerous logs floating upon its surface, we proceeded down the distance of ten miles in about one hour. Fearing to attempt to run the dangerous rapids of Rock Island, we rowed our canoe into a little eddy some distance above, and fastened it to some trees. We then took our baggage on our backs, and proceeded on foot towards the falls, distant eight miles. A number of streams crossed our path, but passing some on logs, and wading through others, we arrived there at three o'clock P.M. ...

Monday, 14th. Attended to the duties imposed upon me in relation to Mr. Rogers' estate...

Tuesday. 15th. Having accomplished our business, we left the falls at two P.M., and returned to our canoe, where we encamped for the night. The river had continued to rise until it was higher than it had been known for thirty years, and we knew it would be almost impossible to ascend with our canoe, yet there was no alternative. The banks were overflown, and we were obliged to pull ourselves up the river by the bushes and trees on the shore, as, the moment our canoe was outside the bushes, in spite of the combined strength of six men and their paddles, she would run astern. Toiling for seven hours, without cessation, except to take two raccoons out of a hollow tree, where they had been driven by the flood, we found that we had ascended three miles only, and being above the mouth of the Pudding river, we concluded to "cache" our canoe in the bushes and try the rest of the way on foot.

We found ourselves in a dense forest, but striking a bee line towards the southeast, after traveling some miles we struck the trail leading from the settlement to the falls, and at dark arrived at the house of a Frenchman near the Butte, and about three miles below Champoeg. ...

Next morning proceeded to Champoeg

and found our trusty horses not far from where we turned them loose. The water had risen to an amazing height; farms were swept of their fences, and farmers suffered heavy losses in grain, the water rising several feet deep in some of their barns. Thomas McKay had recently built a large grist mill, and an old gentleman by the name of Canning (James Cannon) was tending the mill. In the morning when he awoke as he slept in the mill, in the second story, the mill was standing in the centre of a large lake. Some persons at a distance, supposing that Canning (Cannon) must be in a perilous condition, procured a canoe, and sailing high over fields, fences, logs, etc., soon arrived at the mill, and running their canoe into the window of the second story, found Canning (Cannon) perched upon a high box, in one corner of the mill, awaiting some one to rescue him from his danger. No essential damage was done the mill, but several hundred bushels of wheat were lost. The flood coming so suddenly upon the valley, the herds on the bottom lands had not time to make their escape. Horses, cattle, hogs, etc., were swept away and drowned.

This was a high flood, but from the appearance of the country, I am persuaded that it is subject to still greater inundations.

Recovering our horses, we left Champoeg in the afternoon, and arrived at our homes the following evening, relieving our families from the painful anxiety into which they had been thrown for our safety in consequence of our exposure to the flood.[6]

1844

In a letter written December 28, 1844, Peter H. Burnett described the climate of the Willamette Valley as he had just experienced it during the year 1844. He had come in the wagon train migration of 1843, and was a worker and doer. Burnett and McCarver laid out and promoted the townsite of Linnton, Burnett was a member of the legislative committee from Tualatin, and he was elected chief justice of the provisional government.

The climate of this, the lower section of Oregon, is indeed most mild. The winter may be said to commence in about the middle of December, and end in February, about the 10th. I saw strawberries in bloom about the first of December last (1843) in the (Tualatin) Plains, and as early as the twentieth of February the flowers were blooming on the hill sides. The grass has now been growing since about the tenth of February, and towards the end of that month the trees were budding and the shrubbery in bloom. About the twenty-sixth of November we had a spell of cold weather and a slight snow, which was gone in a day or two. In the month of December we had a very little snow, and it melted as it fell. In January we had a great deal of snow, which all melted as it fell, except once, which melted in three days. The ground has not been frozen more than one inch deep the whole winter, and plowing has been done throughout the winter and fall. The ink with which I now write has stood in a glass inkstand, on a shelf, far from the fire, in a house with only boards nailed on the cracks, during the whole month of January, and has not been frozen, as you may see from its good color. As regards rains in the winter, I have found them much less troublesome than I anticipated. I had supposed that no work could be done here during the rainy season; but a great deal more outdoor work can be done in the winter season than in the Western States. The rains fall in very gentle showers, and are generally what you term drizzling rains, so light that a man can work all day without getting wet through a blanket coat. The rains are not the cold, chilly rains that you have in the fall and spring seasons in the East, but are warm as well as gentle. Since I have been here I have witnessed less wind than in any country I have ever been in; and I have heard no thunder, and only seen one tree that had been struck by lightning. If the tall timber we have here were in the States, it would be riven and blown down, until there would not be many trees left. The rains are never hard enough here to wash the roads or the fields. You can find no gullies washed in the roads or fields in this region. [7]

Also in Peter Burnett's letter of December 28, 1844, is one of the earliest descriptions of Mount St. Helens erupting. It contains the reminder that the mountain was then known as Mount St. Helena.

This mountain (Mount St. Helena) is now a burning volcano. It commenced about a year since. The crater is on the side of the mountain, about two thirds of the distance from its base. …On the sixteenth of February, 1844, being a beautiful and clear day, the mountain burned most magnificently. The dense masses of smoke rose up in one immense column, covering the whole crest of the mountain in clouds. Like other volcanoes, it burns at intervals. …On the side of the mountain, near its top, is a large black object, amidst the pure white snow around it. This is supposed to be the mouth of a large cavern. From Indian accounts this mountain emitted a volume of burning lava about the time it first commenced burning. An Indian came to Vancouver with his foot and leg badly burnt, who stated that he was on the side of the mountain hunting deer, and he came to a stream of something running down the mountain, and when he attempted to jump across it, he fell with one foot into it; and that was the way in which he got his foot and leg burned. This Indian came to the fort to get Doctor Barclay to administer some remedy to cure his foot.

1845-1848

The winters of 1844-45 and 1845-46 were mild and rainy, encouraging fruit to form on the trees in April.

The winter of 1846-47 was a winter of blizzards in the Willamette Valley. Heavy snow in January 1847 drifted into and damaged every fence on the Yamhill plain. Late that winter the Columbia froze so solidly that the officers of the British ship *Modeste* played a curling match on the river in front of Fort Vancouver.

During May in 1847, the forests and fields were burning. The smoke was so thick and close to the valley floor that people had to wear neckerchief masks. "It was hardly the rain-kissed May people had come to expect in Oregon. The weather grew unusually hot and dry, pushing ill and speedy winds over the foothills and carrying shrouds of acrid smoke."[8] The hot, dry May was followed by a summer drought so severe that cattle became weakened from extremely poor grazing land, and little or no hay was available to store for winter. The autumn of 1847 was wet and cold, and the winter was bitter cold with wind and snow.

July 1848 was a warm month with some gentle rain. Near the end of December 1848 the Spanish bark *Jo'ven Guipuzcoana* became icebound a few miles below the mouth of the Willamette and remained so until February 1849.

George H. Himes noted in 1902 that casting slurs on Oregon's weather has been common from the earliest white exploration and settlement. He quotes *Oregon Spectator* editor Aaron E. Wait taking exception to the slurs on December 14, 1848: "For the year ending November 30th there have been

240 clear days, 25 days on which it rained or snowed all day, and 101 days on which it rained, hailed, snowed, or was cloudy part of the day."

1854-1865

February 1854. The Columbia River was so full of ice that the steamer *Peytona* took ten days to travel from Astoria to Portland. In mid March, Ketturah Belknap wrote of the Bellfountain-Monroe area: "...we had a Beautiful Early Spring and the weather was all that could be desired, no rain, the roads were quite good, the ground nice and dry..."[9]

December 18, 1854. Rev. Obed Dickinson in Salem noted: "Are enjoying a most beautiful winter. But little rain. The air mild as spring thus far. No frost in the ground; and have not yet seen a flake of snow. If this is Oregon winter it is a most delightful climate."[10]

March 1855. A destructive hail storm passed near Salem. The hail stones were as large as partridge eggs. During the storm, several frail buildings were thrown down.

On March 15, (1859), Editor Bush was complaining about the weather. Cold rain, accompanied by snow and sleet had fallen every day for the past six weeks. Fatalities among cattle were unprecedented. But the summer of 1859 was just as dry as the winter had been wet. Road dust became so deep that travel was unpleasant. [11]

December 1861-February 1862. "After the high water in December 1861, came the deep snow, which stayed on the ground for nearly six weeks. That winter was certainly a hard winter, particularly on stock."[12]

November 1865. In Polk County, the wind blew down several houses, unroofed others, and interrupted telegraph communication with San Francisco.

So the weather in the Willamette Valley went for our predecessors and so it goes 163 years later. It will keep us watching, predicting, wondering.

---

[1]   Hines, Gustavus, *Wild Life In Oregon*, p12.
[2]   ibid., p123.
[3]   ibid., p120-122.
[4]   Bancroft, Hubert Howe, *History of Oregon Vol. II*, p39-40.
[5]   Hines, p130-134.
[6]   ibid., p138-141.
[7]   "Letters of Peter H. Burnett," The *Quarterly of the Oregon Historical Society, Vol. III*, p424-425.
[8]   Applegate, Shannon, *Skookum*, p79.
[9]   Gatke, Robert M., *Chronicles of Willamette*, p127.
[10] Oliver, Egbert S., *Obed Dickinson's War Against Sin In Salem*, p43.
[11] Maxwell, Ben, "Salem in 1859," *Marion County HISTORY, Vol. V*, p10.
[12] Lockley, Fred, *Conversations With Pioneer Women*, p115.

Salem Weather

The highest, lowest, deepest
By Reid Hanson

Salemites like to brag about their weather. Overall we say it is quite mild. In the summer the weather doesn't become too hot and humid and in the winter it rarely is too cold. But we admit that the weather can be rather damp at times.

The following data show the extremes that have been recorded by the Salem Weather Service. Salem weather records go all the way back to 1892, except for snowfall, for which records have been kept officially since 1939.

Of particular interest are the highest temperatures—108 three times; coldest day—12 below zero in 1972; greatest rainfall—4.3 inches December 6, 1933; heaviest snowfall—27 inches January 31, 1937 (although 11.9 inches on February 19, 1993, tops the "official" records begun in 1939).

Also pointed out here are the driest and wettest months; major floods—1861, 1890, 1943, 1964-65 and 1996-97—and biggest storms, topped by the Columbus Day Storm of October 12, 1962.

Floods

According to the US Army Corps of Engineers, flooding usually occurs when heavy rainfall comes with snowmelt, at a time when the soil is either frozen or near saturation.

South Mill Creek bridge during the February, 1890 flood.
MCHS COLLECTION

1861-62 There was heavy snow in November and heavy rain fell in December of 1861. The Willamette River was estimated to be at a crest of 47 feet in Salem. Champoeg was swept away.

1881 In January the Willamette River crested at 36.3 feet in Salem, reaching downtown.

1890 In February flood waters swept away the Marion-Polk County bridge. The Willamette River crested at 45 feet.

1943 January floods did considerable damage following 60 days of heavy precipitation and 26 inches of snow. The Willamette crested at 38.6 feet.

The Circuit Rider statue at the State Capitol was toppled by 1962 Columbus Day storm winds. The Statesman Journal reported the next day that two people were killed in the Salem area during the storm and that the Red Cross estimated damage to Marion County exceeded $8 million. Winds reached 90 mph in Salem and gusted to 130 mph in Newport.

COURTESY STATESMAN/JOURNAL

Downtown Salem during 1890 flood when the Willamette crested at 45 feet.

1964-65 Flooding did $244.4 million worth of damage in Salem during the Christmas week of 1964, reaching a level of 45.3 feet. The flood receded and then rose again in the last week of February 1965, doing a total of $47.2 million in additional damage. One thousand people were evacuated in the Keizer area. The Boise Cascade mill was closed and the Salem Memorial Hospital was surrounded by water. Leading up to the "100-year flood" in 1964 was a snowfall of 12.4 inches in mid-December and 8.16 inches of rain in January 1965. For the November-January period there was a total of 23.58 inches of rainfall compared with an annual total of 36.44 inches.

1996-97 In February of 1996 the devastating combination of a four-day cold spell with 17 degree lows and 35 degree highs, followed by five days of temperatures in the 50s, and continual rain totaling 7.58 inches, brought on a "100-year flood" that carried water over the banks of creeks and rivers in the Willamette Valley.

Snowfall

December 1852 Two to three feet of snow fell "all through the country."

January 8, 1857 Fourteen inches of snow fell in Salem.

January 6, 1862 Twelve inches of snow fell, which remained on the ground for 42 days. The Willamette and Columbia Rivers were frozen over solid.

December 15, 1884 Approximately two feet of snow accumulated by Christmas.

December 9, 1919 Twenty-two inches of snow fell, while the temperature was 6 below zero.

January 15, 1930 Eleven inches of snowfall.

January 31, 1937 Twenty-seven inches of snow

fell and 25 inches of it came down in 24 hours.

Winter 1942-43 Snowfall totaled 23.6 inches.

March 6, 1951 In one day 5.8 inches of snow fell with a total of 10.9 inches that week.

The January floods of 1943 after 60 days of heavy rain and 26inches of snow. Looking east at the inaccessible Marion Street Bridge from Highway 22 in West Salem, shows the Willamette River cresting at 38.6 feet.

Snow piled deep on downtown Salem streets in the January 31, 1937, blizzard. This view is looking southwest at State and Commercial Streets, toward the Capitol Hotel, known earlier as the Griswold Theater built in the mid 1850s and now site of McMahan's Furniture. AL JONES COLLECTION

Weather Oddities

Strongest Wind
On October 12, 1962, the day of the Columbus Day Storm, wind velocity ranged from 58 to 90 miles per hour.

Longest No Rain
■ Seventy-nine days from June 22 to September 10, 1967.
■ Seventy-three days from June 25 to September 7, 1914.

Frozen Willamette
In 1854 it is said the Willamette River froze solid from bank to bank and teams crossed and recrossed the river.
■ On January 13, 1876, the Willamette River was covered with ice.
■ December 26, 1924, saw the Willamette River blocked with drift ice. Two daredevils braved the rough and tumbled formations to cross from bank to bank.

Boat Sinking
On December 29, 1924, the steamer *Relief*, moored at the foot of Court Street, was trapped by crushing ice that broke its back and it sank in 20 feet of water.

Strong Wind
On January 8, 1880, a wind of gale force (between 30 and 65 miles per hour) swept through Salem. Its velocity was not recorded but the fury of its violence carried away the roofs of the old State Capitol and the Sacred Heart Academy.

Huge Snow Drifts
Heavy snowfall on New Year's Day 1915 caused large drifts. The Albany train, consisting of three coaches drawn by three locomotives, started for Salem. At Jefferson they were stalled by drifts and here a fourth engine was added to successfully drag the train, hours late, into Salem. In places snow drifts across the tracks were five feet deep.

Salem's Driest Day
July 12. Since the start of keeping weather records in 1892, no measurable amount of rain has ever fallen on this day through 1997. There have been a few traces of rain recorded but no measurable amount. It seems incredible that no rain has fallen on this day in over 100 years.

All Time High Temperatures

108 -July 23, 1927	104 -July 2, 1942	102 -July 22, 1928	101 -August 28, 1931	100 -June 24, 1925
108 -July 15, 1941	104 -July 18, 1956	102 -July 24, 1928	101 -August 15, 1933	100 -July 9, 1926
108 -August 9, 1981	104 -July 27, 1958	102 -August 4, 1932	101 -Sept. 2, 1934	100 -August 22, 1942
	104 -August 8, 1960	102 -August 2, 1939	101 -August 27, 1935	100 -August 29, 1944
107 -July 10, 1926	104 -July 12, 1961	102 -August 17, 1940	101 -July 1, 1942	100 -July 7, 1945
107 -July 14, 1935	104 -July 31, 1965	102 -June 30, 1942	101 -July 6, 1960	100 -Sept. 4, 1955
107 -August 10, 1981	104 -August 11, 1977	102 -July 30, 1942	101 -August 11, 1971	100 -August 10, 1961
	104 -August 7, 1981	102 -August 14, 1942	101 -July 14, 1973	100 -June 17, 1969
106 -July 19, 1956	104 -Sept. 2, 1988	102 -August 5, 1945	101 -August 10, 1977	100 -August 9, 1971
106 -August 8, 1978		102 -August 3, 1952	101 -August 16, 1977	100 -August 27, 1972
106 -August 8, 1981	103 -August 13, 1920	102 -July 8, 1956	101 -July 17, 1996	100 -August 9, 1977
	103 -July 26, 1939	102 -August 6, 1972		100 -July 21, 1978
105 -August 12, 1920	103 -July 13, 1941	102 -July 22, 1978		100 -July 25, 1978
105 -July 21, 1938	103 -July 16, 1941	102 -July 17, 1979		100 -August 9, 1978
105 -July 20, 1946	103 -Sept. 4, 1944	102 -June 28, 1982		100 -July 15, 1979
105 -August 12, 1977	103 -July 11, 1961	102 -July 25, 1988		100 -May 28, 1983
105 -August 17, 1977	103 -July 30, 1965	102 - August 23, 1988		100 -August 31, 1987
105 -August 7, 1981	103 -July 16, 1979	102 -Sept. 1, 1988		100 -August 3, 1993
105 -June 22, 1992	103 -July 26, 1988	102 -Sept. 2, 1988		100 -July 22, 1994
105 -August 11, 1992	103 -July 21, 1994	102 -July 30, 1994		

Hottest Days By The Month

105 -June 22, 1992	108 -August 9, 1981
102 -June 30, 1942	107 -August 10, 1981
102 -June 28, 1982	106 -August 8, 1978
100 -June 24, 1925	106 -August 8, 1981
100 -June 15, 1966	105 -August 12, 1920
100 -June 17, 1969	105 -August 12, 1977
	105 -August 17, 1977
108 -July 23, 1927	105 -August 7, 1981
108 -July 15, 1941	105 -August 11, 1992
107 -July 10, 1926	
107 -July 14, 1935	104 -Sept. 2, 1988
106 -July 19, 1956	103 -Sept. 4, 1944
105 -July 21, 1938	102 -Sept. 2, 1988
105 -July 20, 1946	101 -Sept. 2, 1934
	100 -Sept. 4, 1955

103 days of temperatures above 100 since 1892

Coldest Days By The Month

-12 -December 8, 1972
-6 -December 14, 1919
-6 -December 9, 1972

-10 -January 31, 1950
-5 -January 21, 1930
-3 -January 20, 1930
-3 -January 30, 1950
-1 -January 5, 1989

-4 -February 4, 1899
-4 -February 3, 1950
-3 -February 2, 1950

Thirty-three days of temperatures below zero since 1892

Five Days Of Greatest Rainfall By Month

2.84" - October 8-9, 1955	3.30" -January 2, 1933
2.36" - October 15-16, 1947	3.07" -January 20, 1972
2.07" - October 1-2, 1951	2.91" -January 3-4, 1956
2.00" - October 17, 1898	2.86" -January 18, 1911
1.90" - October 7, 1893	2.86" -January 3, 1895
3.60" - November 8, 1896	3.16" -February 16-17, 1949
3.11" - November 19, 1897	2.99" -February 1, 1937
3.00" - November 29, 1893	2.97" -February 9-10, 1961
2.82" - November 26-27, 1945	2.93" -February 6, 1996
2.82" - November 15-16, 1950	2.84" -February 18-19, 1968
4.30" - December 6, 1933	3.03" -March 30-31, 1943
3.12" - December 2-3, 1987	2.07" -March 28-29, 1963
2.91" - December 29, 1937	2.05" -March 21-22, 1948
2.72" - December 21-22, 1964	2.03" -March 8-9, 1966
2.52" - December 3-4, 1968	1.96" -March 27-28, 1974

Greatest Snowfall Since 1939

11.9" - February 18-19, 1993
10.8" - January 21, 1943
9.4" - January 25-26, 1969
9.4" - December 5-6, 1972
8.5" - March 2-3, 1960
6.8" - January 18-19, 1960
6.7" - December 29-30, 1968
6.4" - January 29-30, 1950
6.4" - February 1-2, 1989
6.2" - December 1-2, 1985

All Time Low Temperatures

-12 -December 8, 1972
-10 -January 31, 1950
-6 -December 14, 1919
-6 -December 9, 1972
-5 -January 21, 1930
-4 -February 4, 1899
-4 -February 3, 1950
-3 -January 20, 1930
-3 -January 30, 1950
-3 -February 2, 1950
-2 -December 13, 1919

Months With No Precipitation

June -1918
July - 1893, 1896, 1899, 1910, 1914, 1922, 1925, 1926, 1929, 1931, 1933, 1952, 1967
August - 1894, 1900, 1902, 1914, 1915, 1917, 1919, 1928, 1988
September -1975
October -1895, 1917

There are, of course, other interesting records like the highest minimum temperature for a July 22. In 1994, the night time temperature for that date in Salem "cooled down" to 65 degrees.

The high temperatures for July in both 1995 and 1996 reached only 98 degrees, but it seemed hot for July in 1996 because there were 12 days of 90 plus degrees.

Over the years, El Nino, the irregularly occurring atmospheric and oceanic change, has given us unusually dry and/or warm periods in the normally wet, cold months.

The more vivid memory of local citizens in the late 1990s is of especially wet months. But no Autumn rainfall records were set by the "heavy" 1.2 inches of rain on September 15, 1997, nor by the 1.96 inches on November 11, 1995. Neither were 2.80 inches on February 6, 1943, 2.68 inches on February 17, 1995, nor the 2.32 inches for February 7, 1996, records for Winter.

Rainfall By Month

April 1996, at 5.72 inches, was the fourth wettest April since records started in 1892. February 1996, the wettest February on record in 104 years, totaled 13.01 inches. The previous February record rainfall was 12.31 inches. February 5 through 8, 1996, totaled 8.18 inches and three of the four days set records for those dates.

Record Precipitation Years		
1996-97	61.37 inches	
1973-74	61.00 inches	1976-77 was the
1995-96	57.46 inches	driest year with
1982-83	56.88 inches	only 19.52
1937-38	53.10 inches	inches of
1942-43	52.37 inches	precipitation.
1950-51	50.59 inches	
1970-71	49.66 inches	
1994-95	47.85 inches	

Old Chemawa

Indian School entered on national register

By Jordis Schick
Previously published February 1993, Vol.31, No.1

An exciting action occurred on December 16, 1992, when the Chemawa Indian School Site (1885-1933) at 3700 Chemawa Road NE, Salem, Marion County, Oregon was entered in the National Register of Historic Places.

Bill "White Eagle" Wilson has spearheaded the drive for this designation for the past four years, with some help from the Mid-Willamette Valley Arts Council and the Oregon State Historic Preservation Office.

The official description for the listed historic property reads "an irregular area of approximately 78 acres to encompass the old campus area and its sole remaining building, the Health Center of 1907 and the adjoining cemetery and historic institutional farming area." [Editor's Note: The Health Center building was destroyed by fire in December 1995.]

Wilson's ultimate goal is to create the Confederated Tribes of the Willamette which will, in turn, establish a Native American cultural center, museum, resource center, archives, and arts education program in the old medical building at Chemawa.

The Confederated Tribes concept comes from a desire to preserve the Native American culture for the Willamette Valley, not only for Indian children but the general community as well.

Wilson considers the old medical building to be the perfect place because it stands on old Indian grounds in close proximity to a sacred Indian graveyard. The sign at the school's historic cemetery, which contains over 190 burials, was made by students in the old school's metal shop. The same students also made the sign at the Jason Lee Cemetery.

The old campus incorporates a sense of place that is distinct from the new campus to the east.

The mostly flat landscape is enhanced by mature firs, maples and other deciduous trees. The section of Willamette Valley bottom land in the Lake Labish district at the southernmost reach of French Prairie was selected as the Indian School site for its ability to support farming endeavors. For over a century the school engaged in farming operations including a dairy, greenhouses, gardens, and orchards. Currently a Christmas tree farm meets the customary goal and requirements of being a partially self-supporting institution.

Wilson hopes to enhance the park-like setting with the addition of natural plants that would have been indigenous to the site and, possibly establish a seed bank. The paths that led through the old campus as well as the walkways to the various buildings are still there.

The nominated area is the second site of the Chemawa Indian School and was in continual use from 1885 until 1945, with intermittent use thereafter until 1976.

Chemawa Indian School Health Center of 1907.

COURTESY BILL WILSON

The original school was built on leased land in Forest Grove in 1880 by Lt. M.C. Wilkinson, but after some of the wooden buildings there were destroyed by fire, the school was reopened in Salem in 1885. The first generation of wooden buildings here were replaced with a sizable complement of permanent, brick buildings between 1899 and the 1920s. Charles Holmes, who served as the Supervisor of Vocational Education at Chemawa for many years, says these buildings were all of standard army quartermaster design.

Almost all of the buildings on the old campus were razed in the late 1970s after construction of modern facilities, including a new health center. Today, only the old hospital or health center/clinic still stands.

According to the State Historic Preservation Office summary, "Chemawa is the oldest and largest federally-sponsored boarding institution in the Pacific Northwest providing general education and vocational training to Native American students. It is also one of the rare off-reservation boarding schools in the nation."

During the early years, Indian children as young as six boarded at the school. Through ensuing years, students have come from throughout the Northwest, Alaska, the Southwest, and even New England.

The State summary says the high point of the historic period dating from 1885 to 1933 may be pinpointed at about 1927-1930, just after Chemawa became a fully accredited four-year high school, when enrollment reached a record high of 1100, and the number and variety of teaching departments and extracurricular programs were reflected in an array of specialized buildings—some 70 in all—ranging from dormitories to a domestic science building, gymnasium, bakery, industrial arts shops, dairy barn and the well-regarded hospital facility.

Wilson, who is part Cherokee and Choctaw, became interested in the project when he volunteered at Chemawa School after retiring as a state employee. Wilson makes and plays traditional Indian flutes; he also visits schools throughout the state to talk about the history and culture of American Indian tribes.

Salem High School

The origin of Salem's first high school built in 1905

By Suzanne Stauss
Previously published Autumn 1996, Vol. 34, No. 3

Salem's early educational opportunities were a strong factor in attracting early settlers to the area. Oregon historical records from 1840-60 pioneers reveal that they shared the current opinion that childhood education is essential to enhance the quality of adult life.

Formal education arrived in Oregon with the missionaries. The first school began in the fall of 1832, for half-breed boys at Fort Vancouver. John Ball, a member of the Wyeth party of 1832, was the teacher. The Presbyterian and Methodist missions also established schools, believing that education was one of the most important elements of their mission.

On July 5, 1843, at Champoeg, the law of the provisional government of Oregon was amended to state that "Religion, morality, and knowledge, being necessary to good government and the happiness of mankind, schools and the means of education, shall be forever encouraged."

On September 5, 1849, the Oregon Territorial legislature created an irreducible school fund, organized school districts, and granted them the authority to levy a property tax within their district to fund education.

Opposition to taxation was extensive, because many early Oregonians felt that private schools were better suited for their rural existence. The Office of Territorial Superintendent of Instruction was established in 1850. Four years later, a legislative act of January 12, 1854, initiated the reorganization of the Oregon education system to provide free public schools. The Oregon Constitution of 1857 established the Oregon public school system.

Legislative authorization to assume status as a sanctioned university had been granted to Willamette University in 1853. The Oregon Institute, established in 1842, became the primary and elementary school in Salem, as a preparatory department for Willamette. The two served as the academy and college for most of the Northwest.

Only private or subscription schools existed in Salem until public education began in 1858 in accordance with Oregon legislation. Many people were enraged at the prospect of public schools. The *Oregon Statesman* newspaper published the following Asahel Bush editorial on September 29, 1857:

We regret the introduction of that provision into the instrument. Not that we are opposed to common schools in the abstract, for we are not. But Oregon is a very different country. Oregon is too sparsely populated. In our opinion we now have and under the present system for years to come will have schools inferior to those which would spring up under the voluntary system.

Salem's first high school built in 1905.
COURTESY BOB TOMPKINS

Not long before this conflict had emerged, County School Superintendent William Pugh created Salem School District No. 24. In 1857 he had ordered the construction of a Central School. After spending $1,760.30 to build the school, a special meeting was called in August to approve an $800 tax levy to complete construction and include higher grade levels in public education. The first Salem school board meeting took place on April 2, 1858. Later, Robert Horace Down described the meeting as follows:

The annual school board meeting of 1858 was apparently a turbulent one. The leading citizens turned out in force. The issue agitating the community was whether Salem should have a high school. We are not sure what the arguments for and con were. We may be sure of one thing however. Back of all the arguments against the project was the conviction that a public free high school would mean deadly competition for the Oregon Institute, which was the preparatory department of Willamette University. The friends of education had, however, one thing to be especially thankful for. Mr. Bush was at the meeting, converted and devoted to the public school idea. Mr. Bush moved that whatever tax be levied be expended in building a house for a Central High School.

The Bush motion did not pass. I.R. Moores moved to levy a five mill tax to fund country elementary schools only, which passed by a large majority.

By 1875, the school board had worked consistently to develop higher grade levels.

Elementary school grade levels had been defined by then, which would eventually help qualify children for high school. The school year lasted 40 weeks, beginning in September and was divided into three terms of 16, 14, then 12 weeks, with a two week vacation.

In 1878, The Oregon School Code stated the following: "Duties of Directors: To maintain at least six months in each year, in all districts where the number of persons between four and twenty years of age is 1,000, as shown by the clerk's yearly report, a high school, wherein shall be taught, in addition to the common school branches, such other branches as the directors of the district may prescribe."

Only Portland had reached the one thousand school-age stipulation at that time. Salem reached the mark in 1900. Before that, Salem and most other communities had begun "additional grades", an unofficial way to expand education beyond the elementary level. The Salem school board added new required subjects of physical geography, elementary algebra, high arithmetic, composition and rhetoric. They called it the ninth grade.

Parents became determined to expand school to legitimately established grades nine and ten. Most students were graduating at the age of 15 or 16. When college was not in their future, they would pursue a business career. Because opportunities were limited to children of that age, it appeared to be a logical advantage for young people to continue education during that time in preparation for job opportunities and a better life. The school board rejected a motion to that effect.

Most of the opposition seems to have vanished when the decision was overturned in 1901 by a new Oregon law for the organization of district and county high schools. Schools were under the strong leadership of John H. Ackerman, with progressive support from the increasing number of newcomers to our area. Every community had an interest in growing and still recognized educational opportunities as a meaningful attraction to potential residents.

Although grade nine education had existed in Salem for five years, a 1901 Salem special election authorized its existence. During the 1901-02 school year there were 60 ninth-graders with two teachers.

Advocacy for the tenth grade continued. The community considered Salem a highly cultured capital city, but many residents felt that students were not sufficiently educated when they graduated. Opposition came from taxpayers who thought that the high cost of extended grades would benefit only a limited number of young people.

Conventional high school education was probably launched when Luther R. Traver became involved as superintendent of Salem schools. He influenced greater participation in the upper grade levels.

Traver convinced the school board that the tenth grade could be provided without additional expense. The February class of 1903 continued tenth grade work. Twenty students studied higher math and English, modern history and English literature. Traver participated as a teacher and also promoted athletics with help from coach Moser of Willamette University.

All students formed an association to support school literary work, debating, athletics and other activities. Student president was Ted Burton and Lucile Chase was secretary. Students initiated a "popular student" contest to fund a library and purchase books. Paying one penny per vote, people could contribute in the name of any student.

All Salem schools were now seeking higher grade levels, but work was concentrating on the East School, located where Safeway grocery is now (1996) at 12th and Center Streets. Ninth and tenth grades enrolled 90 students in 1902-03, still with only two teachers. All students began every term with a spelling test of words related to "everyday affairs" as regulated by the school district. Scores of at least 90% excused them from taking spelling for the term. Students liked the spelling exams and interest in literary work flourished, along with a healthy social life.

In 1904, Salem was the only city in the United States of comparable size that had not established a high school, and the only principal city in Oregon without a four-year high school. High

schools were operating in six other Oregon communities with smaller populations than Salem. The irony was the fact that Salem had founded the first Oregon public school (a log cabin built in 1850), but failed in progressing toward high school education.

While some people were indifferent to the situation, most Salemites were either bitterly opposed or adamantly supportive. The June 20, 1904, general election resolved the debate. The voting result on the issue of gradually introducing additional grade levels each year was 479 (yes) to 205 (no). Student enthusiasm and involvement soared. The first issue of the monthly high school student newspaper, *The Clarion*, was published in the fall of 1904.

High school facilities were still limited to three rooms in the East School building. More than 50 students crowded each room. There was not a laboratory, library or auditorium. Because enrollment was forecast to reach 300 in 1905, the school board voted to improve conditions.

The class of 1906 was the first to graduate from Salem's official high school program. The first day of school 121 students enrolled, although the number increased to 150 by November.

Students built public respect for Salem High School with their impressive interest and success in academics and athletics. The debating team was well respected. The Drama Club performed *Courtship of Miles Standish* and scenes from Shakespeare without a stage or properties. Boys formed a secret fraternity called Knights of the Mystic Seven. Girls organized a nonsecretive, captivatingly artistic fraternity, The Tam Club.

Football, basketball and baseball teams had winning records. The athletic association had formed a successful football team in 1902. But in 1903, they were still without a field, coach, dressing room, financial support or much game attendance. Although many faculty members were opposed to the idea of football, coach Frank Grannis advanced an interest in football in 1904 with four wins and one loss. Players used the Willamette field and dressing rooms. The freshman class of 1906 selected school colors and cheers—*Rickety blix! Rickety blix! We are the class of 1906!* Coach A.C. Lougheed, of Stanford, proceeded with the successful football team. Ruby Phelps, former head of girls' gymnastics at Willamette, coached an outstanding girls' basketball team.

Perry Reigelman was student body president in 1904-05 and Horace Sykes, *Clarion* editor. Principal was J.M. Powers, a former Wisconsin native.

After extensive research, the school board contracted with Welch and Mauer on April 4, 1905, to build the first Salem High School on the site of the historic Central School, between Church and High Streets. The public endorsed a beautiful fireproof building, designed by W.D. Pugh. Believed to have been at least partially funded by surplus revenue, a district school tax or bond was not necessary for completion. Construction was composed of Newberg pressed brick, with 16 large classrooms, laboratories, and a library. The basement housed bicycle, furnace and rest rooms. The third floor was an unfinished gym and assembly hall with ample seating, stage and acoustics. Unique to the time, a forced-air heating and ventilation system was installed which recirculated air every six minutes. The total cost, including grounds and equipment, was $60,000.

Salem High School was the most modern and convenient school in Oregon when completed. Skilled craftsmen had maximized their artistic talents to finish a gym and assembly hall in Italian style and to widen halls and stairways, make classrooms comfortable and create a beautiful exterior.

Salem High School was dedicated on New Year's night, 1906. Superintendent J.M. Powers addressed the ceremony with the following statement: *I hope that I am no false prophet when I predict that many of you will live to see a thousand students in the Salem High School. The city at this moment has the distinction of having one of the very best public school systems on the coast. You will see the city grow and prosper under the benign influence of a public school system second to none in the whole country.*

Information for this story was collected from *History of Salem High School 1903-1916*, written by Sharon J. Bates in 1957; and *A History of Salem Public Schools 1893-1916*, written by Constance Weinman in 1932.

**Salem High School
First Graduating Class, 1906**

Including Individual Course Study

Rea Utter	German-Scientific
Carrie Magness	Latin-Scientific
Ethel M. Bell	Literary
Marguerite Mers	Latin-Scientific
Genevieve Potter	Classical
Ruby V. Rotzien	German-Scientific
Mabel Magness	Classical
Harvey M. Slater	Literary
Perry P. Reigelman	Literary
Marie Hutchins	Classical
Bertha Duncan	Classical
Della C. Clark	Literary
Elizabeth F. Harding	Literary
Horace Sykes	Literary
Martha Schindler	Classical
Alice Judson	Classical
Helen Phillips	Literary
Fannie Funk	Literary

Sublimity School District Retires

By Suzanne Stauss
Previously published Summer 1996, Vol.34, No.2

 On July 1, 1996, Sublimity School District No. 7 became part of the North Santiam School District. On May 16, the Heritage Museum hosted a day of celebration to honor the retirement and remember the heritage of the Sublimity community. They shared the following information with visitors.

District No. 7 was established in 1854. The first school was a log cabin on the west side of town. The Sublimity post office was only two years old, but one of the first six in Oregon.

By 1857, the United Brethren built Sublimity College, with Milton Wright as head teacher. Wright was to become the father of Orville and Wilbur Wright, the famous aviators.

Tuition for first grade primary students was $5 for the first twelve-week term. As students advanced, an additional fifty cents was charged per subject. Latin and ancient language students paid $9 per term. Higher English cost $7.

Sublimity College closed during the Civil War until February 13, 1865. The college closed permanently in 1870.

However, the Sublimity School District expanded from the original three month term to five months. Teachers were paid $20 per month.

Classes were conducted at St. Boniface Church until the district purchased property for the high school in 1933.

Today Sublimity schools are as important a part of community life as they were in the early days. Descendants of the early Sublimity families remain in the area and continue their historical commitment to education.

St. Joseph College in St. Paul

By Mary A. Grant, Portland Archivist; Archdiocese of Portland in Oregon
Previously published November 1993, Vol.31, No.4

On October 17, 1993, the Archdiocese of Portland celebrated the Sesquicentennial (150th Anniversary) of the opening of the first Catholic school in Oregon. Named St. Joseph College in the European tradition, the curriculum of this school, by today's standards, was intended for primary and secondary grades.

St. Joseph's was built by Father (later Archbishop) Francis Norbert Blanchet in the town of St. Paul on the famous French Prairie in the Willamette River valley. French Prairie is so called because of the nucleus of French Canadians, predominantly Catholics, who had settled there. Retired and former fur trappers and traders, these men had intermarried with Native American women and sought to give their children a formal education. When the school was originally blessed and opened on October 17, 1843, a total of thirty boys were in attendance, sons of farmers except for one boy who was the son of the Grand Ronde Indian chief. As was typical of the day, the boys were resident students at the school.

The first director of St. Joseph's was Father Antoine Langlois of the Archdiocesan clergy. Mr. King served as the principal and teacher of English; Mr. Bilodeau was assistant and teacher of French.

The school was named St. Joseph in honor of Joseph Larocque, a French Canadian former fur trader who retired home to eastern Canada, but who remembered his friends in the Oregon Country by donating 4,800 francs to Archbishop Blanchet for the building of a school in St. Paul.

St. Joseph's is important historically not only to Oregon, but to the region because it was the first Catholic boys' school in the entire Pacific Northwest. Because the fair sex was not to be long forgotten, a typical 19th-century historical parallel soon occurred and a school for women and girls was also built in St. Paul. This "female academy," the first ever in Oregon, was named Sainte Marie de Willamette. It was opened on September 9, 1844, by the Sisters of Notre Dame de Namur, a Belgian religious institute invited to teach in Oregon by Archbishop Blanchet. Because their

Right:
This brick is thought to have been cast in the St. Paul area in 1832.

Below:
This photograph was taken by A.N. Bush in 1912. St. Paul Academy is at the far right. It replaced the Sister's School that burned in 1911.

A.N. BUSH PHOTO, A.N. BUSH COLLECTION • PUBLISHED WITH PERMISSION OF THE OREGON STATE LIBRARY

Sister's School in St. Paul was built in 1891 and burned in 1911. Part of the original 1844 building was in the rear.

building was not quite ready until early October of that year, the Sisters gave their first lessons outdoors. On September 12, 1848, the Sisters opened their second school in the Pacific Northwest in Oregon City.

Unfortunately, the effects of the famous California Gold Rush of the 1840s were felt even in the Willamette Valley town of St. Paul. Due to the loss of financial support because of the fevered exodus of most of the male population, St. Joseph College closed its doors in June of 1849. A few years later the school building served as a hospital during a typhoid epidemic, but it was eventually abandoned.

A second parallel, sadder for the sake of education: Because of the same lack of support, the Sisters of Notre Dame were forced to close Ste. Marie in March of 1852. The following year the Sisters closed their Oregon City school and left for California to continue their teaching tradition there. Neither school ever reopened as such in St. Paul, but what is today the only parochial school in this still largely Catholic city of 322, was opened on February 1, 1861, by four Sisters of the Holy Names of Jesus and Mary in the old school building vacated by the Sisters of Notre Dame de Namur.

For the sake of today's interest in historic buildings and their preservation, it should be noted that the original wood frame buildings of both schools no longer survive, but archaeological tests have been done at both sites which are open fields. The soil yields bricks baked in St. Paul (like those used to build the landmark Catholic church), hand forged nails, pottery shards, and bits of broken glass—all mute witness to what came before.

According to Harriet D. Munnick, the original woodcut below was attributed to Father Nicholas Point in 1847. The captions translated from French are: 1) New brick cathedral and rectory; 2) Convent of Sisters of Notre Dame de Namur; 3) St. Joseph College; 4) Old log church; 5) Jesuit residence; 6)Farm buildings; 7) Blacksmith shop; 8) Mt. Hood; 9) Mt. Molalla (probably Mt. Jefferson). The woodcut shows the second story had been added to St. Joseph College a year or two earlier, to small purpose, because the college was closed in 1849.

Battleship Oregon

By Al Jones
Previously published November 1994, Vol.32, No.4

If the big shiny brass bell could tell its story where it hangs in Salem today, it would ring out a proud account of what it heard and saw on the *USS Battleship Oregon* from 1893 to 1942.

The bell now rests in the drill room of the Navy & Marine Corps Reserve Center, 1015 Airport Rd. SE, where it has been for more years than anyone can recall.

The *USS Oregon's* launching on October 27, 1893, in San Francisco Bay, marked the beginning of a "new" U.S. Navy which had shrunk to only four steel vessels among the wooden ones.

It came to be known as "McKinley's Bulldog" because, after William McKinley was elected president in 1896, the *USS Oregon* rapidly became a tool for enforcing growing U.S. international interests.

When the *USS Maine* was destroyed in the Havanna, Cuba, harbor on February 15, 1898, the *USS Oregon* was in the harbor at Bremerton, Washington. Orders came to Capt. Charles E. Clark to join the U.S. Atlantic fleet at Key West, Florida. Since this was before the Panama Canal was built over the Isthmus from 1904 to 1914, it meant the *USS Oregon* had to churn through 14,000 miles of ocean, around the south end of South America.

In the 68 day trip, the battleship averaged 11.6 knots (13.34 mph), with its coal-fired engines. One nonstop part of the trip was a record 4,826 miles, and the 468 crewmen rationed their own fresh water to feed the boilers.

The *USS Oregon* was handier for use when Congress declared war on Spain April 25, 1898. By the time it reached Cuban waters on May 26, Capt. Clark had word of Commodore George Dewey's destruction of the Spanish fleet in Manila Bay on May 1.

The Spanish fleet at Cuba was trapped in Santiago Bay and the U.S. Marines captured Guantanamo Bay on June 10, which has been a U.S. base ever since.

When the Spanish ships tried to get out of Santiago Bay, the *USS Oregon* pursued the fastest—the *Cristobal Colon*—firing its 13, 8, and 6-inch batteries. The enemy ship beached 70 miles west of Santiago, and the *USS Oregon* helped sink or beach three of four Spanish cruisers. The war brought to an end the Spanish colonial empire that had existed since the time of Columbus.

The *USS Oregon's* next assignment was to support U.S. forces in the Philippines; then it patrolled Asian waters. Its final significant action

Left:
USS Oregon bell.

Below:
USS Oregon is shown leaving Manila Bay about 1900.

AL JONES PHOTO

COURTESY HARRY A. HATFIELD

was to support the controversial 1918-19 Siberian Expedition of the Allies, aimed at the new Communist government.

Decommissioned October 4, 1919, the *USS Oregon* was on loan to the State of Oregon in 1925 for the Rose Festival and remained on the Portland waterfront until ordered to Bremerton to become wartime scrap iron.

The military found a use for its hull as an ammunition barge in Guam in 1945; that hull was scrapped in Japan in 1957.

Besides the bell in Salem, the *USS Oregon's* tall foremast is featured in Portland's Waterfront Park. Two smokestacks and an anchor are in the Liberty Ship Memorial Park; its compass, binnacle and signal flags are in the Maritime Center; and the crystal and silver services (bought by Oregon school children in 1897) are in the Oregon Historical Society collection.

Oregon Electric

Early electric transit systems

By Robert M. Ohling

Previously published May/June 1995, Vol.33, No.2

Advertising "No Soot—No Cinders," a statement the old steam engines could not equal, electric "juice lines," which drew power from overhead cables, hit the country like a storm during the first decade of the 20th century. The enthusiasm was created by visions of another era of transportation after electricity was first used successfully to power intercity street cars in the late 1890s.

While many pictured this power in the wide application of railways, most was actually limited to interurban services—the extension of passenger service into the smaller outlying communities surrounding an urban area, probably in the range of 25 to 35 miles. These lines operated on public streets in the cities and towns, but purchased private right-of-way for their rails in the country. Oregon had one of the few successful electrified railways in the United States.

The Oregon Electric Railway was incorporated May 15, 1906, by its parent company, Spokane, Portland & Seattle Railway. Over the next six years, a railway was constructed from downtown Portland to Eugene, a distance of 142.8 miles. In 1914 a 28-mile branch line was completed to Forest Grove.

The original Oregon Electric track began at Jefferson and Front Streets in Portland and ran on a grade following Multnomah Boulevard past the site of the Fred Meyer/Burlingame development, on south seven miles from the Jefferson Street Station to Garden Home, which was the junction for the line serving Forest Grove.

In 1910, rails were extended north on Front Street to Salmon Street, west on Salmon to SW 10th Avenue, and north on 10th to Hoyt Street to the North Bank Station where SP&S parent company trains arrived and departed. There were stations at 10th Avenue and Stark Street, 10th Avenue and Alder Street, and between 5th and 6th Avenues on Salmon Street.

Construction of this railway was accomplished by man and horse. But this was no big achievement when one considers the harsh environments and unsettled lands through which earlier railroads had to be built.

The Oregon Electric route was laid out to have only minimal grades and to run in as straight a line as possible. However, the route selected was on some of the wettest, poorly drained soils found in the Willamette Valley and this construction required considerable excavation to elevate the roadbed for stability. It also required numerous trestles or small bridges to accommodate the natural drainage.

My interest in the electric railways came about because Oregon Electric happened to purchase some land for a right-of-way from my Great Grandmother Teetze Ohling and my Grandfather and Grandmother Heike and Winnifred Ohling on January 12, 1912. There are three deeds on record which show a total of 12.52 acres; unfortunately, the consideration paid is not shown.

During the construction of this section of the line south of Albany in 1912, a work camp was maintained

This postcard, given to Bob Ohling by his aunt, shows the Oregon Electric Train leaving Salem for Portland. The card, published by the Patton Post Card Company, was postmarked in Salem on March 2, 1911. It was mailed with a one cent stamp.
COURTESY ROBERT M. OHLING

The Oregon Electric Waconda substation and office north of Salem, has thus far withstood more than 75 years of neglect. It served the dual purpose of housing both the transformers and the station itself.
COURTESY ROBERT M. OHLING

The Oregon Electric Cartney Station, north of Harrisburg, is a typical example, providing living quarters for the station agent and his family as well as an office. The only change to this station, moved a quarter mile east of the railway, has been a carport addition.
COURTESY ROBERT M. OHLING

on the Ohling Farm. Large tents were used as barns to house the horses and store feed as well as house the workers.

The Oregon Electric Railway contracted with Portland General Electric to supply electricity from its generating plant at the falls of the Willamette River but, in order to maintain the electricity to operate the trains, a total of eight substations were required for the 142.8 miles of track.

The electricity came into the substation as 60,000 volts of alternating current and through transformers was sent out on the line to operate the train as 1200 volts of direct current. These substations were built of poured concrete with reinforcing rod.

At least four substations are still standing. Two are totally neglected and have still weathered the ravages for 75 plus years. Several, such as the one at Waconda north of Salem, served the dual purpose of housing both the transformers and the station itself.

The 50.7 miles of track from Portland to Salem were completed in December 1907 and is thought to be the first electrified main line in the United States. Passenger service began January 1, 1908, with two trains daily each way. The passenger line ran down High Street and had a station at the southwest corner of High and State Streets in the Oregon Building.

Service to Albany began July 4, 1912. This passenger line ran down Fifth Street and the station still stands at the corner of Fifth and Lyon Streets, used today as the Veterans of Foreign Wars Building. The cost of this station in 1912 was $32,000.

Eugene received service October 15, 1912. The Eugene station, on the eastern edge of the downtown area, is presently used as the Oregon Electric Station restaurant. However, it is actually the second building, built in early 1920 to replace a smaller original structure.

Stations representative of those used on the railway remain at Donald, Cartney, Junction City, and Meadow View.

There were also two spurlines to serve communities not located on the main line. A spur ran from West Woodburn to Woodburn, but there was never a station in Woodburn; tickets were sold in a local drugstore.

The other spur ran six miles west from Gray, south of Albany, to the east bank of the Willamette River at Corvallis. There was a station at this terminus where the passengers debarked the train and crossed the Willamette River, first by ferry, and later by bridge. After the line was abandoned, the station was used by Oregon State University to house the rowing crew.

All told, there were 54 stations between Garden Home Junction and Eugene, a distance of 135.8 miles, making the average distance between stations approximately 2.5 miles.

Oregon Electric passengers enjoyed comfortable surroundings including deluxe rattan seats, shade awnings, opulent mahogany, oak and brass fittings, and overnight accomodations with 8:00 am wake-up calls.
MAXWELL COLLECTION PHOTO #1471 SALEM PUBLIC LIBRARY

Trains were usually made up of two cars and power came to the motor in the lead car through a beam traveling along an overhead wire. The lead car had three compartments—a small operating area in front with a section for baggage and freight, and finally a passenger compartment. The second car was entirely passenger accommodations.

It was a relaxed era of plush and decorum. The wooden passenger cars were opulent showcases with mahogany, oak and brass fittings for the passengers to enjoy from rattan seats. Striped awnings shaded the open decks of observation cars.

With completion of the line to Eugene in 1912, a new service called the OWL was initiated. It was a sleeper which would have berths ready for occupancy at 9:30 pm even though the train didn't leave until 1:30 am. The OWL would meander along at night on a no-hurry schedule setting out a sleeper at Salem, Albany, and Eugene. The businessman could remain in his berth until 8:00 am, get in a day's work, and then return to Portland on another OWL under the same conditions.

Eugene was served with five daily trains. In addition to the OWL, limiteds departed at 7:30 am and 1:30 pm for a four-hour run to Portland, and locals departed at 10:00 am and 6:00 pm for a five-hour run to Portland. The travel time on the limited for the 78 miles from Albany to Portland was two hours and 25 minutes. For the 50 miles from Salem to Portland, the time was one hour and 30 minutes.

The passenger fare in 1912 for a round trip from Portland to Eugene was $3.60. The Salem fare was $1.50, Forest Grove $.75, and Hillsboro, $.60. Revenues from passenger fares peaked at $891,000 in 1920 and finally diminished until, in 1932, the last full year of passenger service, they were only $17,313.

The system also carried light freight on the passenger schedules which was important to the rural areas the line served. Farmers shipped produce such as milk, cream, eggs and veal to the markets of Salem, Eugene, and Portland. The farmers would also receive supplies shipped to them from merchants in Portland, Eugene, and Salem.

On May 13, 1933, the last passenger service ran from Portland to Eugene, ending an era that started 25 years and five months earlier with the first service between Portland and Salem.

There were other electrified lines in Oregon. The earliest was established in 1893 by The East Side Railway Company as a 15 mile interurban

from Portland to Oregon City. It is thought to be the first interurban line in the United States to use electric current generated by water power. This line became the Oregon Water Power and Railway Company and by 1905 it had another line to Estacada. The company moved through a series of ownerships including Portland Railway Light and Power Company and finally became Portland Traction Company.

A 1905 advertisement stated:

Seven Daily Trains Between Portland and Gresham, Anderson, Boring, Barton, Eagle Creek, Currinsville, Estacada, Cazadero; Cars every forty minutes between Portland and Oregon City; Freight Trains daily except Sunday; Milk and Cream Shipments given passenger train service; all cars start from waiting room First and Alder Streets; Sunday Round Trip rates, Oregon City and Canemah Park, 16 miles $.25, Estacada and Points on Upper Clackamas River, 35 miles $.50.

The Oregon Water Power & Railway Company built The Oaks Amusement Park which opened May 30, 1905, two days before the Lewis & Clark Exposition. The $100,000 amusement park was built as a source of revenue for the railway.

The Willamette Valley Southern Railway Company was a 35 mile electrified line built in 1915 from Oregon City to Mt. Angel. The WVSR connected with the Portland Railway Light & Power Company at Oregon City. The original plan for the WVSR was to build through to Salem, but when construction actually began, the terminus was changed to Silverton. The line was financed by farmers and investors in Clackamas and Marion Counties.

Construction never extended beyond Mt. Angel and, after serious financial setbacks, the Portland Railway Light & Power Company took over the line, renaming it the Willamette Valley Railway. This line was abandoned in 1933.

United Railways was established in 1909 running north from Portland to Linnton along the Columbia River to Burlington where it climbed a five percent grade over Cornelius Pass. It became known as the Tualatin Hill Shoo Fly. The line extended to North Plains and eventually to Banks, but passenger service never paid the overhead. In 1911 United spent $500,000 to blast a tunnel beneath Cornelius Pass, but the railway could never compete with the Oregon Electric Railway which made the same Tualatin Valley destinations via the southern route 20 minutes faster. United was eventually purchased by James J. Hill and operated by the Spokane, Portland & Seattle Railway, parent company of Oregon Electric.

Southern Pacific entered the era of electrification by stringing overhead wires along their upper western Willamette Valley routes. Some might have said SP was following this program to keep up with the Oregon Electric Railway. Others might have cited the rapidly growing suburban areas as SP's reason for entering the field.

Southern Pacific painted their cars a smart red and they soon became known as the Red Electrics. The first cars ran from Portland through the upper western Willamette Valley as far as Corvallis in 1914. The big Red Electrics began their run into the valley from Union Station in Portland, proceeding south on Fourth Street through the heart of the business district to what today is Barbour Boulevard.

The Southern Pacific was appealing for patronage of the Red Electrics in 1921 in an attempt to make the operation a financial success. The trip from Portland to McMinnville took two hours and 25 minutes and the round-trip fare for the weekend was $1.70.

Frequent comfortable interurban service probably impelled the first large migration of Portland families to new homes in the southwest suburban areas. Commute tickets cost only a cent and a half a mile, and morning and evening trains moved with capacity loads.

It is interesting to note "what goes around comes around." Today Portland's Tri-Met transit system is once again blasting tunnels through Portland's west hills in an effort to provide fast rail service to the suburbs beyond, although at considerably higher cost.

Salem Made Aviation History

When Charles Lindbergh flew the "Spirit of St. Louis" overhead

By Al Jones
Previously published Summer 1996, Vol.34, No.2

The "visit" to Salem on September 16, 1927, was different from the many made by Charles A. Lindbergh on his three-month, over 20,000 mile tour of the 48 states. An incident here changed his plans.

He was the most famous person in America after his non-stop trans-Atlantic flight in the monoplane, "Spirit of St. Louis." Lindbergh flew from New York to Paris—3,600 miles in 33 hours and 39 minutes.

This tour of triumph began and ended in New York, including landings in 82 cities and overnight stops in each state. Colonel Lindbergh had been at a Portland banquet at the Multnomah Hotel the night before and was due in San Francisco at 2pm on September 16.

He circled Silverton, then Chemawa Indian School before approaching Salem from the north at 7:50am. A blast from the fire department siren signaled his approach. He flew south over High Street while people shouted, and Lindy dropped his message at High and Court Streets. It was retrieved by Frank Watt, a downtown worker, who turned it over to policeman Lou Olson, who turned it over to Mayor T. A. Livesley at his home.

Lindbergh's plan to circle Salem changed when Lindy felt threatened by the closeness of a plane piloted by Harold Adams. Aboard with Adams was the *Capital Journal* newspaper photographer, hoping to get a picture from above the "Spirit of St. Louis."

Lindbergh zig-zagged over South Salem, veered westward over Polk County,

US Postage Stamp commemorating the 50th anniversary solo transatlantic flight.

down the road toward Dallas to out-race Adams, who quit before reaching Independence.

What eventually happened to the message signed by Lindbergh remains a mystery today. It was framed and on display at the *Capital Journal* and later was in City Hall, from where it has disappeared.

It read, in part:

To the City of Salem: Greetings: Because of the limited time and the extensive itinerary of the tour of the United States to encourage popular interest in aeronautics, it is impossible for the "Spirit of St. Louis" to land in your city.

This message from the air, however, is sent you to express our sincere appreciation of your interest in the tour and in the promotion and expansion of commercial aeronautics in the U.S.–Charles A. Lindbergh

Salem had later reminders of Lindbergh's fame. On August 31, 1977, a replica of the "Spirit of St. Louis" visited Salem, 50 years after Lindy was overhead here. Piloted by Bob Davis, the duplicate plane arrived at 3:15pm, circled the State Fairgrounds, dipped to within 15 to 20 feet along the McNary Field runways, circled downtown Salem, then headed for Medford.

Lindbergh's son, Jon Morrow Lindbergh, came to Salem on January 17, 1979, invited for the Celebrity Lecture Series by the Marion-Polk County Medical Auxiliary. He said his mission was conserving the ocean's renewable resources. He said that his father's greatest activity in his last years was conservation.

Salem had earlier looked skyward on June 4, 1911, when Eugene Ely, called the "Bird Man," took off from the Lone Oak race track at the fairgrounds, circled the track while out-racing a motorcycle and a car, and flew around the Capitol dome. Ely became known for piloting the first flight from a ship, flying a Curtiss plane from the deck of the cruiser *Birmingham* on November 14, 1910. Then on January 18, 1911, he landed a plane on the deck of the cruiser *Pennsylvania* in San Francisco Bay.

Another visit stirring an interest in flight was the visit of the Army Air Service pilots on their around-the-world flight. They flew over Salem on September 28, 1924, on their 175-day trip of over 26,345 miles. The pilots were Army Lieutenants Leigh Wade, Erik H. Nelson and Lowell H. Smith.

Ironically, they flew over the State Fairgrounds just one day after Salem's Mayor George F. Rodgers was in a plane crash near the Fairgrounds and three hours before he died in the hospital.

Salem's McNary Field had a ceremony December 5, 1941, when United Airlines added Salem to its air service. Charles Sprague's wife smashed a champagne bottle on the wheel of the "City of Salem" Mainliner. This was two days before the Japanese attacked Pearl Harbor. It also marked the first airmail flight directly from Salem and thousands of first-day covers were posted. The Salem High School band played and there were courtesy flights on the Mainliner.

Also playing roles in Salem aeronautics history is the Eyerly family.

Lee Eyerly founded Eyerly Aircraft Company at McNary Field in 1927, producing the first modern type of plane in Oregon with the steerable nose wheel and tricycle landing gear. He later built the Acroplane, a flight-trainer that became one of the many carnival rides produced by the company.

One son, Harry, was a pilot and "test pilot" for the aircraft simulators and carnival rides.

Salem Flight Firsts

By Al Jones
Previously published Winter 1996, Vol.34, No.4

The urge "to fly like the birds" had for centuries led people to use imagination and mechanical ideas to experiment with hot air balloons and with gliders.

When the Wright brothers finally got off the ground at Kitty Hawk, North Carolina, on December 17, 1903, the word got around to Oregon and to two Salem men who had ingenuity and courage...Ben Taylor and H.H. Scovell.

That feat at Kitty Hawk with Orville Wright at the controls on the first flight lasted twelve seconds and 120 feet. Wilbur then flew 852 feet in 59 seconds on their third flight. There were no wheels on the plane, however. It was the result of three years of testing gliders, using a small wind tunnel to test wing and tail formations. They also got advice from engineer Octave Chanute. The result was to give the Wrights the honor of being first in heavier-than-air flight.

Salem people were fascinated by an exhibit of a Curtiss plane that had won an endurance contest in Los Angeles, achieving 19 miles in 39 minutes. Taylor and Dr. Scovell began tinkering in Taylor's machine shop on what now is Center Street NE near the crossing of north Mill Creek.

Taylor was known to be first in several things. As a mail carrier he was the first mailman who rode a bicycle, which was a high-wheel "bone-shaker," and he installed a generator to provide electricity at his home.

Taylor also was said to be able to sense that a photographer was in the area and appeared in many pictures by riding to the scene.

Dr. Scovell was a "mechano-therapeutist and suggestionist" who offered free consultations at 267 Liberty Street.

When they finally got their "Curtiss model" assembled from odds and ends and bicycle parts, it was towed to the State Fairgrounds for trial the next day, Wednesday, June 15, 1910.

Being about 40 pounds lighter than Taylor, Scovell was to be the first pilot, in the carpet-lined seat. Someone spun the propeller in the back of the craft and away it moved past the wooden grandstand to reach an estimated speed of 25 miles per hour.

At the State Fairgrounds in Salem, Ben Taylor (left) and Dr. H.H. Scovell (right) stand in front of the airplane they assembled in 1910.

COURTESY BEN MAXWELL COLLECTION /SALEM PUBLIC LIBRARY

It did not rise very high, a witness said, and Scovell whirred around the race track, all three wheels on the ground, finally crashing into the guard rail near the three-quarter post.

It was thirty-eight days later, on July 23, 1910, that the repaired craft was given another try. Again it crashed into the guard rail for lack of speed, with Scovell in the cockpit.

Undaunted, they made repairs and tried a third time in about six days. But the newspaper revealed the result in the July 30 headline: *Aeroplane Is Not Success.*

Salem's first look at a successful flight came on June 4, 1911, when Eugene Ely flew from the fairgrounds around the capitol dome in a Curtiss model which today could be called primitive. But,

in this craft, he passed a racing car that was doing 51 miles per hour.

Airplanes gradually grew in popularity and pastures near towns became landing fields while progressive cities built airports. For Salem, 93 acres were bought with funds from a bond issue for the airport. McNary Field was dedicated in 1929 with Lee Eyerly as manager.

The Salem Airport was busiest during the 1948 Vanport flood in the Portland area. Portland flights used McNary Field at a rate of 10,700 flights in 15 days.

United Air Lines flew out of Salem from December 2, 1941, until about 1978. The first airmail went out on the *City of Salem* airplane.

Salem Streets
Curious origins of width & angle

By Al Jones
Previously published Winter 1996, Vol.34, No.4

 There is more than one story about how Salem's downtown streets got as wide as they are—99 feet.

One reason given is that the original survey was done with a chain 66 feet long, with links 7.92 inches long. It was considered too narrow to have streets only one chain wide, so they used a chain and one half, or 99 feet, according to the late Salem City Engineer, Harold Davis.

Another tradition says that 66 feet would have been inadequate for oxen teams and two chains wide would have been too much.

Still another theory was that the wider streets would discourage the spread of fire from one side to the other.

Salem was surveyed again in June of 1861 by Jerome B. Greer and Walter Forward. It set 19 survey control points (monuments) from which exact locations could be measured legally. Most of the monuments are still used.

The point from which all elevations were measured was a brick projecting from the Marion Hotel's northwest corner, 2.78 feet above the sidewalk and 48 feet from mean-low water level of the Willamette River, Davis explained.

And why do Salem streets turn at an angle as they leave the downtown, going north, east or south?

It is because the original plats were laid out with magnetic north as the needle pointed 150 years ago. Later additions were measured by true north which is about 19 degrees different.

Salem's Hotel Argo

By Jordis Schick
Previously published May/June 1995, Vol.33, No.2

The Hotel Argo was built by John H. Lauterman in about 1912. It is not listed in the *1911 Salem Directory*, but is shown in the 1913 edition (when Salem had a population of 18,000) with a Mrs. Mel Hamilton as the "Prop." In the 1915 edition, Mrs. Faud Burke was listed as the "Propr." and the information said it was the newest and most modern hotel in the city.

The 1921 directory listed J.H. Lauterman himself as the "Proprietor" for the Argo—"A modern home at a moderate price with hot water heat, and hot and cold water in every room." The address was 341-345 Chemeketa (placing it at the corner of Chemeketa and Commercial across the alley from the present Penney's). The telephone number was simply 900.

The 1951 directory is the last issue showing the Argo, so Lauterman continued operating it in what was known as the Lauterman Building for many years. After the owner died, Morry Saffron of Salem purchased the L-shaped piece of property (he estimates it was in the late 1950s) and

leased it out for retail stores until J.C. Penney wanted the space for an auto center. Morry remembers the auto center didn't do too well so when the City of Salem wanted to take it over for the Chemeketa Parkade facility about 25 years ago, Penney's gladly obliged.

Morry also recalls the hotel as a nice, middle-grade type of facility throughout the 1930s and 1940s that boasted a fine dining room—the place to go in Salem if you really wanted a good meal.

This postcard of the Hotel Argo's lobby advertises "Excellent Meals in our Famous Dining Room."
POSTCARD COURTESY BOB TOMPKINS

This postcard of the Hotel Argo's lobby is postmarked December 7, 1929. The address-side advertising message reads "A modern home at a moderate rate" and continues "LOOK! PRE-WAR RATES, Rooms without bath—$1.00 and up, Rooms with bath—$1.50 and up, Meals at Popular Prices, FREE PARKING."
POSTCARD COURTESY BOB TOMPKINS

Did You Work At The Cannery?

By Bill Lucas
Previously published February 1995, Vol.33, No.1

In Salem, when conversation turns to work and summer jobs, invariably the first question asked is, "Did you work at the cannery?" If the answer is, "Sure, I worked at Calpack or Hunt's or Paulus Bros., or maybe Oregon Fruit," there follows a period of reminiscing about the good times and the bad, the funny things that happened and the sad, and the good bosses and the ones we thought, at the time, were so awful because they made us work hard and do our job right.

And we all remember our floorlady. "Did you work for Mrs. Dickson? She was the best floorlady I every had." The foremen were there to hand out orders and fix the line when it broke down, but the floorladies kept things going. They answered questions, showed you the easiest way to do your job so you didn't get so tired, and nursed you through your first bout of belt sickness or heat exhaustion. The cannery couldn't and wouldn't run without them.

Cannery work could be hard but, when the summer was over, how great it was to be able to go downtown (there were no malls then) to Bishop's, Miller's, Arbuckle's or one of the other stores to buy school clothes with your "cannery money." If you were lucky you might even get a trip to the "City" to visit the big stores—Meier & Frank, Lipman Wolfe, Olds & King, and Armishaw Shoes. The boys bought Pendleton shirts, white cords that soon got very dirty, and Winthrop cordovan shoes. For the girls it was Pendleton skirts, angora sweaters, and Spalding white bucks or saddles.

If you were careful with your money, there would be enough during the school year for a ten-cent frosty at the Pike now and then or a sundae or soda at the Spa, Ace, or Black and White in Hollywood. Those lucky enough to borrow their folks' car would be able to stop at White's drive-in or the Uptown for a burger and fries. Salem's canneries helped make these things possible for many of us because allowances, if you got one, normally covered only bare essentials.

My association with the Salem canning industry officially began in 1945, shortly after my 16th birthday. In the 1940s, teenagers (and their parents) looked forward to the day they were 16 because it meant "you were old enough to work in the cannery." The most important thing to anyone who grew up during the depression years of the 1930s was to have a job.

Bean dumping and washing at Blue Lake Packers. The three people on the left are not identified. The three on the right are Bob Bohannon, superintendent; Ted Vie, foreman; Elmore Hill, production manager.   COURTESY WILLIAM LUCAS

Like most other kids at that time, I had already been working in the fields for several years before I was 16. We picked beans, berries, fruit, and hops; weeded carrots, beets, and onions; and performed many other jobs on local farms. However, most of these farm jobs were piece work, and we all waited for the day when we would have a steady job at the cannery that paid by the hour.

Both of my grandparents worked at one of the local canneries, Blue Lake Producers, Inc., in what was then the city of West Salem. My grandfather was the plant carpenter and my grandmother, like many other Salem housewives at that time, worked at the cannery during pack season. When I turned 16 it was only natural for me to apply at Blue Lake for my first summer cannery job, but little did I realize on the day I went to work that I would still be there 45 years later.

In 1945, Salem canneries were always in need of workers because World War II had created a labor shortage. Many people in Salem worked their regular job days and then worked a night shift at one of the canneries. Soldiers stationed at nearby Camp Adair also came over in the evening to work a shift. To help save the crops, some Salem stores would close down early so people could go out and work in the fields.

Women unloading a can car at Blue Lake Packers.

COURTESY WILLIAM LUCAS

At times there were so many green beans waiting to be processed they had to be stored at Marion Square in the shade of the trees. The park would be covered with piles of beans in white cotton sacks. For those of us who grew up during this wartime period, these memories of what it was like to live in Salem and work in the canneries are still very vivid.

During and shortly after the war the canning industry in Salem and the surrounding area of Marion and Polk counties grew both in size and importance. In the early 1950s this region of the Willamette Valley would become the largest canning center in the world. Prior to World War II that distinction belonged to San Jose, California, but due to the increase in industry and the advent of "silicon valley," the orchards and farms in that region were being covered with houses, factories, and blacktop parking lots. Many San Jose canneries were forced to close their doors for good and move elsewhere to find raw products.

In 1945 there were 15 canning and freezing plants in Salem alone, with another half dozen in

the surrounding valley towns of Stayton, Dallas, Silverton, and Woodburn.

To understand why this increase in production came to Salem, Oregon, it is necessary to look at several factors. First and foremost, the soil and the availability of irrigation in the Willamette Valley make it one of the most productive farming regions in the world. At one time Marion County produced and marketed more different commercial farm crops than any county in the United States.

Second, the climate in the valley provides the warm days and cool nights that are most conducive to raising quality row crops. Third, there was a good stable workforce in Salem and the surrounding area. And last but not least, canneries of the Willamette Valley had a long and successful history of canning quality fruits, berries and vegetables.

Canneries have been an important part of Salem life for more than 100 years. They have provided work not only in good times, but also when times were hard and work was scarce. They have improved the Salem economy through their payrolls and the supplies and services they purchase. And they have provided the possibility for diversity of crops and increased earnings for the Willamette Valley farming community.

For a business that had such meager beginnings, the food processing industry in the

Salem area has grown until today it encompasses not only canned and frozen fruits and vegetables but also a wide variety of specialty products. It provides employment to over 6000 people with a payroll of more than $50 million. Its products, with sales values exceeding $400 million, are sold throughout the entire United States and in foreign countries as well. It is an industry of which the valley can be justly proud.

When I was asked to write an article about the canning industry here in the valley, I thought it would be a simple task to prepare a brief history of each of the canneries that have operated in Salem and the surrounding towns. After all, I had been around the business for 50 years so I should know all about it. How wrong can you be?

Unraveling the history of our canneries is a little like trying to put together a jigsaw puzzle without benefit of a picture to go by, or knowing for sure if you have all of the pieces.

It is an industry that has always been in motion, people moving from plant to plant; companies changing their names, locations, or ownership; new companies springing up overnight and others disappearing as quickly; and all this with little or no record telling why, when, or how.

Some companies maintained a good account of their history, but most did not. This is especially true of those no longer in business and, for many of the earliest companies, there is no one to provide first hand information of their operation and history.

It has become a fascinating task because I have always had a special interest in the history of the canning industry, and this project provides me with a reason and the opportunity to explore more deeply into the past of that portion of the industry with which I was most closely involved.

I hope at a future date to have unraveled and verified enough of our local canning history to be able to write a reasonably accurate account of what has transpired during the past 100 years. It is a history long neglected that should be preserved so in the future when someone answers, "Sure, I worked at the cannery," it will be possible for them to learn how it all began.

This picture of a vertical pack bean canning line at Blue Lake Packers will bring back some memories.

COURTESY WILLIAM LUCAS

Cinders on Salem

By John H. McMillan
All photos courtesy City of Salem

 Conventional wisdom traces the environmental movement in the United States to the publication of Rachel Carson's *Silent Spring* in 1962 and congressional passage of the Clean Air Act in 1963 and the Water Quality Act in 1965.

Yet, in the Marion County Historical Society archives a report was discovered showing that Salem's City Council was wrestling with environmental issues four decades earlier.

The volunteers found an engineer's detailed study that enabled the council in the spring of 1929 to force two companies to quit spewing soot and cinders over downtown Salem. The fall of partially burned material had been so intense that the *Oregon Statesman* described "soot-begrimed citizens" walking in downtown with their eyes "kept half closed" for protection.

Cinders and soot were not the Salem council's only problem in that last spring before the Great Depression, the *Statesman* reported. The council in the spring of 1929 began developing a municipal water service to replace the Oregon-Washington Water Services Corp., which was delivering not only water but also "vegetable growth" to the citizens. The council ordered livestock—especially goats and chickens—ousted from the city unless neighbors agreed to the farm animals' presence. It awarded the city's first bus franchise, debated possible conflicts of interest in the city's purchases from companies owned by council members, added 96 acres to the new Salem Airport, and authorized the city's first traffic lights.

None of those issues, however, matched for longevity the nuisance caused by the fall of cinders and soot, produced in wood burning boilers at factories along the Willamette River. The council passed Salem's first anti-smoke ordinance in 1923. But enforcement lagged, and cinders, fly ash, and soot continued to fall. The city needed evidence to put teeth into its law.

So the council, acting on the advice of its Smoke Committee, hired E. B. Boals, a professional engineer from Oregon State Agricultural College in Corvallis. It is his report to the council, dated April 29, 1929, that was found in the Historical Society's archives.

He said his tests showed "the soot-fall" over downtown Salem to average 1,400 tons per square mile annually. Compared to other cities, he said, "the intensity of the soot-fall in Salem is decidedly heavy"—worse than the 426 tons that fell on London, England, and the 196 tons experienced by Portland. Only steel-making Pittsburgh, PA., ranked worse than Salem on Boals' list.

![View of the Portland Electric Power Company plant from the roof of the Farmer's Warehouse.]

View of the Portland Electric Power Company plant from the roof of the Farmer's Warehouse. It was observed that this location showed the least cinder fall of any of the locations inspected.

Boals inspected four riverfront factories in Salem: Spaulding Lumber Co., Oregon Pulp and Paper Co., Portland Electric Power Co., and Hanson Planing Mill. The wood-burning boilers at all four, he found, were operated in accordance with the city's smoke ordinance. The smokestacks at all four plants were equipped with spark arresters.

But Spaulding and Oregon Pulp had failed to install cinder removal devices for their smokestacks, Boals found. "Equipment for the removal of dust particles from air or gas streams has been built for many years," Boals said, noting that such devices had been improved during the 1920s because of higher boiler ratings in steam plants, the development of pulverized fuel combustion systems, and municipal regulation.

Spaulding Lumber was located on the river between Trade and Ferry streets, while Oregon Pulp operated between Front Street and the river on Trade.

Boals found both Spaulding and Oregon Pulp to be violating Salem's 1923 smoke ordinance. He recommended that the City Council require both companies "to install equipment for the elimination of a reasonable proportion of their cinders from their smokestacks."

View from the roof of the building occupied by the Oregon Statesman, located about 650 feet from Oregon Pulp Mill.

Such action, he said, would not establish a precedent, reporting that other cities like Eugene and Portland already had invoked legal sanctions against industrial polluters to clean their air.

Boals' report was so persuasive that neither Spaulding Lumber nor Oregon Pulp argued.

Within a month of his report, Spaulding Lumber announced it would convert its steam-driven saws to electricity and abandon its boilers before July 1. Oregon Pulp & Paper said it would buy newly designed cinder arresters that Carl Gerlinger of Dallas would have on the market by August.

The report that forced Spaulding and Oregon Pulp to eliminate their production of cinders included Boals' studies of soot and cinder fall from December 1928 to April 1929.

Simply from observation from downtown rooftops, Boals knew that Spaulding and Oregon Pulp were the principal sources of the cinders—defined as "partly burned combustible substances." Boals said Salem's cinders were "small bits of charcoal."

Boals' initial hope had been to measure the cinders being produced by the two companies' boilers, but the companies apparently balked. "Apparatus for the measurement of the quantity of cinders discharged was constructed but not used because of a difference of opinion as to a point of sampling," Boals wrote.

His evidence came, rather, from cans—six inches in diameter and 10 inches deep—placed on roofs of 10 downtown buildings. The measuring sites:

1. Salem Statesman, Commercial at Ferry, about 650 feet from the two mills.
2. State Street Garage, Front at State.
3. U.S. National Bank, Commercial at State, about 950 feet distant.
4. Eiker's Garage, Liberty at Ferry.
5. Western Auto Supply, Commercial at Court.
6. Farmers' and Merchants' Warehouse, Liberty at Court, about 1,300 feet away.

7. Miller's Store, Liberty at Court.
8. Oregon Building, State at High.
9. Capital Second Hand, Commercial at Chemeketa, about 1,720 feet away.
10. Odd Fellows Building, High at Court.

Boals put out his cans twice—December 8 and February 10.

His first test failed. So much rain fell in December and January that many of the falling cinders had been washed out of the cans.

But after the 21-day second test, Boals found 5.998 grams of soot and cinders in the ten cans.

He emptied his cans and resumed testing until April 6. Translating his measurements, he declared that 7,250 pounds of soot and cinders fell on the block bounded by Commercial, Ferry, Trade, and Front streets during 43 days. That was an average of almost 170 pounds a day. The smallest fall Boals measured was 18 pounds a day on the block surrounded by Court, Liberty, State, and Commercial.

Like many consultants' reports, Boals' document was put on a shelf to gather dust. But why not? It was so well done that its mere preparation led to the solution of the problem Boals had been hired to address. Would that all municipal issues were so easily solved.

View from the roof of US National Bank building, about 950 feet from the paper plant and sawmill.

View from the roof of the Capital Second Hand Store on Chemeketa Street, between Commercial and Front. Distance from the paper plant and lumber mill was about 1720 feet.

Mahonia Hall

A house that hops built: Thomas and Edna Livesley

By Jordis Schick
Previously published August 1994, Vol.32, No.3

In honor of our upcoming Hop Festival & Hops 'n History Exhibit, it seems appropriate to tell you something about the man who built Mahonia Hall, Oregon's official governor's mansion, in this issue of *Historic MARION*

Long known in Salem as the Livesley House, Mahonia Hall was originally built in 1924 for Thomas A. and Edna Livesley. And the Livesley family occupied it for the next 34 years, until the property sold in 1958. With a ballroom on the third floor, an organ, and a wine cellar and billiard room in the basement, the beautiful, half-timbered Tudor house was designed to accommodate the lifestyle of a leader in the community.[1]

Overall design is attributed to the office of Lawrence & Holford, and more specifically to Ellis Lawrence, who was also the founder and first dean of the University of Oregon School of Architecture. He was an architect noted for his ability to successfully mix historical stylistic details with a modern approach to function and exceptional craftsmanship.[1]

According to the National Register of Historic Places nomination form prepared by the Oregon State Preservation Office[2] (a status granted to Mahonia Hall in May 1990):

Thomas Albert Livesley (1863-1947) was a progressive mayor of Salem and State Legislator during the years he occupied the house. Mr. Livesley was also a highly influential and world renowned grower and broker of hops.

He was in the forefront of social reform for the welfare of workers in the hop fields, as well as an innovator in the practice of the latest scientific and technical advances in hop agriculture in the State of Oregon during the first half of this century.

Mr. Livesley was also a noted philanthropist and civic leader. He served as mayor of Salem from 1927 to 1931 and was State Representative for

Marion County during the 1937-1939 session.

The Livesley residence was also the site of many charity teas ...for worthy organizations ...(which) Mrs. Livesley oversaw.

In his book *South Salem Past*, David Duniway[3] notes Thomas A. Livesley was known in Oregon as the "hop king." His father Samuel had also been a prominent hop dealer, first in Wisconsin and, after moving to Seattle, one of the Pacific Northwest's largest.

Mahonia Hall—the house that hops built.   AL JONES PHOTO

"Livesley," Duniway comments, "began his career in Salem in 1894, and in a few years acquired a ranch of 260 acres." Robert C. Clark, author of *History of the Willamette Valley*, is quoted by Duniway as saying Livesley is reputed to have been the largest grower of hops in Oregon.

He established an export trade with England," Duniway reports, *and his most prosperous year was 1915, when he handled and sold 40,000 bales of hops, amounting to 16 million pounds.*

He was president of the Canadian Hop Growers, Ltd. of Sardis, British Columbia, and materially promoted the industry in Canada as well as the United States. His ties with Canada were through his wife, Edna De Beck of Vancouver, British Columbia, whom he married in 1909.

Livesley was also president of T.A. Livesley & Co., a company that had Oregon holdings in 1924 consisting of four hop ranches in the Salem area with a total of 840 acres of hops under cultivation. Altogether, T.A. Livesley & Co. grew on their own land about one million pounds of hops in the early 1920s—about one-tenth of the hops grown in Oregon annually and about one-thirtieth of the annual production worldwide.[2]

Also one of Oregon's largest hop brokers during the first half of this century, Livesley sold even more hops than he grew. His business was approximately 60 percent brokerage and 40 percent growing. In the aforementioned year of 1915, for instance, he exported approximately 20 percent (primarily to England), and sold the other 80 percent directly to large breweries in the U.S. Much admired for his business acumen, Livesley's office was a major outlet for hops grown locally. It was also typically crowded with growers, waiting for his word on when to sell. Wisely, Livesley shifted his attention to his export markets during prohibition.[2]

An example of the leadership Livesley contributed to the movement to provide good living situations and social services for seasonal field workers in the hop industry was his Lakebrook Farm in 1924—the first in Oregon to provide a day nursery for the youngest children of workers; morning school, playground and recreational activities for older youngsters; medical aid; etc. The pioneering efforts of Livesley and other Salem area hop growers during the 1920s garnered national attention for Salem and Oregon during this period (when the provision of social services was a new labor phenonemon in the U.S.).[2] During World War II, German prisoners of war were encamped in a stockade at Lakebrook to ease the shortage of manpower on the homefront.

Both Duniway and the National Register nomination note that T.A. Livesley, Inc. erected and owned the First National Bank Building[4] at 388 State Street in 1926-1927. Livesley also served as director of the bank for a brief period. Upon his death in 1947, this prominent Salem landmark was renamed the Livesley Building in his honor. The building, listed on the National Register of Historic Places in 1986, was later known as the Capitol Tower and is today the beautifully restored Capitol Center.

Livesley was also vice president of Oregon Linen Mills, an industry he secured for Salem.

Active in the Democratic party, Livesley served,

too, as Salem's mayor and state representative. He was known as "The Good Roads Mayor" because his main priorities included many bridge, street, alley and sidewalk improvements. At least 13 permanent concrete bridges were built during this period "in the interest of economy and civic beauty."[2]

During his four-year tenure, other major projects accomplished included extending fire protection and building two new fire stations; upgrading the sewer system; constructing three new playgrounds, the Salem Airport, and a refuse incinerator plant; installing street lights and traffic lights downtown; and the adoption of building codes.[2]

Livesley was adamant that Salem accomplish development with concern for the beauty of the city—so much so that he vetoed the downtown street lighting system initially because it did not provide an ornamental system that would be "in keeping with our progressive program of beautifying Salem generally."[2]

In addition, Livesley was determined to provide Salem with a more efficient and business-like city government. He is credited for his repeated efforts to establish a city council-manager form of government (and lived to see this finally accomplished in 1946).[2]

Livesley served as a director of the YMCA for many years and as chairman to the committee that raised the funds for its fine building; was president of the original Illahee Country Club; and belonged to the Elks, both the Salem and National Chambers of Commerce, Commercial Club, Salem Golf Club and Congregational Church.[2]

The hop community honored Livesley on his 81st birthday in 1944, stating in a commemorative brochure that he *Started from scratch without parental advice or financial assistance, self-educated without the facilities of high school or college, he has gained the highest honor of good citizenship. His philanthropies all through life have been ceaseless, continuous and most generous, materially helping and relieving the sick, poor and distressed. He has gone forward when others have turned back, optimism his choice and victory his achievement.*[2]

After the Livesleys, subsequent residents of Mahonia Hall have included Salem realtor Ben Colbath (1958-1961), radio station owner W. Gordon Allen (1961-1965), and Dale G. and Glinda Parker. Iral D. and Gwen Barrett, the owners of Supra Products, Inc., purchased the property from Mr. Parker in 1974 and lived in it until selling it to the State of Oregon for the official governor's mansion in 1987.[2]

---

[1] Joy A. Beebe, *Mahonia Hall Reference Book*, April 1992.

[2] *Nomination Form for National Register of Historic Places*, Oregon State Historic Preservation Office, submitted March 14, 1990, section 8.

[3] David Duniway, *South Salem Past*, p 39.

[4] According to the *Mahonia Hall Reference Book*, Lawrence also designed this building, as well as the classic Elsinore Theater, Elks Club, and Masonic Building in Salem.

Meier & Frank

Reminiscences of a salesgirl

By Annabell Prantl
All photos courtesy Gerald Frank

In today's world of gigantic shopping malls with their endless array of small shops and department stores placed strategically in almost every town of any size in Oregon, they suffer from a monotonous sameness. Few people remember the days when one outstanding store so dramatically dominated the retail business in Oregon that it took on a personality all its own. The gleaming white terra-cotta edifice that covered an entire city block in downtown Portland between Alder and Morrison and 5th and 6th Streets, was the home of Meier & Frank, a department store second to none. It rose thirteen stories above the ground. Ten floors were devoted to merchandise. The rest housed the offices, the employee's cafeteria and locker room, a marking room and a candy making operation. The basement held three more floors of merchandise and deep in the bowels of the store was the heat plant. It was a giant boiler that came off an ocean going ship. It provided the steam heat for the entire building.

Those ten floors, along with the basement, filled with merchandise were a wonder to behold. There was everything ranging from men's and women's clothing to suit every price range, to furs, jewelry, cosmetics, home furnishings, oriental rugs, restaurants, bakery, deli, candy shop, fruit and vegetable market, beauty salon and more. If Meier & Frank didn't carry it, it was practically nonexistent. The buyers combed the world for the best merchandise at the best prices. Portlanders were so accustomed to this smooth running, great store, that it was taken for granted. To them, it was always there. It was a landmark.

Little was ever spoken about its bumpy humble beginnings. Not many businesses that had their beginnings before Oregon became a state ever moved on into the twentieth century, let alone

The first Meier & Frank store was located at the Portland corner of Yamhill and Front Streets in 1873.

surviving long enough to celebrate a hundredth anniversary. It was in the days of the middle 1850s after the California gold rush had peaked and was on the wane, that the then 24 year old Aaron Meier from the Bavarian village of Eisenstadt, Germany,

Aaron Meier

came to America. After a long and arduous trip, he made his way to the small village of Downeyville, California, and went to work for his brothers who owned a dry goods store.

One can only surmise that business had slowed since the height of the gold rush to the point where there was not enough to keep three brothers busy. So Aaron went north on foot with a pack mule bearing yard goods, ribbons, laces and other notions to sell to the settlers. There are those among the descendants of Oregon's pioneer families who point out that their forebears remembered the very personable, compassionate young Aaron Meier. It would seem that he often gave away as much as he sold. The pioneer families were most happy to give him a meal or provide him with shelter for the night for he often left ribbons and laces as payment.

He probably restocked his merchandise in the small town of Portland at the end of the run. The next year he came with a wagon load of wares. After that, he didn't come anymore. They missed his visits and often wondered what had happened to him. Later they learned that in 1857 he had opened a store at 137 Front Street, near Yamhill, in Portland.

Several years passed. Aaron Meier's little store seemed to be on a firm path to success. By 1863, the business was doing well. He had enough confidence in his business partner to leave him in charge and return to Germany to visit his mother and possibly find a wife. Eligible ladies were in short supply in the west at that time. He met with success and married Jeanette Hirsch, the daughter of a grain buyer, who was eleven years his junior.

When they arrived in Portland, the following year, the living that was supposed to be theirs had vanished. Aaron's business partner whom he had trusted, had bankrupted the store. One can only imagine the devastating effect this had on the young bride who had traveled so far from her

home and family. In those times this kind of disaster sent many a young bride back to her homeland to seek refuge in the bosom of her family, never to return. We may never know precisely why she stayed, perhaps that Civil War in the east made her wary of a trip on the high seas. Her husband was broke, but perhaps she received a

Jeanette Meier

dowry when she married and this was the means of starting over. She rolled up her sleeves and worked along side her husband to rebuild the business. As time went on, her determination to succeed exceeded that of her husband and left no doubt in the minds of their employees who was in charge. She was called by her first name, with a German accent, of course, "Shanette."

In 1872, on a buying trip to San Francisco,

Sigmund Frank

Aaron met a young German music teacher by the name of Sigmund Frank. Meier offered him employment as a clerk in his store which Frank accepted. He must have proved himself to be a loyal, hardworking employee because in 1873, with the approval of Shanette, he was made a partner in the business and from then on the store became Meier & Frank. Tragedy struck in that same year. This time the store was destroyed by a fire that swept through the business district of Portland. Once again the Meiers with the aid of Sigmund Frank were forced to start over or give up altogether. Before the fire, there must have been a substantial following of good and loyal customers who liked trading at Meier & Frank, or starting over would have met with failure. Again the store was rebuilt and business moved forward.

It seemed that Aaron Meier had just the right touch with the customers. He remembered everyone from his days on the backwoods trails of Oregon. Tales of encouraging his old customers from out on French Prairie to bring butter and eggs to his store to trade have been told through several generations. Butter was wrapped in cold cabbage leaves to make the long trip to Portland. At the journey's end, the customers were treated very well. After the trading was done, as an inducement to return to his store on their next trip to Portland, the men were often given gifts of tobacco and the ladies received coffee and candy.

Jeannette Meier had weathered the storm of coming to a strange land. With the business devastated by bankruptcy and fire, she understood how fragile a business could be. The specter of disaster always lurked close by. Who knew what might happen next. She went to the store every day. She also scrutinized every event in the personal lives of her family. She must have had control of the purse strings, for none of her children dared marry without her approval. The marriages she approved seemed more like business mergers. "In unity there is strength. A house divided against itself cannot stand." She firmly believed in these mottos with all her heart.

As the business grew, Shanette brought brothers, half-brothers, nephews and cousins to Oregon to work in the store. At that point in time, there were many con artists about in the west who had a good line, but once they hit their mark, they disappeared in the vast wilderness of the west never to be heard from again. It was no wonder that she wanted to surround herself with her own family whom she felt she could trust.

As the years passed, the Meiers had three children, Fannie, Abe, and Julius. In 1885, Fannie and Sigmund Frank were united in marriage, but only after the approval of Mrs. Meier.

Aaron Meier died in 1889 at the age of 58. At that time his partner, Sigmund Frank, took over as manager of the business.

The Willamette River overflowed in 1894, inundating parts of Portland, and Meier & Frank was flooded with three feet of water. Four years later, in 1898, Meier & Frank moved uptown into an elegantly appointed five story building which boasted two elevators and many other modern innovations. No longer a country store, it emerged as an elegant department store with a fine reputation for selection and service.

The expanded business thrived. Every few years there were expansions and additions to the building and the business. A warehouse that covered a city block and a garage that housed the delivery trucks also followed.

Upon the death of Sigmund Frank, Abe Meier

became president and held that position until his death in 1910.

Shanette passed away in 1925 at the age of 82. She left her family with a great legacy and a tremendous responsibility. Her contribution to the development and well being of the state of Oregon cannot be measured.

Julius Meier held the title of president from 1930 to 1937, although he also served as Governor of Oregon from 1931 to 1935.

It was during the great depression that Meier & Frank made a final expansion on the Fifth and Sixth Street site which began in 1930. By 1932 it was completely remodeled, covering an entire city block. It rose majestically thirteen stories above ground and three floors below

This is the edifice that most Portlanders remember.

My memories of Meier & Frank began as a child of the depression days. I remember my mother making at least one trip to town during the Christmas season to take my brother, my sister and me to the toy department which covered one whole floor. It was a wonder to behold. (The rugs and draperies gave up their space and were scrunched up on another floor to make room for Santa Claus and his loot.) Portlanders were not interested in redoing their homes when Santa was in town anyway.

The mechanical elves depicted in Santa's workshop in the large outdoor display windows on Fifth and Alder were a sight to delight the hearts of the children of Portland. There were so many people on the street one had to wait a turn to get close enough for a good look.

I graduated from Commerce High School in Portland in 1941. The country had not fully recovered from the great depression. I knew I must work. I secured employment for a few months in what I consider to this day the most miserable, depressing small office on the face of the earth. Years later the owner of the business went to federal prison for mail fraud. I was elated to leave there and vowed I would never seek office work again. What probably influenced me to apply for work at Meier & Frank was a story that was often repeated by my mother and my aunts. It concerned my mother's youngest sister. In the days before World War I, she had gone to business school and had learned to operate a comptometer, an early day calculator. She had tromped all over town looking for work for many days and one evening came home in tears, lamenting her bad luck, unable to find employment. My grandfather was a streetcar conductor who had been with the traction company since the days of the horse drawn cars and knew the Meier family members from way back as they all had ridden with him many, many times. He said to my aunt, "Stop crying. Tomorrow we go to see Julius."

The following day they went to the office of Julius Meier, who was in a position of authority. After the usual greetings, my grandfather got to the point, "Julius, this is my daughter, Edna. She needs work."

"Why, yes, Harry. What can she do?"

"She can operate a comptometer." Julius Meier hired her on the spot. She went to work the next day. He looked out for the old time Portlanders. This was not an isolated incident by any means. He was noted for it.

In the fall of 1941, I went to apply for work at Meier & Frank. At that time their employees numbered over 3,000. Surely there was something there I could do besides the dreaded office work. The employment office was on the twelfth floor, the line was as long as two city blocks. One had to get there early in the morning to even get an application blank. After that was done, we were told that they were not hiring anyone that day. In high school, we had a class in how to find a job. It was a case of go back, go back, go back some more. I remember going back for six days, getting into line. When I reached the employment office, Miss Moore, who did the hiring, began to recognize me along with a half dozen others. One morning she told us to take a seat. We were getting close. It wasn't long until she said, "You, you, you, and you, come with me. I have a call for help in the wrapping department." She skipped over some, so I was delighted when I was one of the "you's" that was hired.

A delightful lady by the name of Victoria Krueger gave us our indoctrination and training. We worked six days a week. Our hours were from 11:00 a.m. until 6:30 p.m. or until all the packages were wrapped. We learned that smiles and pleasant voices were a must. What customer in her right mind would shop in a store where the help went around with sour faces. She told us a story about Mr. Kiernan who was head of personnel. One time he had to make a decision between two ladies that were applying for the same job. One had an impressive resume from past employment and a serious countenance. The other girl was a blonde with big blue eyes and a radiant smile. He and his assistant discussed which one to hire. His assistant leaned toward the

lady with the resume. Mr. Kiernan was quoted as saying, "I know, I know, but I'll still take the blonde with the winning smile and the big blue eyes."

Meier & Frank had a reputation for having the most agreeable sales staff in Portland. To be a Meier & Frank girl was considered very special.

The place where I was to be employed was called the transfer desk. It was in the lower basement with a sign on the door that said "Employees only!" Here all the small purchases that were to be delivered came down a shoot that ran through the store.

Along with the unbelievable in-store sales, Meier & Frank did a brisk mail order business, sending hired shoppers around the store to personally fill the customers' orders. It took six of us wrapping hundreds of orders a day to keep up. I soon advanced to assistant at the transfer desk, and labeled the mail order packages. Then when my boss quit her job to get married, I was put in change.

World War II began while I worked at the transfer desk. Aaron Frank, son of Fannie and Sigmund Frank, was now president and general manager of the company. His sons, Richard and Gerald, were both in the service, and I addressed many a package of sweets to them from their father. Their mother died while they were in the service. Her personal belongings came into the wrapping department to be packed for storage. The lady who packed them knew Mrs. Frank as she lived in Garden Home not far from the Frank's estate. There was much sadness in the store at that time.

After Hitler was defeated in Europe, Gerald Frank returned home. He finished his college education and then went to work as head of the mail order department. His brother, Richard, headed up the sporting goods department.

Gerry was very much liked by all. His smile and ability to put everyone at ease was well known. He also had a mischievous side to his nature. One could surmise that running the mail order department didn't tax his intelligence. The store had a vacuum tube system that carried sales slips, money and so forth to the various offices and wrapping stations throughout the store. It was not unusual for Mr. G. to drop coins in the tubes without putting them in the carrier. They made a dreadful racket and it took Jack Berry, the repair man, to get them out. I can remember him walking through the store shaking his head and saying, "He's at it again." One day while the elderly lady who coordinated the mail orders was at her post at the transfer desk, some papers came down in a carrier from the mail order office. When she opened it, a big, dark, spring-loaded play rat leaped out of the carrier. She jumped and screamed, putting her hand over her heart exclaiming, "Oh, that Gerry!"

Part of my job was to search for lost packages that somehow were late getting to the delivery. Each department, and there were over a hunded of them, had a number. I finally got tired of looking them up on the list that I had. I obtained of copy, took it with me on my lunch hour for several days and committed it to memory. It simplified my work to know where packages came from on sight. I also worked lunch reliefs for the cashiers in the various departments all over the store.

Many of the employees that worked in the great store were there for many years. A job was a precious thing, especially where the working conditions were good. There were two buyers that were probably the most whispered about of all, Miss Cooley and Miss Hanley. Miss Cooley was head of the book department. I can visualize her yet. She had red-grey hair drawn in a bun, wore glasses and went around her department on a dog trot. She was sharp tongued, but knew every book she had in stock. It was rumored that she was so old that she had swept out the store on Front Street when packing crates were used as display counters. I remember hearing her speak once. She said, "I may be an old maid, but there is nothing in life that I have missed." One comment she made that I never forgot, "There is dignity in work! Hold your head up high."

Miss Hanley was a frail little lady. I remember her assistant, Miss Head, longed for the day that she would retire. When Miss Hanley came to work in the morning, Miss Head was obliged to help her off with her boots and coat. Miss Hanley would go to her office, take a little nip out of a flask of spirits she kept in the bottom drawer of her desk and then take a nap. When her aches got the better of her, Miss Head had to fill her hot water bottle. She also had to go to the employees lunch room and bring Miss Hanley a hot lunch. Still, occasionally, the aged buyer could be seen waiting on customers on days when she was feeling well. She and Miss Cooley were great friends and often went on vacation together. It was rumored that they often visited bars and went to places where angels feared to tread.

Before the war with Japan ended, I moved to sales. I became a corsetier in the foundation department, fitting bras and girdles. It was considered a trade back then and once learned could keep a person employed for the rest of her days, if necessary. Even in tough times, corsetiers were in short supply. The pay was much better than that of my friends from high school who had office jobs, because we worked on commission. The department consisted of a staff of 22 sales girls headed up by a buyer and an assistant buyer. The department grossed a million dollars a year. It was busy, to say the least.

Fortunately, I did know how to sew, which helped. On my first day of selling, someone gave me a run down on the sizes, and hung a tape measure around my neck. When I asked if someone would show me what to do, I was told that the customers would teach me all I had to know. It was true, but that was doing it the hard way. I'll never forget my first customer. She had selected a latex satin girdle to try on. She got into it, but we couldn't figure out which was the front or back of the thing as the garters weren't sewn on in the usual place. I finally asked the assistant buyer which was the front or the back and she couldn't tell either. It wasn't long until my customer got the giggles. "Frontwards or backwards, I'll take it," she said. We both laughed 'til the tears rolled down our faces.

I was the youngest person in the department and was terrified for days, for each customer had a new set of figure problems; but somehow I persevered and became quite proficient.

Now I began coming to work at 9:00 a.m., before the store opened. When we entered, the doorman bid us good morning and handed us the store's daily bulletin. We had better have a big smile for him and a bright "good morning" or we were required to go outside and come in again and give the proper greeting.

Meier & Frank encouraged its sales staff to build personal followings. Once I got the hang of things and knew what I was doing, I built up a personal following to the point where I had enough customers who looked me up when they came to town so that most of my day was spent waiting on ladies who I knew and liked. Many were from very prominent Portland families. One of my co-workers remarked to me one day, "You laugh and visit with your customers all day long and have a good time. We go around dead serious, running our legs off and I'm not so sure at the end of the month that you don't come out better than we do." Judging by the low rate of returns I had, in comparison with hers, she was probably right.

During the war years, Meier & Frank held bond drive after bond drive. Hollywood celebrities often performed in the auditorium to packed houses to promote bond sales. So outstanding were the results that the store received an award for the most outstanding support of the war effort, surpassing larger stores in the east.

The employees also donated blood regularly to the Red Cross. I was a member of a group of M & F sales girls that solicited blood donors in the foyer of the Broadway Theatre. Giving blood was so new to the public that oftentimes patrons would turn pale at the mention of it. However, there were brave souls who signed up.

Meier & Frank never treated its employees like second class citizens. Before unemployment benefits were common in the work place, M & F had a welfare department. We employees weren't a sickly lot. If we had problems it was with our feet. In the rare event that an employee suffered a lengthy illness, the welfare provided a portion of his or her pay until that person could come back to work. I remember when we were first offered full medical coverage. Meier & Frank must have been one of the first in the city of Portland. The cost was fifty cents a month. After a year, the cost went to a dollar and stayed there for many years. The employees were referred to as the store family with the slogan, "We take care of our own."

After the war was over the company sponsored some wonderful activities for us, a gigantic family picnic in the middle of summer, and a winter and spring dance. All of these affairs were punctuated with fabulous door prizes. I won on two separate occasions, a radio phonograph combination and a TV. During ski season they also sponsored a ski bus to Mt. Hood. We rode all the way to Timberline and back for $1.00. The ski group could also have a bus for a summer one day trip. Every department could have a Christmas breakfast in the Tea Room restaurant at no expense to us.

Aside from the employees' events Meier & Frank provided, the major corset companies such as Warners, Formfit and American Lady often held evening fashion showings in Portland's finest hotels for our entire department. These were fun affairs and were always preceded by cocktails and sumptuous dinners.

When Meier & Frank held their spring and fall fashion extravaganzas in the store's auditorium, they were staged for the employees before work. I never missed a one. They also held, in the dead of winter, Aloha Hawaii week. The main floor was like a tropical garden loaded with beautiful flowers from the Islands. This, too, was highlighted with a beautiful fashion show which was my favorite.

The auditorium also housed the fall rose show and the orchid show. It was filled with demonstrations during Oregon Products Week.

After the war, the Rose Festival once again became a yearly Portland event. Meier & Frank always had a gorgeous entry and the prettiest of the young female employees were chosen to ride on the float. The store closed during the parade, and we all sat in the windows on the Sixth Street side and enjoyed the beauty of the event.

Meier & Frank was not a place for the faint hearted or those who were afraid to work. It was fast and hard. There were new special sales every few weeks: factory closeouts, inventory clearances, irregular merchandise (slightly flawed), and sales that preceded holidays. The customers came in droves. In some business circles it was referred to as the pressure cooker. The buying power of the store was second to none in the nation. While many stores and chains bought on consignment, M & F paid in cash for every purchase.

Woe be unto the buyer who didn't get her invoices for merchandise received from the manufacturer to the office for immediate payment to take advantage of the 30 day discounts. This played a big part in the store's profits. When all was said and done, one and a half percent of the gross income represented the net profit.

Of course, the most famous of all the sales were on Friday. Merchandise was advertised in the Portland papers with a question mark where the price should be. It was called "Friday Surprise." There were customers that shopped on no other day, enjoying every minute of the wild melee the sale promoted. However, there were customers that avoided Friday like the plague, wanting nothing to do with it. Saturday was always the biggest day of the week.

Although the store had four banks of elevators, as the years went by, and the crowds increased, getting the customers to the upper floors became more and more of a hassle. In 1950, the escalators were installed. They solved the traffic problem that would have soon cost business.

In the early nineteen fifties, Meier & Frank was ready for a bold new move. Plans were in the works for their first branch store. Salem, our state capital, would be the site of the new venture. The project would cover a whole city block. Mr. Gerald Frank, now in his early thirties, was to become the general manager of the new store. He had slowed up considerably on the hijinks. For some time he had managed the center aisle. This was a series of sales counters that ran through the center of the main floor from Fifth to Sixth Street. Sales items from all over the store found their way to these counters. When the store opened in the morning, especially on Friday, it was bedlam.

It was all so exciting. All year, (1954) there were new people who had been hired as group sales managers coming from Salem to work in the Portland store and receive training and experience. Many included in those going to Salem as managers were already employees of the Portland store. When all were hired, there were seventy three. I was hired as group sales manager for the foundations and ladies uniforms. It was so exciting to be part of the new venture. On June 2, 1954, the *Oregon Statesman* published the the news story below.

Oregon Statesman • June 2, 1954

Civic Dignitaries Attend Ground-Breaking Rites For Meier & Frank Store

Aaron M. Frank, president of Meier & Frank Co., gave a ceremonial start to wrecking operations on the downtown site of a new Salem store Tuesday as his company officers and civic dignitaries look on.

Details of the $8,000,000 store project were given out as the ceremony unfolded at the old front entrance for the high school building on Marion Street, dating back a half century.

Frank took off his coat, donned a construction helmet and climbed a stepladder to remove the lantern-fixture over the north entrance of the school which had served in recent years as a center of school, county, state and federal offices in Salem.

Meier & Frank has bought the entire school block bounded by Marion, High, Center and Church Sts., and other property nearby.

Sharing the top honors at the ceremony was Gerry Frank, young bachelor son of Aaron Frank who will manage the Salem store.

Young Frank is planning to build a home on Candalaria Heights where he has purchased a large view lot at Crestview and Downs.

Older son Richard Frank also was on hand for the ceremonies, along with other M & F officers, including Lloyd Eckhardt, A.E. Rosenberg, Allen E. Meier, Clinton Eastman, Joseph Thursh, Leslie Sherman and others. Chester R. Duncan of the Portland firm was master of ceremonies.

Others playing a part in the ceremony included Associate Architect James L. Payne, Salem; Mayor Alfred W. Loucks and Mayor-elect Robert F. White; Edwin H. Armstrong, representing Gov. Paul Patterson; officers of Meier & Frank Co., Emma Deering, M & F employe for 62 years with only two days' absence from work; Salem Chamber of Commerce President William H. Hammond; a band composed of Willamette students; the Rev. Louis White, who gave the invocation; Albert Wiesendanger, Keep Oregon Green executive, who received a gold charge-plate as the oldest M & F customer of Salem in the company's books.

Its nearly 160,000 square feet of area "will be a complete entity in itself, a complete department store," and will have covered and roof parking for more than 700 cars. Inside will be more than 75 departments, both selling and service.

There are to be seven public entrances, four on the main floor which will house the men's, youths', children's and women's ready-to-wear departments, and a restaurant.

Home merchandise of all kinds, a beauty shop and an auditorium for civic use will be on the second floor; special service departments on the mezzanine.

Marking, storage, power and air-conditioning facilities and employees quarters will be in the basement.

A spiral four-level covered garage and roof deck are to be correlated with the store itself. The structure will be of reinforced concrete, with mosaic tile and brick facing, and an entrance terrace with planting areas at Center and High Streets, flanked by covered walkways.

Silver Birch trees now there will remain in the parkway.

There are to be both elevators and escalators; a combination of fluorescent and incandescent lighting; acoustical ceilings; resilient floor-covering. Design will be contemporary.

Architects are Welton Becket and Associates, Los Angeles, and James L. Payne, Salem.

Wrecking of the old high school building now on the site of the new store is underway by E.S. Ritter & Company. Actual construction is expected to begin September 1, with completion scheduled a year hence.

Merchandise in the Salem branch would represent the best lines from both the upstairs and the basement Portland departments. For months we attended classes in advance merchandising, lectured by the top executives in the Portland store.

Life became very hectic the last few months before the Salem store opened. I was still selling, working in the buyer's office and attending classes. My commission was dropping so finally I asked Mr. Frank if I could be put on salary and he immediately responded. Meier & Frank paid for our move to Salem. I moved the week before the store opened.

It was evident that this store was going to be just beautiful when finished. It was set to open October 27, 1955. However, part of the store was finished and part was not. There was less than a week left before the grand opening. I was shocked at how much there was left to do. Some departments had fixtures. Mine had nothing but a stock room and a few unfinished fitting rooms. Workmen were still struggling with the floor coverings. Further more, the merchandise was being held up because the new Salem store had a different set of department numbers than those assigned to the Portland store. Merchandise was being sent to the wrong departments and the dock

Meier & Frank under construction in Salem on November 12, 1954.

workers who were trying to get the merchandise where it belonged were going crazy. One weary, bewildered dock worker with a large packing box of merchandise on a hand truck wandered over to the foundation department and asked, "You wouldn't know where this belongs would you? I trucked it over to the drug department and they said it doesn't belong there. Is there anybody that knows where this stuff belongs?"

I could see what his problem was. They put the Portland department numbers on the merchandise and had not included the new Salem store department numbers. I had a good memory back then and from my days at the transfer desk so long before, I could still recall all the department numbers from the Portland store. I was able to straighten him out as I had also memorized the floor plan for the new store. From then on, he brought the boxes back to me for identification. It wasn't long until his boss on the dock came and asked me if I could come to the dock and identify where more merchandise went as they had a terrible pile up on the unloading dock. "If you could just come for awhile." Up to that point, I had received no merchandise for my department so I agreed. I was out there about a half hour, and they were able to unload several large trucks from Portland. At that point the foundation buyer from Portland came charging out on the dock. "Miss Hermle, get back to your department. You have merchandise to put away!" The head dockman pleaded my case, but her voice only grew louder and louder. Finally he quietly said to me, "You'd better go back to your department. We know where you are, we'll find you."

Above is the 1954 ground breaking ceremony in front of the old Salem High School. From left to right is father Aaron Frank with his sons Richard and Gerry.

Below is Salem High School as it appeared in 1924.

There was one box of merchandise that took about 15 minutes to put away. Rather than send the Portland buyer into another tirade, I moved out to where I could watch my department and the dockmen that were trucking in merchandise could see me. I directed traffic for the better part of two days. Rather than stand like a wooden Indian waiting for my stock to arrive, I felt useful and needed.

The night before the grand opening, very little merchandise had arrived in my department. I had no fixtures and only a little merchandise. Nine-thirty that night, the fixtures and counters arrived. There was little that could be done except to unpack and try to keep it in some kind of order. By midnight I was exhausted. Tomorrow was another day, even if it was the big day, so I went home.

On October 28, 1955, the day after the grand opening, the *Oregon Statesman* newspaper published the story at the bottom of this page about the opening ceremonies.

A steady stream of huge floral bouquets of congratulations streamed into the store early on opening day. Wherever there was something missing, we placed a bouquet. After the speeches were given in the outdoor foyer of the store and the ribbon was cut, the public entered. I doubt that anyone noticed what was unfinished. The store was a thing of beauty to behold. The sweet scent of flowers filled the air. Salemites were

ecstatic with their beautiful, upscale store with three floors of parking plus the roof which in all accommodated 1000 cars.

It took several months before one could say that the building was finished, but when it was, it was elegant from one end to the other. Along with beautiful light wood fixtures and glass, my department had imported blue silk shantung draperies that must have cost a fortune. And the Crest Room, across the aisle which housed the most expensive ladies dresses and gowns, had imported silk wall coverings in the fitting rooms.

Crowds of people attending the Meier & Frank grand opening in Salem on October 27, 1955.

Oregon Statesman • October 28, 1954

Business, Public Leaders Speak at Brief Ceremony

An array of officials, both public and private, including television-radio singer Vaughn Monroe, were on hand Thursday to help open Salem's new Meier & Frank's department store.

An estimated crowd of 75,000 surged through the doors at shortly after noon when Mrs. Julius Meier, widow of the former Oregon governor and late president of Meier & Frank, cut the ribbon.

Store manager Gerry Frank was master of ceremonies at the brief program prior to the ribbon snipping.

He introduced a list of guests and visitors including contractors, architects, store board members and officials with their wives, and public officials including Gov. Paul Patterson.

Aaron Frank, Meier & Frank president, said that in addition to building the $8,000,000 store in Salem the firm had also acquired property in surrounding blocks, "which will be developed in due time."

He pledged the Salem store would carry on in the "same outstanding tradition and the same ideals," which had developed the Portland store into one of the best-known on the Pacific coast.

Kent Attrich, project architect of Los Angeles, assured the visitors that the Salem Meier & Frank's store "is the most modern and up-to-date in the West."

E.P. Platt, company vice-president, said the store boasted the largest and broadest array of merchandise in any store in the Pacific Northwest.

Also introduced were James Payne, associate architect of Salem; L.H. Hoffman, Claude Post and E.R. Viesko, all contractors; Ritchie Turner, Salem store superintendent, and other officials.

Mrs. Ludwig Hirsch and Mrs. W.H. Holmes, officials' wives, cut the huge 700-pound birthday cake, symbolizing the birth of the new store. The cake was distributed to visitors.

The Rev. Wayne Greene, president of the Salem Ministerial Association, gave the invocation. Flag raising was handled by Boy Scout Troop 1 of Salem.

Although the four-level store was in readiness for the throngs, the staff of 500 clerks, carpenters and others labored feverishly up until the opening hour in last-minute work.

Hundreds of bouquets of flowers, gifts from well-wishers and associates in business, dotted the store.

The best of the best was the only way to describe it. The Oregon Room restaurant decor was reminiscent of our Oregon forests, done in green with wood trim. It abounded with greenery and flowers.

Downtown areas all over the nation were beginning to deteriorate, but with the coming of Meier & Frank to Salem, eventually other companies moved in close, feeding off the foot traffic. The beautiful store started a revival of the downtown area.

The night scene of Meier & Frank, looking toward the store front.

Although the Salem store had sales that coincided with the Portland store, it was never as hectic. I was used to a much faster pace. I enjoyed my job so much, at times I wondered if I was truly earning my paycheck. The building was air conditioned, which at that time was a luxury.

It was the custom in the foundation department to have manufacturers' representatives come to the department to consult with customers who had fitting problems and help the sales girls learn how to fit new garments that came on the market. Every month someone was scheduled to come. The events were advertised in the Salem papers and also announced on the in-store PA system. One time in particular I remember. The Portland buyer scheduled a fashion model to come in and model foundations and girdles from a well known line. The model was to be presented in an afternoon fashion show, with a commentator. There was to be a daily drawing for a free garment. I remember making the comment that I didn't think Gerry would go for someone wandering around his elegant store in her underwear.

I thought about it the rest of the afternoon. We could dress her in a negligee that covered her and add lace flounces at the bottom of the garment. Then we could group the chairs in a semi-circle so she would not be visible to passers-by. Late that afternoon, I made the proposal to Mr. Frank. He made a little groan, but I assured him we would stay in the department, and she would be discreetly covered. He gave his permission with some reservations.

Then I decided to give the affair a real touch of class. I asked Lillian Rudy, who was fashion coordinator in the Salem store, to do the commentary. I asked Gerry if I could borrow Lillian for an hour every afternoon for the duration. He gave an exasperated sign and agreed. Disaster struck, Lillian came down with the flu and wouldn't be back to work for a week. What was I to do? So again I spoke to Mr. Frank. He looked me square in the eyes and said, "Well, I guess you'll just have to do the commentary yourself, won't you!" and he wasn't smiling. He whirled around and left. He'd had it with me and my fashion show.

I hadn't done any public speaking since high school when I placed second in the city of Portland in the American Legion oratorical contest. One thing in my favor, I was an expert on the subject matter. Every afternoon we had an excellent turnout. The ladies seemed to enjoy the presentation and applauded vigorously. Afterwards, they came and shook my hand. On the first day one lady remarked that I was the best commentator that she had ever heard. I probably had answered many of the questions about fitting that she had always wanted to know. The rest of the week went well and I enjoyed the event.

Meier & Frank was nearing its hundredth anniversary. In 1956, the company held a contest open to employees for a slogan that was to be used henceforth in their advertising. There was a cash prize. I entered. After the contest ended, at an early morning store meeting Gerry announced the winner and read the winning slogan, "Pioneering for your better tomorrow." My entry contained one more word that I had considered leaving out. I was disappointed, but then Gerry announced another prize, "First honorable mention, goes to an employee of our store, Annabel Hermle." With a big smile, he handed me a white box from a florist shop. I opened it, and it contained the biggest orchid I had ever seen, done up elaborately with appropriate ribbons. "Well, pin it on," he said. I was speechless. It covered my shoulder. I went back to my department after the meeting and my sales girls had the same reaction I had. Their eyes lit up when they saw it and vowed it was the most beautiful they had ever seen and looked rather longingly at it. I wore it most of the day and every customer commented on it's beauty, enjoying the story of how I came by it. Later in the afternoon, I got a bright idea. Why not share it. I looked at the clock. Each of my sales girls could wear it for one hour. Never was there a corsage that made more people happy. Later that day I had occasion to go to Mr. Frank's office and he asked, "Where's your corsage?" "We're sharing it. Each of my girls is wearing it for one hour." He smiled his approval.

I worked in the Salem store for just short of a year. I left to get married. My future husband was a farmer and a widower with two small children to raise, and life moves on. If ever in my life I suffered from mixed emotions it was then. It was like reading the last chapter of a great book. Should I read it again or move on to something else? I had spent a year in what was then probably one of the most elegant stores in the U.S. and I loved every day of it. Gerald Frank was one of the kindest, most fair persons I had ever met. He had a way of bringing out the best in his employees. I remember thinking at the time that some day he would be swept into politics and leave the store. Mentally, I gave him about two years. I was wrong. He stayed with his lovely store

for ten years and might have been there yet if not for the fact that there were those among the descendants of Jeanette and Aaron Meier that wished to sell their stock. When the stock buy out was complete, Meier & Frank became part of the May Company with some of the descendants still playing a roll in management. No doubt, "Shanette" was turning over in her grave. Gerald Frank resigned as manager and became administrative assistant to his long time friend, Senator Mark Hatfield. I once referred to him in a letter as a Washingtonian, and he promptly replied that he was an Oregonian, first, last and always.

The Salem store was only the first in a progression of new stores to bear the name of Meier & Frank, six more in Oregon and Washington, five of which came after the stock buy out.

Working at Meier & Frank was the ultimate education, and it was as was told to me the first day I began selling when I asked in my bewilderment, "What should I do?" The answer? "The customers will teach you." And they did.

Author's Note: *My thanks to Mr. Gerald Frank for allowing me to use materials from his files.*

Patton Brothers

Picture postcards

By Suzanne Stauss
Previously published Summer 1996, Vol.34, No.2

 In 1909, Salem area residents were participating in the height of the national craze to mail and collect picture postcards. From about 1907 until 1912 it was trendy to send several postcards when traveling. Day trips were no exception and local people often returned home before their postcards were delivered to neighbors and friends. Picture postcard albums were fashionably displayed in every family parlor. People took great pride in the quality and quantity of the cards inside.

Some of the most popular picture postcards were manufactured in Salem by the Patton Postcard Company. Hal Patton had developed an interest in cameras and photography at an early age. Hal and his brother, E. Cooke, were already in the

book and stationery business when they decided to open the Patton Postcard Company in 1908.

The business was located at 320 State Street. At that time, Salem buildings were often built with a 10-12 foot space between them. The Patton building was constructed in one of those vacant spaces which made it narrow, like a hall. That is why the card gallery on the main floor was named Patton Postcard Hall. The wholesale postcard business operated upstairs.

An estimated 5,000 cards were on display for purchase in the hall. Racks of cards were mounted side-by-side, stretching from floor to ceiling. People traveling to Salem from the outlying areas visited Patton Postcard Hall to select cards to mail back home. Most cards were priced at two for a nickel.

The interior picture of Patton Postcard Hall located at 320 State Street, shows E. Cooke Patton working with clerk, Mrs. Helene Hogan. The picture was taken about 1916.

COURTESY BOB TOMPKINS

Tom Cronise was the original photographer for the Pattons. It was not long before Eugene Lavalleur arrived in Salem and soon established his reputation as a perfectionist with his photography for the Patton Postcard Company. Lavalleur had an extraordinary talent to plot engaging but candid photos. He was known to stay at one site for an entire day, with his camera in position, waiting for the perfect light on his subject or a natural motion. Contents of Patton postcards indicate that Lavalleur's $15 per week expense allowance carried him throughout Oregon, southern Washington and into western Idaho. It is a curiosity why Lavalleur did not take pictures of the exterior of the Patton postcard business property. Speculation is that Lavalleur preferred to photograph the unknown, rather than objects he saw routinely.

Lavalleur used 5" x 7" glass negatives so that he could crop any photo to attain the best composition without having to enlarge his prints to be postcard size. His larger format and method helped make Patton postcards appear very detailed. Attempts have failed to locate the original negatives from which Lavalleur printed Patton picture postcards.

Because the negatives have never been found, it is presumed that James Cooke discarded them when he purchased Patton Book and Stationery Store from Hal and E. Cooke many years later. (It

is only coincidence that James Cooke spells his last name the same as E. Cooke Patton spells his name.)

Picture postcards were usually produced by Lavalleur in the basement of Patton Postcard Hall. The Patton brothers sent some photos to Germany for color lithography and press printing.

Germany had been manufacturing postcards long before it became an industry in the United States. German printers had more experience, sophisticated lithographic equipment and advanced techniques than West Coast companies. And labor was cheaper. Some Patton postcards were printed in Chicago. However, the identification "Patton Postcard Company" appears on the left edge of the address side of their cards.

The Patton Brothers Postcard Company enjoyed it's greatest success during the first few years of operation, employing two or three salespeople who traveled to several cities. Sales began to decline when Americans were preparing for World War I. Competition from the Portland Post Card Company and Mitchell Card Company of San Francisco also had an effect on sales. They could sell cards for $1^1/_2$ cents each, a penny less than Patton Brothers. In 1912, E. Cooke and Hal Patton closed Postcard Hall and resumed the Patton Book and Stationery Store. Lavalleur continued the picture postcard business under the name of West Coast Postcards.

Today, historians have rekindled a national interest in postcard collections as a significant resource. Patton postcards are highly regarded for their historical value. The Patton brothers supported Lavalleur's creative picture compositions to include pragmatic elements in every image. Because most Patton postcards were produced as direct black and white photo prints (or mezzotints), the elements of every picture are well sustained. Pictures that Patton brothers sent away for printing were subject to alteration. Lithographers routinely distorted pictures by eliminating legitimate telegraph lines, street and store signs, trees or woodpiles and replaced them with backgrounds of clouds and foreign mountains or foregrounds of unknown people, automobiles and landscapes. Consequently, the content of Patton postcards is a creditable source for historical research because of their legitimate subject matter. Viewing Patton postcards with a magnifying glass reveals details that are not found on most other cards.

Looking east, up State Street from the intersection of Commercial Street, Patton Postcard hall is on the right, below the arrow. AL JONES COLLECTION

The Patton Family

E. Cooke and Hal Patton spent their entire lives in Salem. Their grandparents were E.N. and Eliza Cooke, and their parents were T. McF and Frances Patton. These 1852 Salem pioneer families were involved in the civic and social structure of the community. As children and as adults, the Patton brothers extended their family history of community involvement while enjoying successful and amusing lives.

The Patton family home was located at 883 Court Street.
COURTESY BOB TOMPKINS

For example, the fiftieth birthday celebration of ex-State Senator Hal Patton on January 12, 1922, was one of the most unique social events in Salem history. Two-hundred men who had grown up with the Patton brothers, or worked together for Salem development, made rehearsed presentations about the importance of the past, relating stories of dignity, courage and humor. The celebration was restricted to men only and was held in the Shrine mosque over the J.C. Penney store on Liberty Street.

E. Cooke Patton had become fascinated by magic and hypnotism during a two-year visit to Kobe, Japan, when he was 14. He pursued his interest in hypnotism as an adult hobby. Although it was not medically acceptable at the time, E. Cooke did assist Dr. Mark Skiff, a local dentist, by hypnotizing patients at their request to reduce the pain of dental work. He was also known to produce shows of his hypnotism and magic at Salem churches and schools.

The Patton legacy of community enrichment still exists. E. Cooke Patton's daughter, Mrs. Luella Patton Charleton, lives in Salem and is respected for sharing her heritage.

Paulus Saloon

Downtown Salem on State Street

By Jordis Schick
Previously published May 1994, Vol.32, No.2

The picture below, provided by William G. Paulus, Salem attorney, dates to about 1890. It shows his grandfather's saloon at 102 State Street.

Bill thinks the first J.K. Gill store (a firm that began life in Salem) was the original occupant of the building. However, since the late 1880s, it has housed taverns. At one time it was known as Talkington's; it later became the Pioneer Club or Palace. More recently it was Videl's. Now it is called Weber's Too.

Somewhere along the line, the building's street number was also changed—to 356 State—and the three upstairs windows became four after a couple of fires.

The baby in the upstairs window is Fred Paulus, Bill's uncle who passed away in 1991. The woman is Bill's grandmother (and Fred's mother) Elizabetha Nees Paulus who originally came from Neustadt, Germany. The gentleman is Bill's grandfather (and Fred's father) Chris Paulus who arrived in Oregon from a German community in Grafton, Wisconsin. One item sold in the saloon (as shown in the signs on the pillars next to the entrance) was H. Weinhart Lager Beer.

Elizabetha and Chris married in 1888. Two of their six boys were born over the saloon—Fred and Bob. Bill says he was told Elizabetha made Chris sell the saloon (he owned both the building and the business) because she did not think it was a fitting occupation for a man with children. Chris then became a builder which must have provided a fine influence because the boys all grew up to be outstanding citizens. Fred Paulus served as Oregon's deputy state treasurer for over 40 years. One of his biggest claims to fame was initiating the timely reforestation of Oregon's Tillamook Burn area where trees are now once again becoming harvestable.

When Fred died, he left the building pictured and most of his estate to Willamette University and the Salem Hospital. The building was later sold to Weber's.

Three of the six Paulus boys—Bob, Bill (the present Bill's father), and George, operated the Paulus Brothers Packing Company in Salem for many years, the largest cannery in Salem when the Willamette Valley was the canning capital of the world. Otto Paulus, another son, was a prominent Salem lawyer and a member of Oregon's House of Representatives. Ted Paulus became a Grants Pass businessman. Ted recently celebrated his 90th birthday in Grants Pass.

At the time of this photograph, the Paulus family lived "over the store." Norma Paulus, Bill's wife, has some of the flowerpots in the picture. Norma and Bill's son, Fritz, has the gold watch his great-grandfather is wearing.

Salem Public Market

Where the city still meets the county every Saturday

By Jordis Schick
Previously published February 1995, Vol.33, No.1

Salem's secret shopper's paradise celebrated its 50th birthday in 1994 and it's time we spread the good news (and the good goods) beyond its unpretentious doorway—especially since the market also bears the distinction of being Oregon's oldest continuously operating farmer's market!

What regular customers have known for years (and believe me, there are regulars) is that if you are willing to get up on Saturday morning and go down to the modest building at the corner of Rural and 12th Street SE between 8:30 a.m. and noon, the closer to 8:30 the better, you will find fresh produce to die for, straight out of the fields and probably picked that morning, as well as beautiful fresh and dried cut flowers, bedding plants, home-made baked goods now produced in "licensed" and "inspected" kitchens, unusual specialty products like Oregon hazelnuts and field-fresh honey, and old-fashioned handcrafted bibs, aprons, knitted caps and mittens—all of the things you rarely see in today's "Made in Taiwan" world.

The sellers who rent the stalls and the shoppers who load up say they become addicted to the Saturday morning ritual.

It's all fine and dandy with Donna and Robert (Bob) Heilman, who live out in the Lake Labish area near Brooks. The Heilmans have been part of the market since its beginnings. Bob's father, William Heilman, was one of the original vendors back in 1943.

The Heilmans: Robert, William, and Donna.
AL JONES PHOTO

The modest exterior of the Salem Public Market building gives no hint of the flurry of activity that occurs there every Saturday morning.   AL JONES PHOTO

And, since William celebrated his 102nd birthday December 25, 1996, I guess years of hard farm labor and fresh farm food must bear some relationship to longevity.

William still helps his son and daughter-in-law get produce ready for the Public Market stand on Friday nights, although he has quit working every Saturday morning.

Bob and William say the idea for the market was promoted by Albert Gille, who was on the Salem City Council, Ronald E. Jones Sr., a state representative and senator from 1935 to 1943 and also a Brooks area onion broker (whose brand was "Pride of Lake Labish"), and L.O. Arens, with the State Industrial Accident Commission.

During World War II and gas rationing, these men (and possibly others) placed a classified ad in the Salem newspaper saying people who lived in the city were interested in getting a farmer's market started because they couldn't get the gas to go get fresh farm produce. The ad suggested that farmers (who did get gas coupons for their trucks) could fill a special need by bringing their produce to city dwellers instead, and asked any farmer interested to contact the writers.

Both William Heilman and his son, Bob, who had just graduated from high school at the time, remember piling their ton-and-a-half flatbed truck with surplus produce and driving down to Marion Square for the first public "tailgate" market that fall. There were quite a few farmers who responded, about 20 to 25, and they parked alongside the square on the south side.

The Heilmans say they sold sweet corn, squash, beans, beets, carrots, and wonderful Oregon Delicious watermelons. And they point out the difference in prices between then and now. Carrots and beets sold for 10¢ a bunch; big stalks of celery and lettuce were 15 cents.

The farmers came from all of the surrounding communities—Silverton, Stayton, Turner, Aumsville, even the Roberts area. Since many farmers didn't know each other at that time, it was a good chance to get acquainted as well as talk "shop."

William Heilman had moved to his Lake Labish farm in 1936 from Tigard, where his father had a 48-acre farm on Beef Bend Road, now unrecognizable amidst the sea of "Street of Dreams" houses and upscale apartments. William's father, Emil Heilman, of German ancestry, was himself born in Tigard. In 1918, young William married Anna Gaarde, the daughter of John & Matilde Gaarde of Tigard where a street bears the Gaarde name. To make ends meet, he worked a daunting schedule, daily at the Kraft Dairy and, before and after his regular job, shouldering his normal share of the farm chores. Before Anna's death at the age of 96 in 1993, the Heilmans celebrated their 71st wedding anniversary.

One memory William shares is of helping his father build a wooden barn out of whole timbers cut right on their Beef Bend farm. The barn was meant to last for many, many years and would probably still be standing today were it not for modern development.

In the early 1920s, William's father owned a piece of land in the Brooks area and William traveled back and forth to help farm it. From time to time his father even talked about having his son grow onions in the area.

When a neighbor mentioned a place for sale in the Lake Labish area in 1935, William hightailed it down to Chester Cox at the Ladd & Bush Bank, who arranged a loan.

The farm was full of stumps then, that the senior Heilman had to clear. The Lake Labish area was also full of the old beaver dams from the pre-drainage days. Bob Heilman says he has heard nettles grew as high as a man on horseback in the early days. You couldn't see over them!

The lake bed boasts wonderful soil, a rich combination of river silt and peat. But Bob says he has watched the ground level sink several feet since the family moved there, and knows the soft deep dirt in the old lake bed can easily eat up both people and farm equipment. The soil is also highly flammable; if a fire gets started it travels huge distances underground and it almost takes a miracle to put it out.

According to Bob, this fine Lake Labish soil also crumbles when exposed to air, which is why water is such an absolute necessity for maintenance. In earlier days, the lake's drainage ditch and laterals furnished the water. Today wells must be dug but, fortunately, underground water is still plentiful.

In 1949 Robert Heilman married Donna Jefferson, daughter of another notable pioneer farm family that still farms in the Middlegrove, North Howell area. Delos Jefferson, Donna's great grandfather arrived in Oregon in 1848.

The Heilman family now owns about 30 acres of Lake Labish land, much of it leased out to other farmers. Bob and Donna live on the same acreage that belonged to Emil Heilman, William's father, way back when. William still lives in his own house on the other side.

After that first winter hauling produce to Marion Square, two farmers, Fred Steiner and Martin Reuter, went together and purchased a lot at the northeast corner of Union and High where

A customer discusses honey with Walt Nichols.

Jennifer Bevier, a granddaughter of Mrs. Carlson (a longtime vendor) helps out at David Bielenberg's booth. Jennifer says the market gets in your blood; she doesn't feel right unless she's there on Saturdays. It also must get in your stomach. Jennifer was pictured at age 10 in the Statesman Journal digging into the free strawberry shortcake the market serves at a celebration held each June when the berries ripen. AL JONES PHOTOS

a carwash is now located. Then all of the farmers took up a collection to buy materials to put up their own building, a rough open-air structure that they used until 1946, when property values zoomed upward after the war, and the two who had purchased the property sold the land out from underneath the building.

The farmers once again combined forces and tore the building down piece by piece so it could be rebuilt at the present location. They also made sure the land wouldn't be sold out from under them again by forming a non-profit corporation. The $100 each chipped in to pay for the site has long since been paid back.

The farmers who formed the original corporation are listed in the first record book: Bob Heilman, G.B. Smith, L.D. Johnston, Ruth Bressler, Mabel Higgins, J.K. Crabtree, Louis Frohmader, Mrs. John Van Lydegraff, J.L. Zielke, Fred Steiner, and Martin Reuter. Mrs. Charles (Catherine) Barsch was the secretary for the group for many, many years.

The building has since been enclosed with metal siding and reroofed. It has also been painted and the group has replaced the old wood boiler with a gas furnace. Louis Johnston pulled the original wood stove out of the Leslie Methodist Church on South Commercial before it was torn down.

Today there are 33 members in the Public Market organization although not all are active. The market has both double and single stalls and all must be rented in advance. Prices, which used to be $1 per week, are now $6 per week for five to six feet of counter space. Vendors cannot buy and resell items; produce sold is to be produced or grown by the vendors themselves.

Over the years several managers have served the market. The first was Louis Johnston, next Fred Steiner, and then Mrs. Ruth Bressler, who served for a long time. Robert Heilman followed Ruth. He was followed by Rose Michalek, who also managed the facility for many years before her retirement at the beginning of 1991 when Donna Heilman, the current manager, took over.

Other things have also changed. Farmers can no longer sell fryers, eggs, and other fresh animal products since all such items must now have expensive processing licenses. Even the baked goods sold must now come from licensed kitchens with licensed scales, all of which doesn't come cheap. A new scale costs about $75 and there is also a yearly fee for usage and inspection.

For a period of time after the regulations were first changed, there was such a hullabaloo about

Gerda Schifferer, Cloverdale Flowers.

AL JONES PHOTO

the Public Market having to end its sales of home-baked bread that Irvin Mann of the state Department of Agriculture, at Gov. Tom McCall's direction, modified the initial ruling to permit bakeries producing goods only one day a week to continue operating if they displayed a sign saying they were not licensed or inspected by the state.

A tongue-in-cheek comment appeared in the July 15, 1972 *Oregon Statesman*:

The State Department of Agriculture is preparing to modify its regulations to permit farmers' wives to bring their baked goods to the Salem Public Market for sale on Saturday mornings.

A sign must be posted near the stand, however, reading "These products were prepared, processed or manufactured on premises not licensed or inspected under Oregon law."

Wouldn't it take far less space and be just as accurate to put up the sign which attracted the customers there in the first place? It would read "Home Made."

The attraction still holds true today. People still shop at the market principally for things either home grown or home made. And fortunately, despite ever increasing regulations, farmers and customers are still holding on to the tradition on Rural Street.

Today's vendors, more like one big happy family than separate businesses, include:

- The Heilman Family—Robert, Donna and daughters Carol, Joyce and Sharon. They offer fresh seasonal produce, dried flower arrangements, and handcrafted jewelry.
- Daum's Produce—Gary, Kathy, Aaron, Jill, and Grandma. Seasonal produce. At present a big seller is apple cider, winter apples, squashes, etc.
- David Bielenberg—Seasonal vegetables, dried flowers, fresh cut flowers in the spring and summer, also hanging baskets of fuchsias and geraniums, and bedding plants.
- Jeanne Whitener—A veteran of over 25 years who operates the booth with her daughters. Hand-sewn items including T-shirts and sweats; also dried floral and seasonal nursery stock.
- Jo Bielenberg—Flowers and both summer and winter vegetables.
- White's Produce—Nuts, vegetables, fresh and dried fruits, home-baked goods.
- Cloverdale Flowers—Gerda Schifferer and daughters. Dried and fresh flowers in season and seasonal produce.
- Never Enough Thyme—Marion Wirth and Roseanne Boldine. Ceramics, dried flowers, and some handicrafts like bibs and candles.
- Agnes Carlson—A family affair, with a daughter and her mother-in-law and grandchildren all participating. Fresh produce and plants in season. Also hand-sewn, knitted and crocheted items.

- Sugar Cube Bakery—Steve & Pearl Ellis. Home-baked variety breads, cookies, and also a mean salsa—Steve's own concoction, either mild or hot.
- Gopher Broke—Joan and Jim Kirk. Specialists in miniature roses (including scented varieties), orchids, and healthy medicinal house plants.
- The Brittle Kittle—Royce and Naomi Powell. "The Brittle with the Cushion Crunch"—soft peanut, hazelnut and almond nut brittles, distinctively boxed.
- Walt Nichol—Honey, honey sticks, honey mustards, jams & jellies, bee's wax candles, anything to do with bees. Walt keeps the bees in Salem, West Salem, Albany, etc. Farmers welcome the pollination they provide.
- Hunt's Hazelnuts—Bruce Hunt. Hazelnuts from in-the-shell to chocolate-coated candy, coffee, syrup, pancake mix, flour, oil, and butter; also gift packs in wooden boxes. Recipes and free samples are provided!
- Cookie Mamas—Barb Watkins. Every kind of cookie, muffin and breakfast roll for Sunday morning treats.
- Trudy Goin—Arts & crafts, seasonal vegetables, fruits and berries.
- Shirley Walle—Products created from earth-friendly natural materials. Dream catchers, rose petal beads, herbs, candles. Also miniature water colors that Shirley paints.
- Alma Lockhart—Popular double terry kitchen towels to hang over oven and refrigerator door handles, seasonal vegetables, including shallots, and berries—all grown with no spray. Also handicrafts during winter months.

Lake Labish

A brief history
By Eleanor Morgan
Previously published February 1995, Vol.33, No.1

 All that now remains of the 10,000 year old peat bog known as Lake Labish are rich agricultural fields and a ditch that flows into the Little Pudding River. But in the late 1830s, when Thomas Moisan, an employee of the Hudson's Bay Company, settled in the area, Lake Labish was nearly ten miles in length and about one-half mile wide at the widest point.

At that time, the lake's depth varied from one foot to eight feet with drainage to the east and the west. On a northeast axis that ran from what is now the northern edge of Keizer to Parkersville, Lake Labish formed the southeast edge of the area known as French Prairie.

The ecosystem surrounding the lake was rich and varied. In the shallow areas willow, alder, ash trees, vine maples, cattails, and cottonwoods

Lush Lake Labish soil on the Heilman farm.

COURTESY DONNA HEILMAN

could be found. Surrounding the lake were groves of pines and oaks. The lake also supported thriving animal populations—mainly deer, beaver and ducks—as well as a wide variety of insects and a breeding ground for frogs.

The first surveys of the lake were undertaken in September and October of 1851. These showed the township lines and subdivisions and they were filed in Oregon City in 1852 and refiled in Eugene City in 1862. They appear to show only three land claims abutting the lake: James Webb and John Quigley in T2W and William Parker in T1W. The plats were again signed off as being correct copies of the originals in Portland in 1925.

The first attempt to drain the lake commenced in 1875 when the Marion County Court authorized a ditch two miles long through the lake's center. In the 1890s, attempts were renewed to drain the lake into the Pudding River on the east, but a big impediment—provided by a dam at Parkersville on the north end of the lake, used to run a grist mill and log mill owned by the Wattier family—stood in the way.

In 1913, A.F. Hayes, a millionaire from California, saw the potential for cultivating the lake bottom and, after purchasing a large acreage, organized other landowners. A goodly sum of money was paid to the Wattier family to destroy their dam and mills and, by the spring of 1914, the lake bottom was under cultivation. Land that had sold for $1.00 an acre was now selling for $1,000 an acre.

According to Bob Ohling, a Salem-based farm appraiser, Lake Labish acreage values peaked out in 1985-86 at about $8,000 to $10,000 an acre. A hybrid onion was developed about then that could also be grown in the upland areas. Today the going price is around $3,500 an acre and, since most of the area's farmers don't hold really large acreages, it is now getting harder and harder to farm profitably.

The 1927 *Soil Survey of Marion County*, published by the U.S. Department of Agriculture, discusses the soil in and around Lake Labish, saying it consists principally of peat, also known as "beaver-dam soil," Wapato silty clay loam, and Willamette silt loam.

The pamphlet continues:*The main area of peat extends northeast from Chemawa Indian School and is known as Lake Labish. This area is about nine miles long and ranges in width from an eighth to a quarter of a mile. The surface of the Lake peat is practically level.* The crops in cultivation then as now were mainly onions, celery, and peppermint.

This brief history reveals nothing of the rich and varied cultural history of the lake that touches on every aspect of the Keizer-Salem area. Pieces of the story are scattered all around us—in the stories of families, in multitudinous government documents, in the documents of private enterprise, and in our newspapers and libraries.[1]

---

[1] A delightful account of Lake Labish that furnishes much additional information was written by George Strozut, Jr. entitled *Black Gold: The Story of Lake Labish.* It is in *Marion County HISTORY,* Vol. 5, 1959, p 47-49. Strozut points out one thing still apparent to anyone driving on I-5. He says: "On the east side of the Portland highway onions are grown to 'strengthen the breath' but on the west side of the highway acres of mint are grown to 'sweeten the breath'!"

Teasel Has A Story

By Sybil Westenhouse
With thanks to Judith Sutliff
Previously published August 1993, Vol.31, No.3

As autumn comes to the Willamette Valley the word teasel brings a familiar picture to mind, since collecting teasel along with other grasses and weeds to dry for winter arrangements is a common weekend project. That two-foot stalk with a conical head of straight, pliable spines found in roadside ditches and in uncultivated edges of fields is wild teasel, *Dipsacus sylvestris*.

Another teasel, much less commonly found, is *Dipsacus fullonum*, or Fuller's teasel. This cultivated plant, light green in color, grows about six feet tall and produces twenty or more cone-shaped heads. These heads are up to one and a half inches wide and vary from two to four inches in length—with stiff yet flexible hooked spines. It is the hooked outer end of each spine that makes this a specially valued teasel.

Over the centuries, as cloth makers worked to improve the appearance of their finished woven product, somehow they discovered unevenness, knots, and other irregularities could be altered or hidden by napping—that is, by gently raising the surface fibers and then trimming those fibers to an even length. Napping is done by passing a tool with a rough yet slightly yielding surface lightly across the dampened woven fabric face.

Perhaps cloth makers in Grecian times discovered the usefulness of the hooked spines on Fuller's teasel. Certainly by the 15th Century,

This authentic Fuller's teasel is planted at the Thomas Kay Woolen Mill site.

AL JONES PHOTO

English cloth makers were using it in their industry. The original napper's tool was a hand held paddle with an average of 12 to 14 teasel attached vertically across the face. Two of these paddles at a time were used by workmen to lightly catch the dampened woolen fiber tips and lift them up while the fabric was tautly held in place on a frame. After receiving as many as three passes with the weft and the same with the warp, followed by trimming, the fabric took on a nicely uniform appearance and would be much softer, smoother and even warmer because air pockets form in the napping process.

When the first gig (a mechanized teasel napper) was introduced in England and the skilled handnappers saw the end of their trade looming, they fought the changes through their guilds. Thus in 1551 gig mills were outlawed, and it was not until the mid-1880s, 300 years later, that English woolen mills replaced the skilled craftsmen with rotary napping machines run by semi-skilled operators.

Other woolen manufacturers around the world and particularly those in the United States had begun using the rotary teasel gig much earlier. A.J. Sawtell, born in England, had grown up learning the business. When he and his sister Mary emigrated to America in 1858, they packed the family dishes in teasel seed, hoping to grow the plant and follow the business here. Sawtell bought 310 acres a few miles north of Molalla where he raised, harvested and sold teasel for the next 39 years.

Dipsacus fullonum is a biennial, resembling a cabbage plant the first year, then shooting up a six-foot center stalk with many side branches, each of which produces a head which blooms out white, then matures to form the many spiked teasel. The center stalk forms the "king" or male flower for the plant and it will become the biggest teasel. During flowering, it produces pollen which showers down over the 20 to 30 female teasel, fertilizing the seeds. If the king is removed before pollination, the other teasel will not produce fertile seeds but will grow to a larger size. Where the branches meet the main stalk a cup-like depression is formed. This may hold a quart of water and this liquid is necessary for perfect teasel to form.

When a teasel head is mature, it is cut with a six-inch stem, then carefully dried in shallow layers in a shed, remaining there for several months. In early spring the stiff leaf spikes around the base of the teasel head are cut off and the stem is shortened to three inches. The teasel are now ready for sizing and sale.

At the woolen mill the uniformly sized teasel would be placed in rows on a drum, held in place by the stem inserted in a hole in a crossbar, and the cloth would be passed over them. The teasel frequently need to be removed to clean the fibers out that have broken and become caught in the spikes or for replacement of a worn out teasel.

A very informative display panel on teasel gigging and the hand tool, with illustrations, is available at Mission Mill Village Museum. Contact Curator Judith Sutliff for information.

"Molalla—The Sawtells, First Teasel on West Coast Sown in Clackamas County," *Everything's Fine-O in Mulino*, September 1991

Elizabeth Leadbeater, "Teasels," *Handwoven*, November 1981, pp 54-55.

Alzina Loveless, "The Teasel Industry in New York State," *Shuttle, Spindle and Dyepot*, Fall 1977, Issue 32, Vol. VIII #4, p 71.

Kay Antunez de Mayolo, "Teasel Tools," *Shuttle, Spindle and Dyepot*, Fall 1982, Issue 52, Vol. XIII, #4, p 10-11.

E. Rigby and H. Libeler, "*Dipsacus Fullonum*: Fuller's Teasel," *Weaver's Journal*, Fall 1983, Issue 30, Vol. VIII, #2, p 58.

White House Restaurant

Circa 1905

By Jordis Schick

Previously published November 1993, Vol.31, No.4

The photograph below was taken about 1905 inside of the White House Restaurant, located at 362 State Street in Salem in the space now occupied by part of the Cooke Stationery Company.

After Emma Judson Crouser kindly donated this picture and others to MCHS for our research files, Reid Hanson, an MCHS member, did considerable background research. And it really whetted his appetite.

He believes the white-haired gentleman is William P. George, proprietor, and that the employee dressed in white is John McDonald.

Some of the information he gleaned from old Salem directories follows. Evidently the George family lived for many years in the rooms above the restaurant.

1902 • The listing for 106 State (old numbering system) shows Wm. P. George as owner and Lee T. George, Wm. R. George, and Wm. R. George, Jr. (who were all waiters) living above the restaurant.

1905 • The listing shows Lee T. George, waiter; Wm. P. George, proprietor; and John McDonald, farmer. Lee and John board elsewhere.

1907-1908 • The listing of 362 State (new numbering system) shows Wm. McGilchrist & Son as proprietors, but it still shows Wm. P. George and Lee (or Levi?) George as a clerk. They both now reside elsewhere.

1909-1910 and 1911 • Wm. McGilchrist & Son are still listed as proprietors.

1913 • It seems the George family has regained ownership. Wm. P., Levi T. & Jesse are listed as proprietors. Jesse has a wife named Elva and lives on Church Street. Wm. P., Laura A., and Jesse R. and Chalmer L. (students) live on 14th St. Levi rooms at 148 S. Commercial; and Opel and Pearl George, who both work at F.W. Woolworth Co., board at 522 N. Church.

From 1915 all the way through 1931, various Georges are still listed as proprietors. It appears Wm. P. and Laura moved back over the restaurant in 1917. There is the Jesse with a wife named Elva, and a Jesse R. George shows up in 1915 along with a Wm. P. Jr. in 1917. Chalmer goes to dental school and marries Grace. Jesse R. marries Lenore. And Isabel, John D. and Lee T. George also live with Wm. P. & Laura above the restaurant.

In 1932, The Spa Restaurant was listed at 382 State, a few doors to the East. But we still have Georges at 360-1/2 State—Hazel L., Isabel, Jesse R., Wm. P. and Laura, and Wm. P. Jr.

The interior of the White House Restaurant (circa 1915) located at 362 State Street in Salem. The man dressed in white is John McDonald. Second from left is probably William P. George, proprietor. Others included are believed to be Levi T. George, Jesse George, Jesse R. George and William P. George, Jr. The boy on the counter stool may be John David George.

COURTESY
EMMA JUDSON CROUSER

Babe Ruth

By Al Jones
Previously published August 1994, Vol. 32, No. 3

Babe Ruth had two busy days in Salem in 1926, making kids happy in his many appearances. He knew the feelings of the ones he visited in the institutions because George Herman Ruth, in his childhood in the slums of Baltimore, had been a homeless, neglected, delinquent youngster.

When he insisted on visiting the children who couldn't see him at the new Capitol Theatre in two Pantages Vaudeville matinees, his hosts took him to the State School for the Blind, School for the Deaf, Chemawa Indian School, and the reformatories. Included also were the penitentiary and the flax plant there.

At the reformatory he urged the youths to "do the best you can at all times. Bet your life you can do it, and if one mistake is made, don't let that prevent you from correcting the error and keep on trying to do right."

He autographed many baseballs and bats in those two days as Salem people got to meet the famous King of Swat, the Bambino, or the Babe.

The 200-pound star with the thin legs and small feet had hit 47 home runs in the 1926 season with the New York Yankees, the seventh season he led the league. It wasn't known then, but in the next season he would hit 60 homers, just one more than he hit in 1921.

In compiling a lifetime batting average of .342, Babe Ruth slugged 40 or more homers in 11 seasons. That was when a major league season was 154 games, whereas today (since 1962) a slugger has 162 games in which to add up home runs.

For the record, the all-time highest total of homers was 61, by Roger Maris of the Yankees, done in 162 games in 1961.

Adding to Babe Ruth's fame was his ability to pitch the baseball, left-handed. That's how he broke into major league ball as a pitcher for the Boston Red Sox in about 1913.

In his first three full seasons he won 64 games, helping the Red Sox win three pennants. In the 1916 World Series, Ruth won the second game against Brooklyn, 2-1, in 14 innings. In the 1918 Series, he pitched 29 consecutive scoreless innings against Chicago.

When Ruth visited in 1926, Salem had a population of about 22,000, with J.B. Giesy as mayor. The Capitol Theatre had opened on October 5, the Elsinore Theatre opened on May 28, 1926.

Also in 1926, the Salem YMCA erected its building and the Oregon Linen Co. and Western Paper Converting Co. plants were built. Streetcars were being phased out. By August 1927, busses were taking over.

Babe Ruth's final season was 1935 when, at age 40, he hit three homers in one game just a week before the last game. He died of cancer August 16, 1948, a legend who will be remembered as long as baseball players hit home runs.

While here, Babe Ruth autographed this horsehide for Kenneth McDonald, address unknown.

COURTESY AL JONES

Horses: They're Off!

By Jim Martin
Previously published August 1993, Vol.31, No.3

That thought was on the minds of many residents around Fort Vancouver as Saturday, July 25, 1846—the day of the Oregon Country's "first public exhibition on the 'turf' " —approached.

A race course, one mile in extent, was lately laid out upon the plains adjoining the Fort, and riders could be seen, for days previous, coursing and training, with keen and anxious countenances, the *Oregon Spectator* informed its readers.

The weather proved very favorable, cool and dry, and as the hour (one o'clock) approached, vast multitudes moved to the scene of action, the Oregon City paper added.

An "elegant" reviewing stand had been erected at the finish line. From this vantage point, Peter Skene Ogden, ranking official of the Hudson's Bay Company at Fort Vancouver, was to render his decisions as judge of the races with "happy temperament, pleasantry and firmness."

Ogden was joined on the platform "by numerous friends and a brilliant circle of the fair sex."

Also present were Lieutenant Neil Howison, commander of the U.S. Navy schooner *Shark*; Captain Thomas Baillie of *HBMS Modeste*, a sloop-of-war; and their officers.

The *Modeste* had been stationed in the Columbia River since November 1845, to protect British interests should hostilities erupt with the United States over the northern boundary question. The crew had maintained harmonious relations with settlers from both nations, although some Americans remained wary.

The *Shark* arrived in July 1846, on orders of the U.S. Pacific Squadron commander, Commodore John D. Sloat, to report on trade, shipping and general development of the Oregon Country, and to keep an eye on the British.

A treaty setting the boundary at the 49th parallel had been signed June 15, 1846, at Washington, but the news had not yet reached Fort Vancouver. The people who gathered for the race, however, were able to forget the issue and enjoy the occasion.

A noble array of horses were on the ground, tastefully decorated, and arranged by the committee to contest the different handsome prizes, the *Oregon Spectator* commented. *The gaudy and 'jocky' dresses of the riders were much admired...The heats, particularly that for the 'Ladies' Plate,' were eagerly contested and great prowess displayed by the riders.*

It was gratifying also, that these sports passed off with regularity and éclat, and without any serious accident," the account continued. "*A handsome pavilion was pitched in the center of the race course, where the officers of the Modeste entertained at dinner a numerous circle, among whom were the officers of the Shark, and much happiness and good feeling prevailed.*

"Alas," the paper informed its readers, the list of horses, owners, riders, heats and prizes was found "too lengthy for insertion."

Oregon State Fair Beginnings

By Al Jones
Previously published August 1992, Vol. 30, No. 5

Oregon's first State Fair was staged for an obvious reason—to exhibit the magnificent bounty of this state's harvest season and to honor our agricultural industry.

But before the first event took place in October 1861, County Agricultural Associations had been organized, starting with Yamhill in 1853; Marion and Polk in 1854; Linn in 1856;Lane, Jackson, Benton, Multonomah and Clackamas in 1859; and Umpqua Valley in 1860. These groups and the *Oregon Farmer*, our first farm newspaper, called for a state fair and a meeting was held in Salem on October 20, 1858, that resulted in the Fruitgrowers Association of Oregon.

The State Agricultural Society was organized and merged with the Fruitgrowers September 10, 1860.

That first State Fair in 1861 was on a four-acre site on the north bank of the Clackamas River, about two miles below Oregon City. It lasted four days and even had a track for horse racing, which was the primary entertainment along with equestrian events.

The terrible flood of 1861 helped convince the board it should look for a larger site to accommodate larger crowds, away from a river that floods. The Marion County Agricultural Society's offer of the Marion County Fairgrounds was accepted.

John Minto, an 1844 Oregon Trail immigrant who became a leader in many statewide activities, donated $1200 for a board fence around eight acres of the 55-acre grounds. Minto also introduced purebred Merino, a hardy fine-wooled white sheep. In the 1880s this helped shift the emphasis in livestock judging from size and condition of flesh to pedigree and quality.

The exhibits of livestock, poultry, grain, fruit, vegetables and equestrian events drew larger and larger crowds from more and more corners of Oregon. They came in their wagons, carriages and on horseback, usually camping in the oak grove west of the Fairgrounds.

Horse racing always was a main attraction, and bicycle races were added in 1895, prior to the availability of autos, tractors or ferris wheels. In 1895 the Fair was also extended from four to ten days.

Although jurisdiction over the State Fair started with the State Agricultural Society, in 1885 the Legislature gave the Board of Agriculture control.

In 1951 control shifted to the new State Fair Commission; in 1977 it again shifted to the Executive Department.

The Fair was held on Sunday for the first time in 1927, without horse racing because of opposition of some churches. It opened on Labor Day rather than late September in 1933.

The following list highlights construction during the years on the State Fairgrounds, which now total 185 acres.

1929 Grandstand erected; capacity 6500; cost $150,000.

1934 Restaurant pavilion; new concessions building; oval racetrack.

1939 New restaurant, stock barn addition, 650-seat horse show barn.

1976 Jackman-Long Exposition Center dedicated; pavilion replaced 4H-FFA barn.

1987 Livestock Pavilion replaced fifty year old barn; cost $2.4 million. New L.B. Day Amphitheater used for Fair; capacity 9000.

1989 $1,100,000 beef barn built on east side of grounds, replaced old barn which burned that year.

1995 Cascade Hall was remodeled to accommodate various sized groups for conferences and other indoor meetings.

Other State Fair Highlights

1905 No State Fair because of Lewis & Clark Exposition in Portland.

1933 Parimutuel wagering allowed for first time. Rodeos and parachute races added.

1934 Jason Lee Day held on Saturday, 100th year after his arrival in the Willamette Valley. Indian village built.

1943-1944 No State Fair because of World War II. The Army leased the Fairgrounds to bivouac personnel as did other military services. Willamette Cherry Growers used the grounds in 1943 for a Mexican labor camp.

1953 Fair Commission approved sale of beer but Governor Paul Patterson rescinded Act.

1961 Huge cake, 16 feet by 16 feet, cut on Capitol steps marking 100th birthday of first State Fair. A ninety foot Thor missile was on exhibit at the Fairgrounds.

1967: On July 31, fire destroyed the 1913 Commercial Building and the 1891 Natural Resources Building. But the Fair went ahead, using tents.

The Master Bread Junior Band

By The Honorable Richard D. Barber
Previously published May 1994, Vol.32, No.2

It occurred to me as I was reading a quarterly edition of *Historic MARION* that subject matter from the 1930s just might already be of historical interest to someone.

I am referring to the Master Bread Junior Band, which was organized in Salem in about 1935 and was sponsored by Hillman's Master Bread Bakery.

My initial contact with the band took place in about 1937. At a family gathering in Salem, my cousin Fern Colwell Riffe was playing piano, her sister Faye Colwell VanCleave was playing violin, my uncle Jack Sperling was on alto saxophone, and my cousin Jim Welch was playing clarinet. (Coincidentally, Jim Welch worked for Langendorff Bakery until retirement.) I became entranced with the music (at age nine), but particularly with the clarinet, and told my parents.

My mother, Doris L. Barber, played the piano as a child and my father, Merrill L. Barber, played valve trombone and mellophone with the City Band in Dallas, Oregon, most of which formed the Company "L" Band that went to France during World War I. (P.D. Quisenberry also played in the band in Dallas.)

Following up on my statement of interest, my parents talked with cousin Jim and a Cavalier metal clarinet was purchased from him for $15.

They also followed up by calling Joe Hassenstab, director of the Master Bread Junior Band, and I was enrolled to practice weekly with the band for a fee of $1.25 per month.

It was mostly a "boy's band" as portrayed in Meredith Willson's *Music Man*, but some of the girl drum majorettes also played instruments. (Later on, the McClintock twins, Gloria and Barbara, were in the band.)

Hillman's Bakery was located at the southwest corner of the intersection of Broadway and Market Streets, presently (May 1994) the home of the Salem Fraternal Order of Eagles. We rehearsed in the meeting room at the south end of the second floor.

Just a block away was Barber's Market (guess who owned it!) next to the Pollyanna Eat Shop, owned by Tad Shinkle's parents. Tad played tuba in the band. Both the Barber and Shinkle families lived in apartments behind the shops, where Tad and I had adjoining basement bedrooms. The Pollyanna Eat Shop was named after one of Tad's sisters; his other sister is Mary Alice (now Beard) who lives in Salem. (Tad Shinkle himself now owns the Marie's Salad Dressing Company and he has homes in both Sacramento, California, and Salishan on the Oregon coast.)

But I digress. To get back to the band, the state colors, blue and gold, were adapted in our uniforms and we performed for several state events, including the dedication of our new Capitol on October 1, 1938.

During the pre-World War II days, the band participated in such events as the Portland Rose Festival Parade, The Newberg Berry Festival, the Woodburn-Brooks Onion Festival, the Mt. Angel Flax Festival, the Lebanon Strawberry Festival, Sheridan Phil Sheridan Days, Oregon City Territorial Days, the St. Paul Rodeo, the Molalla Buckaroo, and daily parades in Salem during the Centennial Celebration in 1940.

Some of the players who do not appear in the picture come to mind, such as Jim Bradshaw, who was Superintendent of the State Hospital for awhile; Wayne Struble, an architect who lived in Medford for several years but is now back in Salem; Dick Hill, who retired as a builder with Lloyd Hill & Associates; and the previously mentioned Tad Shinkle.

Joe Hassenstab died in 1987 at the age of 86 in Seal Beach, California. He and his wife Mary owned and operated the now defunct Hollywood Theater in the late 1940s and 1950s until they retired and moved to California. The Master Bread Junior Band, which he originated, later evolved into the award winning Salem Junior Band with numerous local musicians as members.

Largely through the efforts of Marjorie Young and her brother Norman, who now lives in California, most of the members of the Master Bread Junior Band pictured have been identified. They are: **Front row**: *1-Jim Apple, died in WWII, 2-Daniel (Sugar) Boone, 3-Jerry Clay, 4-Pat Bond, 5-Marjorie (Marjean) Potter Young, 6-Lynn Locaner, 7-Dannie Verhagen, 8-Francis Windishar, 9-Max Maude, retired builder/developer living in Maui, Hawaii, 10-unknown, 11-Jerry Hassenstab, 12-Jim Noyes, 13-Glen Klein, 14-Bob Hagedorn.* **Second row**: *15-Norman Potter, 16-Darl Davis, owner of Davis Auto Parts in Salem, 17-Darrell Woodward, 18-Richard Barber, 19-Darrell Simm, 20-Oren Johnson, 21-Ray Miller, 22-Verne Boock, longime worker at Valley Motors and Skyline Ford, 23-Jim Bunnell, now back in Salem, 24-William (Buster) Wilson, 25-Carlos Woodward, 26-Bob Hjort, 27- Jack Weisser, retired lawyer now living at Illahe, 28-Lane Cooper, 29-Joe Hassenstab (band leader).* **Third and fourth rows**: *30-Jerry Apple, 31-Milton Savage, younger brother of Ernie Savage of The Junior Bootery, 32-Jerry Rogers, 33-Don Noll, 34-Bob Payne 35-Bill Maude, also died in WWII, 36-Glen Armpriest, Jim Armpriest's younger brother, 37-Jim Rogers, 38-Louis Bradford, 39-Dave Melson, 40-Dick Givens, retired from the gasoline business, 41-Bob Bradford, 42-Donald Earle, 43-Morris Hunsaker, retired CPA who lives in Salem, 44-Virgil Banks, 45-Donald Fleck, 46-Tom Faught, 47-Donald Baal, 48-Bob Macey, 49-Bob Jones, 50-Guy Jonas, died in Seattle several years ago but was the first Democrat to ever be elected to the legislature from Marion County, 51-LaVerne Hiebert, retired WOSC professor.*

Politicians Visit Salem

By Al Jones
Previously published Autumn 1996, Vol.34, No.3

Salem has been a natural attraction for visitors for several reasons. It is the capital city of Oregon, with a governor, legislators and other officials to meet. It has Willamette University, which has drawn many celebrities of sports, education, politics and music.

Salem is on the north-south railroad from Portland to California, and on the highway that once ran conveniently through the downtown area.

Among the famous visitors have been at least 16 United States Presidents, or men who would become President later in history or who had been in that highest position. Add to the list about a dozen candidates who campaigned here, but did not get elected to the Presidency.

The Presidential visit has not always been a one hundred percent welcome event, like the time that President Benjamin Harrison came here on May 5, 1891. Harrison, a Republican, had to come face-to-face with a Democratic Oregon Governor, Sylvester Pennoyer.

President Harrison was on tour on a train from Eugene to Portland, but Pennoyer did not want to meet the President at the depot and was quoted as saying, "If he wants to see me, he could come to my office."

It was reported by some that Pennoyer's staff persuaded the governor to yield. When a parade started from the depot to the capitol, the fourth carriage contained the President, Mrs. Harrison, Governor Pennoyer and Mayor P.H. D'Arcy.

The crowd was estimated at 20,000, although the Salem census showed that about 12,000 people resided in Salem. The others came from neighboring towns and farms.

At the capitol, Pennoyer's welcome to the President included this: "Upon this occasion all party differences are forgotten, and the citizens of our state hail your presence here...we were gratified when we learned of your intended visit."

Pennoyer had even more negative feelings toward President Grover Cleveland, who also was a Democrat.

This issue was over the Chinese exclusion act of 1893, when President Cleveland sent advice to Pennoyer to "employ all lawful means for their protection."

Pennoyer's reply was, "I will attend to my business, let the President attend to his."

President Taft standing in a Pierce Great Arrow on Court Street near Church. Salem Public School teacher Grace W. Wheelock leads children in singing "America."

*Left Photo:
President Truman at Salem
Airport in 1948.*

*Right Photo:
President and Mrs.
Eisenhower appear at the
Salem train depot in 1952.*

Salem Visits From U.S. Presidents, Candidates and Political Activists

Susan B. Anthony: Leader of the Woman's Suffrage, Temperance and Antislavery movements spoke in Salem on September 15 and October 9, 1871.

William Jennings Bryan: "Silver Tongued Orator," populist Democrat, three time `presidential candidate (1896, 1900, 1908) visited Salem during 1895 State Fair; March 27, 1900, as candidate; July 23, 1919, as Chautaqua orator; Sept. 16, 1924, campaigning for presidential candidate John Davis.

George Bush: Campaigned in Salem as vice presidential candidate on Reagan ticket on May 14, 1980.

Jimmy Carter: While campaigning for U.S. President, visited Salem on April 26, 1975, and May 22, 1976.

Charles Colson: Known as President Nixon's "hatchet man" in the Watergate scandal of 1972-73, Colson repented and became a prison counselor who spoke at the Oregon State Penitentiary October 24, 1979.

Thomas E. Dewey: Republican presidential candidate who lost to Franklin D. Roosevelt in 1944, and Harry S. Truman in 1948, campaigned in Salem May 4, and September 27, 1948.

Abigail Scott Duniway: Woman suffragist, Oregon Trail immigrant at age 17, taught school in Eola (West Salem) at age 18; fought 40 years for women's voting rights; first woman to vote in 1914 on state issues.

Dwight D. Eisenhower: Campaigned for his U.S. presidential candidacy at the Salem train depot on October 7, 1952.

Barry Goldwater: Republican presidential candidate opposing Lyndon Johnson, campaigned here on April 7, 1964.

Samuel Gompers: American Federation of Labor (AFL) leader from 1886-1924, visited Salem in 1902.

Ulysses S. Grant: As former US. President, visited Salem in October 1879.

Benjamin Harrison: Toured Salem and the Chemawa Indian School on May 5, 1891.

Warren G. Harding: Arrived by train on July 28, 1923. After eating spoiled shell fish in Alaska, he was mortally ill while here and died on August 2 in San Francisco.

Rutherford B. Hayes: Arrived in Salem in September 1880 with his wife, Lucy, en route to Portland from Jacksonville, Oregon.

Herbert Hoover: Having lived in Salem as a child from 1888-91, Hoover made his last return visit on August 5, 1955.

Hubert H. Humphrey: Campaigned in Salem against Richard Nixon on April 22, 1959.

Jesse Jackson: Activist and minister spoke at Salem's First Methodist Church on January 12, 1988.

John F. Kennedy: Visited Salem as a U.S. Senator from Massachusetts on October 21, 1959. He returned to Salem to appear at the Oregon State Fair on September 7, 1960, during his presidential campaign.

Robert Kennedy: Appeared April 18, 1968, at the Marion County Courthouse and May 18, 1968, while traveling by train through Salem. Kennedy was assassinated June 5 in Los Angeles.

Ted Kennedy: Campaigned for his brother, U.S. presidential candidate John F. Kennedy, September 7, 1960.

Eugene McCarthy: U.S. Senator, campaigned in Salem for: Hubert Humphrey May 14, 1975, and October 20, 1976; Jimmy Carter May 4, 1988, and Mike Kopetski May 13, 1992.

George McGovern: Appeared at the Oregon State Fair on August 28, 1971, and May 19, 1972.

Walter Mondale: Vice presidential candidate on Jimmy Carter ticket, campaigned October 4, 1980, at the home of Oregon Governor Bob Straub.

Richard Nixon: As Vice President, visited Salem February 13-14, 1959, for the Oregon Centennial. On April 25, 1968, campaigned for President at Salem's McNary High School.

General John Pershing: World War I commander, came to Salem by train on January 21, 1920.

Dan Quayle: Vice President under George Bush, visited Salem in September 1990.

Ronald Reagan: Visited Salem on February 7, 1975, as governor of California and on May 23, 1976, while en route from Portland to Corvallis.

Franklin D. Roosevelt: Visited Salem in 1932 as part of his train campaign for his first term as president.

Theodore Roosevelt: Spoke in Salem on the State Capitol steps and in Marion Square Park on May 21, 1903.

General William Sherman: Former Civil War Commander of the Union Army, visited Salem in 1876.

William Howard Taft: Participated in a parade in downtown Salem on October 12, 1909, while traveling south from Portland.

Harry S. Truman: Arrived 11am on June 11, 1948, at Salem airport on his way to see the Vanport flood. He returned to Salem by train at 4:20pm.

Earl Warren: Former California governor, later U.S. Chief Justice, was in Salem on May 9, 1952.

Woodrow Wilson: Arrived by train September 18, 1919.

"Venus Victorieuse"

The uproar was glorious!
By Mary E. Eyre
Previously published May/June 1995, Vol.33, No.2

As time marches on, we become very interested in stories from the past; incidents that at the time of happening received much discussion but which have faded with the years. One example of this is the story of Salem's encounter with the work of the great artist Renoir which received nationwide attention in the columns of *Harper's* and *Time*. The page from *Harper's* (1953) has lain in my scrap book ever since and fell out as I searched for something else. I quote first from the *After Hours* column of that magazine.

"The capital city of Salem, Oregon, is at loggerheads with a piece of nude sculpture—a hassle that is in the best entrenched tradition of American art patronage. This time the trouble has been caused by a Renoir, and the question is not merely one of decency. Indeed, decency has beclouded the issue of suitability. As usual. Here

Statue of Venus by Renoir.
COURTESY PORTLAND ART MUSEUM, PORTLAND, OR; ACC.NO. 56.15, GIFT OF MR. & MRS. VICTOR M. CARTER; TITLE: VENUS VICTORIEUSE, CAST BRONZE BY PIERRE-AUGUSTE RENOIR, C. 1916.

is the story as I received it from a friend who lives out that way."

An obscure elevator man who worked in the State Supreme Court Building had wanted to do something to honor the gallant souls who founded Oregon. In 1938 this man, Carroll L. Moores, died and left his life's savings of $25,000 to pay an annuity to a friend, with the residue for a monument or memorial to be erected in memory of the early Oregon pioneers. By 1953, the sum, prudently invested, had grown to $34,000. Expert advice was summoned—Thomas C. Colt, Jr., Director of the Portland Art Museum, and Pietro Belluschi, Dean of the School of Architecture of

M.I.T. (formerly lived in Portland). They found that Salem was already supplied with statues of pioneers, culminating in the one on the top of the Capitol building. Why not pay homage to the pioneers more subtly? Colt and Belluschi suggested the purchase of a statue called "Venus Victorieuse" by Renoir from the Valentin Gallery of New York for $18,000. Salem would be among the few cities of its size (pop. 44,000) to possess a work of this distinction, so universal in spirit and appeal.

This made sense to the trustees; Venus was bought and paid for, and her picture was published. The resulting outburst was terrific. The *Capital Journal* called her "fat and naked." Sports fans said she had a sturdier figure than the outfielders of the local ball team. Women's clubs thought it undignified. Defenders were drowned out— Frederick Littman said this was a distinctive rather than a routine way of honoring. Colt said she was symbolic of "woman as the mother of the race." Art teachers tried to get in a few words; so did ex-Governor Sprague. But the uproar grew. People whose only acquaintance with Carroll Moores was probably going between floors on the elevator decided that Carroll never would have approved this.

Reluctantly, the Pioneer Trust Bank as trustee gave in. Mr. Henry Compton of the bank said, if necessary, he would pay for Venus. The trustee set up plans for a competition, and Venus went to California.

Mr. Putnam of the *Capital Journal* was far too sophisticated to be shocked, but he loved a good fight and this was a beauty. His concluding comment was, "Harper's is just another art lover sneer at Salem for rejecting an unsuitable memorial to Oregon's early pioneers. It was not prudery on the part of Salem citizens. The valuable free national publicity for Salem is appreciated and offsets the gibes, for most of our citizens prefer sneers to Venus as a pioneer memorial."

An answering editorial in the *Statesman* concludes, "If we want to capitalize on this publicity, perhaps we should set up a base, bearing the label "Venus Unvictorieuse." The *Capital Journal* also presents a letter from the Council of the National Sculpture Society emphasizing the unsuitability factor."

The competition brought quite a number of entries. I remember being particularly pleased by the one from Mary Elizabeth Kells MacCollum; but the public vote gave the preference to the work of Avard Fairbanks of Salt Lake City who also has one called "Pioneer Mother" on the campus of the University of Oregon. The Salem choice is called "Guidance of Youth" and presents Pioneer Father (with hoe), Pioneer Mother (properly attired with skirt sweeping the ground) and Pioneer Youth (I think he is carrying a lantern). This group, sited in Bush Park's southeast corner quite off the beaten path, strides eastward rather than to the west.

"Venus Victorieuse" was purchased by Victor M. Carter, businessman and art collector of Los Angeles, who loaned her to the Los Angeles County Museum, to San Francisco, and finally to Portland Art Museum where she was purchased and remains.

Many think she was the female pictured when Portland Mayor Bud Clark, in a prank, posed for a poster calling on Portlanders to "expose" themselves to art. However, the charming statue used for the poster was actually "Kvinneakt," Norwegian for "nude woman," sculpted by Norman Taylor of Seattle, Washington. It is located at SW Fifth and Washington in downtown Portland.

EDITOR'S NOTE: It seems the original "Venus Victorieuse" (until recently in the second floor Portland Art Museum gallery where she remained remarkably unvilified) has found a home where she is really appreciated. An artist's rendition, pictured on the cover of a museum publication, shows "our" Venus occupying the central place of honor in the Museum's new main entrance foyer.

Willamette's Football Centennial

How it all began in 1894

By Al Jones
Previously published November 1994, Vol.32, No.4

When Willamette University formed its first football team in 1894, it was short on players, equipment, experience, and opponents. In fact, the sport still had rules so lax that Willamette's president, Willis C. Hawley, was eligible to play.

The college yearbook, the *Wallulah*, recorded that Hawley "wallowed in the mud with the rest of the squad, and by hard work and faithful training aspired to be center on the first team."

He was 30 years old, had earned five degrees since 1888, and his future would include being U.S. congressman from 1907 to 1934 and co-author of the high tariff Hawley-Smoot Act of 1930.

Willamette called for "ambitious and energetic young men" to turn out for football in 1894. That was a week after Salem YMCA revealed plans to organize a team and order two footballs from Chicago—then almost round or "melon" shaped, fashioned from rugby.

Willamette's team lacked helmets, shoulder pads, hip pads, or matching uniforms. On September 23, 1894, the *Oregon Statesman* reported that a forthcoming meeting would be to purchase "suits and other needed paraphernalia."

Nevertheless, the WU yearbook wrote, "This '94 team brought new life and enthusiasm into Willamette."

WU and the YMCA played a series of "practice" games, using the rules that had evolved from the earliest days on the east coast, shifting from rugby.

Scoring in those days was different, conforming to changes in rules brought to Salem from the east. In Salem in 1894 a touchdown counted five points, and a point-after-touchdown was one. A decade earlier, in 1883, a touchdown back east was worth only two, and a "goal" or extra point was four. In 1884 a touchdown became four points. This was changed to five in 1898 and finally to six in 1912. The point after touchdown dropped to one in 1885.

The only inter-collegiate game WU played that first season was against Pacific College (at Forest Grove) which the *Wallulah* said was won over the Quakers by a large score.

Another WU gridder of note was Isaac H. Van Winkle, a 24-year-old right guard. He later became dean of the College of Law and state attorney general.

The next year, Willamette's opponents included University of Oregon, two losses; Monmouth (now WOSC), "severely beaten" by WU; and Oregon Agricultural College (now OSU), when WU "buried the farmers under a big score."

In 1894 Willamette University's first football team included the school's president—Willis Hawley (fifth from left in the back row)—as a player.

Salem YMCA Celebrates Centennial

By Al Jones
Previously published November 1992, Vol.30, No.6

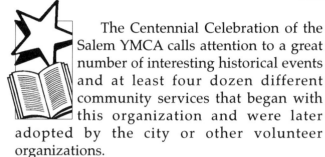

The Centennial Celebration of the Salem YMCA calls attention to a great number of interesting historical events and at least four dozen different community services that began with this organization and were later adopted by the city or other volunteer organizations.

It all started when the Salem YMCA was incorporated on March 18, 1892, about the same time some Willamette University students took part in the first basketball game played in the Northwest.

Salem's first YMCA board included four men who were area leaders: President Herman S. Gile, who headed the Willamette Valley Prune Assn., Pheasant Fruit Juice Co., Phez Loganberry Juice Co., and H.S. Gile & Co.; and board members Frank N. Gilbert, banker and father of A.C. Gilbert, inventor of the Erector set; Wylie A. Moores; and J.A. Van Eaton.

That first basketball game was held on the third floor of the State Insurance Building. It occurred soon after James Naismith invented the sport in Springfield, Massachusetts, at a national YMCA conference attended by two Willamette University students who returned with much enthusiasm.

In the first game in Salem was Frank E. Brown, a first-year student in the Academy of Willamette

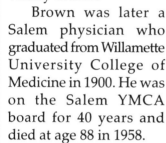

Dr. Frank E. Brown at the time of his marriage in 1898.
COURTESY AL JONES

University, which was then a three-year preparatory course before the four-year liberal arts university course.

Brown was later a Salem physician who graduated from Willamette University College of Medicine in 1900. He was on the Salem YMCA board for 40 years and died at age 88 in 1958.

One time Brown described the primitive rules they had back in 1892 for the basketball games they played in that small gym in

A group of YMCA boys are shown leaving the YMCA in 1924 for an educational tour. The YMCA was then located on the northwest corner of Commercial and Chemeketa. The building was also the site of Salem's first basketball game in 1892.

COURTESY AL JONES

Activity time on a trampoline.

COURTESY AL JONES

downtown Salem. He said a team could have up to 10 players and dribbling and running with the ball were prohibited. However, a player could catch his own pass.

The referee started the game with the centers lying on the floor—arms extended and hands on the ball; they scrambled for it at the whistle.

A foul counted one point without shooting a free throw; two fouls would disqualify a player.

Players took turns climbing a ladder to get balls out of the peach baskets.

The YMCA nationally directed basketball from 1892 until 1897.

Buildings

The YMCA has occupied various locations over the years in the following buildings:

Patton Block: A building east of the original Ladd & Bush Bank building (on the west side of the alley) on the second floor.

Gray Building: The northwest corner of Liberty and State.

120 Commercial NE: In 1897, over a hardware store on the east side.

Hughes Building: In 1898, south side at 144 State Street.

Commercial & Chemeketa: In 1901, northwest corner.

685 Court Street NE: Present location, dedicated in 1926, with the Youth wing added in 1956.

Community Services

The four dozen community services originally initiated by the Salem YMCA are:

1892 Both basketball and football introduced to Salem.

1907 Naturalization classes.

1910 Swimming pool built, teams formed.

1913 Relay race, Salem Y beats Portland Y, Salem to Portland.

1921 Employment Bureau, helping 15,000 by 1933.

1921 Leadership training course.

1921 Learn-to-swim classes under lights.

1921 Softball league organized, also baseball.

1921 Sunday School Athletic League.

1921 Boys' camp begun.

1922 Cherry-pickers' and hop-pickers' camps opened, offering child care for migratory workers.

1922 Public playgrounds, taken over by city in 1933.

1922 Willson Park gospel meetings.

1922 Oregon Historical Pagent staged.

1922 Hiking Club formed, later became the Chemeketans.

1922 Vacation Bible Schools held.

1922 Hobby and Pet shows.

1930-31 Sponsored Salem Symphony, Dr. Hans Seitz, director.

1930 Biweekly art exhibits held.

1930 Salem Gleemen Chorus formed.

1930s Volleyball League begins.

1937-47 Marble tournaments.

1941 Men's Garden Club.

1942 Salem War Chest raises funds.

1940s Adult Bible course.

1942-45 Military servicemen housed in YMCA, also WU Navy V-12 men.

1946 City Police Baseball Team.

1947 Alcoholics Anonymous groups formed.

1947 Chess Club formed.

1948 Youth Legislature begun, continues today.

1950s Father and Son sex education.

1952 Fencing classes.

1953 Film Forums.

1956 Camp Silver Creek pool opens.

1957 Salem Marriage Clinic.

1968 Little Brother program, also Yokefellows.

1960s Parent-Child Counseling, also Investment Class and Kids' Wrestling.

1960 Parents Without Partners groups.

1970s Mini-bike program for junior high boys and girls.

1973 Men's Health Club.

1974 Kindergarten opens.

The Barlow House

By Jackie Schulte
Previously published May/June 1995, Vol.33, No.2

Not only was the construction of the Barlow Road an important achievement in itself, but its existence meant that the bulk of immigrants in the succeeding years would in all likelihood move on into the Willamette Valley, rather than remain above The Dalles out of sheer fear of going down the Columbia River on flatboats, or, perhaps, thread their way across passes on the right bank leading into the Puget Sound area.

With each passing year that immigrant wagon trains arrived, the choicest farm lands of the Willamette Valley were claimed...[1]

Captain Samuel Kimbrough Barlow, in 1845 the head of a newly arrived immigrant party, whose experiences in building the first wagon road in Oregon are widely known, chose land in southern Clackamas county. When the Oregon Donation Land Act was passed in 1850, Sam Barlow's D.L.C. covered 640 acres of rich land near the confluence of the Molalla and Willamette Rivers.

Sam Barlow was 55 years old when he arrived in Oregon, "the old man" by 1845 standards. His family consisted of one daughter, married and with a family of her own, his wife Susanna Lee, and four unmarried children. William, the oldest son, was 22.

The older Barlow sons played important roles in building the road around Mt. Hood, "The Barlow Road", for which their father and Philip Foster of Eagle Creek are credited. William's memoirs refer to his receiving several hundred dollars in payment for his work on the road.

The two oldest sons are listed as tending the toll gate with their father during the years that it belonged to the family. After the partnership with Foster was terminated, Sam Barlow was commissioned Justice of the Peace for Clackamas

County in 1850 by the governor of the Oregon Territory.

William Barlow was a most successful farmer and merchant in the Barlow area as well as Oregon City. During the gold rush he shipped barrels of his wheat flour by boat to the mining areas of California, and made more money than if he'd found gold! He and his brother-in-law also had a steamship company in Canemah (south of Oregon City) and built twenty shallow-bottomed steamers for use above the falls in the upper Willamette.

The William Barlow House, Barlow, Oregon, 24670 South Highway 99E, Canby, Oregon 97013. Virginia L. Miller, the fourth owner, has been the owner-occupant-restorer since 1973.   SKETCH COURTESY VIRGINIA L. MILLER

The Oregon City *Spectator* ran this ad for William Barlow:

We have a large and select assortment of Cooking Stoves of the 'New World' and 'Premium' patterns of all sizes, a complete assortment of furniture; also doors, pots, kettles, etc., which I am offering at prices much lower than they have ever been sold in the Territory. Also, a good assortment of Parlor Stoves. I have also recently on hand a full and carefully selected stock of Queensware dishes (Wedgwood). 'Small profits and quick returns' is my motto.[2]

It was William Barlow, successful farmer, merchant and businessman, who built the historic Barlow house.

The Italianate mansion, well over one hundred years old, has not been in the Barlow family since 1905. Interior decorator Virginia Miller bought the house and one and a half acres in 1973. As an interior decorator, and in an attempt to achieve authenticity in the restoration, Virginia researched the Barlow families, the time period, and all information about the property.

On the exterior a roofed, wrap-around porch, added in 1908, has been removed and the original Barlow front porch has been restored. The house is now painted in the original colors, as substantiated by Alfred Staehli, restoration architect with the Historic Preservation League in Portland.

Doors and windows have been relocated and even with the addition of a few "creature comforts" (a bedroom closet, for instance), the house shows the results of all Ms. Miller's efforts. It is magnificent, but inviting and warm.

During restoration, it was discovered the house was of "balloon" construction, meaning the upright rough-cut studs were nearly 30 feet long, stretching from foundation to rooftop.

The remaining outbuildings, wash house, well house, carriage house, and gardening shed—all of various ages— now support ancient grapevines, beauty bushes and climbing roses that pick up the colors of the mansion, surrounding potted flowers and garden borders.

The interior, for many years undergoing restoration and change (with a few modern touches in the country kitchen) feels completed. Some of the carpeting was in the original house, and some of the Barlow family furniture came with the house. Other pieces have been located and purchased at auctions or from parties who sold it back to Ms. Miller.

She has ingeniously filled the house with furniture, dried flowers and art work of the period of the Barlow families, much of it her own creation.

---

[1] Oscar Osburn Winther, *The Old Oregon Country*, p 114-115.
[2] Ruth McBride Powers, "Oregon's Early Furniture and Furniture Makers," *Marion County HISTORY, Vol. XI*, 1976, p 14.

The Buchner House

Historic Notes by Bonnie Hull
Previously published November 1992, Vol.30, No.6

The Walter Buchner House, the historic name of the house at 1410 Court Street NE, which was the site of two fire deaths in late September 1992, was built in 1914 by Walter and May Buchner.

Buchner was born in Waukesha, Wisconsin, in 1864 and came to Oregon with his family in 1872, settling on a farm in Marion County.

Walter Buchner grew hops on 160 acres south of Salem and, in 1903, established a feed store and mill, building most of the plant and installing machinery.

May N. Newsome was a Marion County native who married Buchner in 1896. They had two daughters, Dorothy and Ruth, and lived at 1410 Court Street until 1942. At that time the house was converted into apartments.

Even with the heavy rental use over the last 50 years, the house still retains its Craftsman detailing and visual interest. Neighbors in the Court-Chemeketa Residential Historic District are hopeful that the Buchner House will have a new, quiet life.

The Walter Buchner House   AL JONES PHOTO

Birthday Thoughts

Historic Notes by Bonnie Hull
Previously published August 1993, Vol.31, No.3

The summer of 1993 marks the 100th anniversary of the remodeling of the Waller-Chamberlin house, at the moment in the care of Roger Hull and myself.

That summer of 1893 the old Waller farmhouse was picked up from its original site on State Street and moved to the corner of 17th and Court Streets NE by Martin Chamberlin and his wife Rose Weller Chamberlin. Martin's sister Mary Chamberlin Waller and her husband O.A. Waller were moving to a smaller house out near the fairgrounds after raising their family in the house that missionary pioneer Alvin Waller had built on his donation land claim.

Mary had great feeling for her father-in-law and for the house "where we spent so many years in Grandpa Waller's suburban home as long as he resided in Salem," she wrote in her journal on October 25, 1908. I like to speculate that these feelings of Mary's played a part in the house being saved and moved by her brother, Martin Chamberlin. When Alvin Waller died suddenly in December of 1872, he had been laid-out in the front parlor and the funeral procession began at home and moved down State Street. Mary's babies were born here.

Martin and Rose moved the house, raised it up high, added a large addition on the back, and essentially changed the Gothic farmhouse into a grander Victorian lady. They put a new double door in front and a fancier porch along Italianate lines.

Martin died in 1903 leaving Rose with some debts, the house, and several acres of land from the Waller Donation Land Claim. Since Rose's real attachment was to her own family home, the Weller house, which stood on Liberty Street NE, she subdivided her acreage into Chamberlin's Addition and moved our house around the corner to its current site facing Court Street NE.

I had planned to invite you all to celebrate in the garden this summer, but our 1993 lives leave us too busy for such an event. I content myself with thinking of Wallers, Chamberlins, Sherwoods, Waters, McElhinnys, Bradshaws, Lebolds—all who sheltered under this roof and took care of this house through the years.

A birthday toast to you all!

Waller farmhouse

AL JONES PHOTO

A Case In Point

By Jordis Schick
Previously published February 1994, Vol. 32, No.1

If you want to see a textbook example of a splendid 1859 pioneer farmhouse restored to its former glory, the William Case House on Case Road near Champoeg is a good place to look.

What you see today is the result of a 17-year (and ongoing) project undertaken by Wallace Kay Huntington, one of Portland's finest landscape architects, and his lovely wife, Mirza Dickel, an equally talented interior decorator. The project began when they purchased the house and about eight acres surrounding it from the family of Mrs. H.J. Arendt in 1977.

At that time the house was in a total state of disrepair but, Huntington says, they discovered "its bones were good" because the interior proved sound despite years of neglect. Huntington thinks the unusual design of the home was the biggest contributing factor, but some longevity is also due to the excellent quality of materials used and the skilled workmanship.

Case, a carpenter, is thought to have based the L-shaped, one-story, Greek Revival plan on houses he had seen in Louisiana. One OHS account even says he copied his grandfather's house in Nachatoches, Louisiana. Although Huntington doesn't know how accurate this is, there evidently were Cases in Louisiana.

The brick pier design Case used for the foundation allowed air to flow freely underneath the house to keep it cool—and dry. Identical doors and windows, placed opposite one another, also helped this air flow. Huntington says the design proved to be ideal for Oregon's climate because it is probably what prevented the house from succumbing to dry rot, and allowed the interior to remain as solid today as the day it was completed 135 years ago, even though it was uninhabited for a long period of time.

According to an article by Dale Schmidt[1], William M. Case was born in Randolph County, Indiana, in 1820. He set out for Oregon with his family and one black slave woman in 1842 but they were delayed and didn't arrive until 1844—after crossing the plains with covered wagons and ox teams.

Evidently Case first built a log cabin on his property, but began constructing his unusual home almost as soon as the cabin was done. He was interrupted by the California Gold Rush in 1849-1850, so the house wasn't completed until 1859—after his return. But he must have struck it rich in California, because Huntington's research indicates Case purchased a complete sawmill in San Francisco and had it shipped to Oregon where he reassembled it on Case Creek, which runs through the property behind the house.

Since building materials were virtually nonexistent at that time in Oregon, Case, like all settlers, had to depend on his own ingenuity and his land claim's resources. Unlike most others, however, he created his own center of technology. He used his own sawmill to finish lumber cut from trees on the property. He built a brick kiln to fire his own bricks. He even constructed a forge so the hardware, including many large square nails, could be hand-forged. He also went on to build many neighboring barns.

Wallace Kay Huntington, a Portland landscape architect who also happens to be a Salem native, is shown standing at one end of the William Case House near Champoeg, which he and his wife, Mirza Dickel, have painstakingly restored. AL JONES PHOTO

William M. Case House
circa 1859
In 1845, 24-year-old carpenter William Case and wife Sarah arrived from Indiana and settled the French Prairie site. The farm became a center of technology in our valley, and on its 1500 acres there were barns, a sawmill, brick kiln and forge. Case's energy and skills became legendary. At this house, finished as Oregon became a state, he provided information and hospitality to farmers, circuit riders, and territorial legislators. Its unusual size and style, with its peristyle of 31 doric columns, best exemplifies the spirit of the classic temple among Greek Revival buildings in the Oregon Territory.

The upper left photo shows one of the thirty-one porch posts. To the right is content of the sign at the Case House entry gate.

The unusual style Case chose for the home's plan includes a wide porch that extends almost all the way around the house. It has thirty-one pillars, supposedly one for each state in the union at the time the house was built. Case improvised a lathe to turn the many posts he cut from whole trees on the property.

The restoration work, Huntington says, showed Case used quarter logs for the posts, probably because whole ones would have split.

Huntington also discovered an entire row of the columns along one side of the porch do not really bear any weight because huge beams do the job instead. Curiously, he also found spacing between the columns varied as much as 18 inches. Perhaps exact placement was not really measured.

The entire house is built with wooden dowels and square nails, including the solid two-inch doors, which are about nine feet tall (possibly because Case was over six feet tall himself); the 10-foot tall double-hung windows; and the cupboards, which are the original ones. Huntington says nothing sticks or sags to this day.

The interior is one room wide and has 11-foot ceilings. On one side of the L-shape, six small bedrooms open onto a central hallway with a curved ceiling and a door at the far end opening to the porch. Huntington and Dickel have turned one bedroom into a bathroom (not original to the house) and are using two others as dressing room-cum-closets since bedroom closets were not built into most homes in the 1850s.

The rest of the house includes a large dining room, a lovely large parlor with fireplace, a second living room with fireplace (where the front door is now located) and an enormous kitchen. There are quilting frame hooks in two of the rooms, and the kitchen has hand-forged hooks in the ceiling that Huntington says were used to tie up wood so it could dry out during the winter months.

All of the floors in the house are old growth, wide fir planks with a wonderful dark patina. Dickel says it is the result of years of oiling which

The view of the front parlor shows the hearth where restorers used the backsides of the original bricks. Mirza Dickel also found old handmade bricks still being sandcast in Vancouver, which were used for the fireplace surround. The 1820s clock has wooden works. The door leads to the only closet in the house.
AL JONES PHOTO

This is the newest part of the garden, designed by Huntington as sort of an outdoor amphitheater with a gazebo he calls his "folly" (because of the cost) as its central feature. The entire garden is a series of "rooms," each with its own ambience.

AL JONES PHOTO

have now made the floors just like the hardest oak. Throughout the house Dickel has combined pieces of original furniture that she and Huntington have been lucky enough to find, or have been given, with other pieces authentic to the period, in consummate taste.

Ruth McBride Powers[2], in an article she wrote for *Marion County HISTORY* in 1976, says that

The bedroom shows one of the original Case beds, rather long for that period (although standard today), probably because of Case's height.

AL JONES PHOTO

Wm. Case employed at the farm "a young German boy named John Hofer, who had spent two years in New Orleans in the shop of a furniture maker. Learning of his talent, Case employed Hofer to make furniture for his new house. John Case liked to sleep out-of-doors, and had Hofer make wheels for his single bed, to be wheeled in and out on the porch according to the weather."

One kitchen wall in the house is hung with many authentic old kitchen tools (which Dickel claims she is still using today). The kitchen opens to the log-constructed utility or woodshed space, an enormous 40-foot long wing with whole log beams spanning its width. One huge door was used for hauling in farm implements.

The house has a big attic, which was used for hired hands. And the property includes the well and firepit where the Cases heated water for bathing in the old washhouse. (The firepit is now used as a barbecue.) The Cases' towel and drying rack is still on the porch of the main house next to this site and Huntington and Dickel know it is original because they have a picture taken when the building collapsed. The old smokehouse has been completely replicated with its original beams—well preserved by years of smoke.

The original red exterior color of the house has also been duplicated by Huntington and Dickel. But he confesses he was stumped when it came to figuring out how the big wooden gutter worked and had to invent a whole new system (there was a pattern for almost everything else). Lyle Warren, a master craftsman who also restored houses for Ruth Powers, worked with Huntington and Dickel for about a year before they could move in.

The grounds surrounding the house, a tribute to Huntington's expertise, are also enchanting, with beautiful trees and shrubbery interlaced with profusions of perennials. It is rather heartening to see the indigenous plants growing willy-nilly despite Huntington's effort to tame them. Other plant materials, many chosen because they are native to the Northwest, are tucked along meandering pathways, and delightful surprises greet you around every corner. Obviously Huntington enjoys working with, and not against, nature. Flowers creep between paving stones, vines climb up posts and spill over eaves, espaliered treasures cling to walls, and herbs and vegetables mingle right among prime rhododendrons and other prized shrubbery. The whole garden is separated into various outdoor rooms, each with a different focus or wonderful work of art.

My husband, Hal Schick, and Al Jones from MCHS accompanied me when Huntington and Dickel graciously conducted a tour just for us. They do occasionally open the home by special arrangement so, if you ever have the opportunity, I hope you will make it a "case in point" to go. I promise it will be worth your while.

It will also make you appreciate the profound patience and effort that goes into a preservation effort like this—especially when the people involved obviously understand its meaning and value and consider it a privilege, not a burden, to be able to assume stewardship of a real historic treasure.

---

[1] Dale C. Schmidt, "The Case House," *Marion County HISTORY, Vol. 10,* 1969-71, pp. 15-17.
[2] Ruth McBride Powers, "Oregon's Early Furniture and Furniture Makers," *Marion County HISTORY, Vol. XI,* 1972-76, pp. 4-19.

The Little Gem Store

Historic Notes by Bonnie Hull
Previously published Spring 1996, Vol.34, No.1

 A recent afternoon reverie had me thinking about how things looked in my childhood and how much things have changed. I was thinking of the bank, the doctor's office, the train station, the food store, the hardware store. I began to remember the numerous little stores located around our neighborhood—the "Mom and Pop" stores. The kids really knew these stores and what treats they had and which was the nicest place to "shop" (if you can call buying a Fudgcicle shopping).

In our Salem neighborhood today, at the corner of 17th and Chemeketa Streets, sits a much beloved little store, once called "The Little Gem." It is a tiny room lined with shelves and has a gabled roof hidden by an Italianate false front—much like the numerous buildings lining the streets in the frontier towns. Probably built in the 1920s, the store fills the front yard of the 1906 house on the corner. A succession of owners lived in the house and operated the store: the Wilsons, the Clarks, the Nelsons, the Largents.

When we moved to our house in 1980, the big sign proclaiming "The Little Gem" was still on the front. Later in the'80s an artist rented the store for a studio, but kept the sign inside, up on one of the shelves that had once held groceries. As the research began on the Court-Chemeketa Residential Historic District, we found a photo of the Little Gem store in its heyday.

Though our neighborhood loves the Little Gem and thinks of it as community property, of course it is not. The current owner of the house behind the store wished to raze the Little Gem in

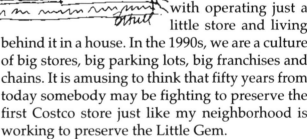

order to put on a larger porch. The neighborhood has been in an uproar, and as a result, an extraordinary solution is being proposed for relocating the Little Gem to a neighbor's back yard. Here it would be put on a temporary foundation until space can be readied for it at the Riverfront. A visitor's information center perhaps?

A small amount of money has been earmarked by the neighborhood association (NEN) to help defray the costs of moving and relocation. Donations are sought and volunteers will shore up the building so it can survive.

As I think about all this activity for such a small and ramshackle building, I find my head crowded with thoughts:

The world around us changes so fast, and often without our even noticing, that it makes us want to hold on to a few things that indicate what our past was like.

The recent three-year study of transportation woes in Salem probably indicates (my interpretation anyway) that smaller places to which people can walk wouldn't be a bad thing.

Today people wouldn't be content with operating just a little store and living behind it in a house. In the 1990s, we are a culture of big stores, big parking lots, big franchises and chains. It is amusing to think that fifty years from today somebody may be fighting to preserve the first Costco store just like my neighborhood is working to preserve the Little Gem.

Editors Note: During the winter of 1996-97, the Little Gem store was moved from its orginal foundation and temporarily stored in a neighborhood backyard.

Saving the Yew Trees

By Jordis Schick
Previously published November 1994, Vol.32, No.4

Two rare Irish yew trees were moved to a new site at the northeast corner of the State Library after Harry Demaray, a longtime MCHS member, discovered them next to a vacant house on Homestead Road (adjacent to Minto-Brown Island Park) that the Salem Fire Department planned to burn as a training exercise.

Demaray, a member of the city park board, estimates the trees to be about seventy years old, apparently planted soon after the house was built in 1917.

After several attempts to move the trees bogged down in bureaucracy, Jess Eastman, landscaping supervisor for the Capitol grounds, decided to accept them if it involved no cost to the state.

Roger Greer of Greer Brothers agreed to transplant the trees for $600 and the U.S. Marine Corps Reserve Engineering Company A unit removed the concrete walkway for the tree spade.

A remarkable book, *The Yew Tree, A Thousand Whispers*[1], by Hal Hartzell, Jr., gives a complete biography of the species—its botany, ethnobotany; its mythological, legendary, and historical connections; its use in literature; and, of course, an exploration of the present controversy over harvesting massive amounts of yew bark to produce taxol, a new treatment for cancer.

It mentions a few fairly large yew trees in the Northwest and particularly one in Marion County,

which stood on the edge of downtown. Known as the Deepwood Yew, this tree, measuring eight feet ten inches in circumference in its prime, met its demise in the early 1990s. The Deepwood Yew was a male tree that had been a member of a large grove in the past century—in the area known as Yew Park, where Dr. Luke A. Port began to build his elegant Deepwood Mansion in the 1890s.

"Elsewhere in Marion County, the Marion Yew at Parrish Gap, twelve feet four inches in circumference, was known as one of the largest yew trees in the state," according to the book. It was fatally injured by a split into its heartwood during the Columbus Day storm in 1962, although it lived seven more years.

The largest known living Pacific Yew is in Lewis County, Washington, near Mt. Rainier. It stands seventy feet tall, with a girth of fourteen feet ten and a half inches, and is probably near one thousand years old.

The book reports that Oregon's champion is "a twisted behemoth leaning precariously over a cliff twenty feet above the Tualatin River in Washington County." It is thirteen feet four inches in circumference and is estimated to be one of the oldest trees in Oregon.

The Fortingall Yew, situated in a churchyard at the entrance to Glen Lyon, Perthshire, Great Britain, is deemed to be three thousand years old—"as old as the time of Solomon—the most ancient piece of vegetation in Europe." According to a placard in the stone church there, Pontius Pilate was born in a nearby Roman camp and suckled at his mother's breast beneath the old yew's sacred boughs.

In the Pacific Northwest, the Kalapuya Indians hunted game with bows and arrows and yew wood was thought to be the best available for this purpose as well as for ceremonial purposes. Kalapuya women also dug camas with yew saplings, fire-hardened into sharp, stout, indestructible digging sticks. When the woman died, her digging stick was stuck in the ground to mark her final resting place.

Today the last remaining national stands of yews in the Northwest are threatened with extinction because we found another use for the yew when its bark was discovered to contain taxol, the most promising anti-cancer drug in view. Since the trees are few and slow to grow, this has resulted in a major conflict between the needs to harvest and to husband the resource.

According to National Cancer Institute (NCI) sources, sixty pounds of dry bark are needed to produce two grams of taxol, or one treatment. Since the average harvest is estimated at six pounds of dry bark per tree, it requires ten large trees to produce one taxol treatment. Consequently, the demand for yew bark has risen dramatically.

At the same time, it has become apparent there is a finite supply of yew trees and destroying trees for a mere five or six pounds of bark is stealing from the future.

The book points out the great need for alternatives to bark as a source of taxol, and then cautions that time is running out for the natural species as well as for cancer patients since many obstacles remain to the creation of a coherent, renewable taxol production plan.

On the last page of the book are these fitting words: "Our ancestors revered this tree above all others in the forest. Current events would imply that they had good reason; certainly English poets from Chaucer to Eliot thought so."

𝕄

[1]Hal Hartzell, Jr., *The Yew Tree, A Thousand Whispers, Biography of a Species*, Eugene, Oregon: HULOGOSI Press, 1991.

Vanishing Architectural Landscape

Historic Notes by Bonnie Hull
Previously published May 1993, Vol. 31, No.2

 On a summer afternoon in 1975, Roger Hull and I went to tea at Professor Emeritus Marian Morange's home on Market Street near Lansing Avenue. The initial talk was of France and Claus Sluter's *Well of Moses* at Dijon, but when we sat at the table for our tea accompanied by a bowl of fresh raspberries and cream, the talk turned to gardens.

During a tour around the outside of the small neat house she had lived in for years, we were delighted by the yard with its combination of deep shade and bright garden space. Professor Morange and her colleague, friend and neighbor Gail Curry had lived and gardened in their two houses at that spot for a long time…since "Market Street was called Garden Way." As a relatively new

Salemite (we arrived in 1970) I was charmed to think of "Garden Way" as it was described by Professor Morange—a small and quiet two-lane street soon turning into a dirt road out into the countryside. No freeway then, no Lancaster Drive development, no gas stations, malls, etc.

On an errand one morning in March of this year I was saddened to see that lovely garden corner and the two houses of the two friends being bull-dozed flat—all the roots of the trees and berry bushes in a tangled mess. I offer this remembrance of a warm summer afternoon, the taste of fresh-picked berries and cream served in delicate china bowls on a flowered cloth, in memory of Marian Morange, dead for several years now. And in memory of all the lovely little houses and gardens we have lost. It isn't as small a loss as it might seem.

𝕄

Starkey-McCully Block

New life after 127 years

By Jordis Schick

Previously published November 1994, Vol. 32, No.4

The Starkey-McCully Block, built in 1867, was well researched by David Duniway in 1978 for the nomination form he submitted to the National Register of Historic Places.

Originally the building was a two-story unpainted brick masonry structure, rectangular in plan, with its major 120-foot frontage extending north from Court Street, in the heart of Salem's business district.

Duniway says it appears to have been one of the first commercial buildings in Salem to use architectural cast iron in large areas for its expanse of 17 bays with display windows and openings. Its ground story arcade, which extended the entire 120 feet, was manufactured by Oregon Iron Works of Portland and was formed of conventional, highly embellished elements—including Corinthian style capitals topped with pineapple motifs to mark the store divisions.

In 1978, only three of these original five (the northerly ten bays, or 60 feet) were recognizable and still contained elements of the castiron arcade. These—at 223 Commercial NE, a single space created by two former stores, and 233 Commercial —were the subject of Duniway's nomination.

Duniway believed the southerly 50 feet of the building were incorporated into a radical remodeling in about 1920. Another revamping occurred in 1937 when second story window hoods and upper cornices were removed. The second story openings at 223 Commercial were also superficially blinded, or filled, with "decorator panels" at this time—so only the four second story windows above 233 Commercial remained intact, although they, too, were altered from casement to double-sash in about 1915.

According to Duniway, the ground story space at 233 Commercial is distinctive for its original pressed metal ceiling. He also found an array of paneled finish work upstairs, unchanged since the space was converted to a Forester's Hall shortly after 1917.

The cast iron used for the building's ground floor was deemed most significant because it is the oldest architectural cast iron manufactured in

situ anywhere in Oregon.

The first iron in the state produced from locally mined ore came from the blast furnace south of Portland which commenced operation as Oswego Iron Company in 1867. Between 1854 (which marked the first use of architectural iron in Portland commercial structures) and the advent of Oswego Iron, the planning of iron-fronted buildings in Portland, Oregon City and Salem depended on San Francisco foundries.

By 1867, however, four Portland foundries were busily meeting increased demands for architectural iron. Among these was the Oregon Iron Works which manufactured the ground story front and second story cornice and window cornices for the Starkey-McCully Block.

Oregon Iron Works was established in Portland in 1863. Shortly after the Starkey-McCully project was finished, a foundry and iron works was organized in Salem. It began operation as Salem Iron Works in 1868.

Duniway reports there has been severe attrition of the once extensive array of iron-fronted buildings due to massive clearances and redevelopment projects. The Starkey-McCully Block not only has the oldest-known, ore-made,

This closeup of the outer corner column at 233 Commercial NE shows some of the elaborate ironwork. You can also see the manufacturer's mark for Oregon Iron Works at ground level.

AL JONES PHOTO

Above is the 1908 view, taken during an IOOF Parade in Salem on May 21. It shows the northern portion of the Starkey-McCully Building on Commercial Street NE. The Belle Confectionery is the light-colored storefront. Watt Shipp, The Bicycle Man, is to the south and Stone's Drug Store is to the north. The right photo shows the new entry which opens to the stairway leading to the apartment in the restored building.

cast iron architectural elements still in place, it is also the second oldest of a half dozen brick buildings antedating 1870 still standing in Salem.[1]

In the original design, Duniway comments, furnished rooms in a hotel-like operation occupied the second floor above the five ground level stores. Only two of the original occupants have been identified—Nicklin & Company, a general store selling groceries, dress goods and hardware; and Mrs. Snyder's Millinery Shop.

By 1894 there were two groceries in the southerly two stores partially financed by William Anderson. In May of that year one of these—Gilbert, Patterson & Company—had a serious fire which damaged neighboring establishments. Duniway identified the northerly three occupants as E.S. Lamport's harness shop (established as early as 1878); Charles G. Given boot & shoe maker; and Charles Hellebrand's restaurant (1889).

A record of occupancy traced through Salem City Directories, beginning in 1886, shows E.S. Lamport continued in business at 223 Commercial from 1878 to his death in 1912.

Other occupants included Watt Shipp & Co. sporting goods (later sold by the owners to manager William Everet Anderson who, in turn, eventually sold to his manager Harvey Fox. Fox, in turn, sold to his employees, and they are still operating as Anderson Sporting Goods in another downtown Salem location today); Quackenbush Auto Supplies (1921); F.W. Pettyjohn & Co. automobiles (1924); The Nash Furniture Co. (1928-1945); Coast to Coast Stores hardware (1947-1949); and Valley Furniture Co. (1951-1956).

The store numbered 233 was occupied from 1889 through 1893 by Charles Hellenbrand's Restaurant; J.W. Thomas, general merchandise (1893); Ben Forstner & Co., drygoods & clothing (1891-1896); Steven C. Stone, physician & druggist (1902); Claude S. Belle, confectioners (1907-1913); Peetz Furniture & Glenn L. Adams, wallpaper &

paints (1915); Fletcher & Byrd, dealers in paints, oils, seeds, feed, etc. (1917-1924); Jacob A. Rise Co., harness & shoes (1926-1934); Coast to Coast Stores, hardware (1945-1955); Norris Paint & Varnish Co. (1964-1975); and was owned by Nancy Gormsen of Nancy Gormsen Interiors from 1977 until the Joneses purchased it in 1991.

The upper floor of the block, designed as a hotel, had been rented as apartments and shops by 1894, according to Duniway's research. By 1921 the upstairs space over 233 Commercial had been remodeled as the meeting hall for the Foresters of America, Sherwood Forest No. 19. From 1928 through 1934 it was occupied by the United Sign Co., and in 1938 through 1942 it was converted to the Star Apartments. From 1945 to 1951 there were up to four renters including Dr. George P. Hoffman and the shoe merchant, Arthur L. Rise.

The Gormsens pur chased the building in September 1977, through Pioneer Trust Bank, from the estate of Arthur & Bernice Rise, a brother and sister who had evidently inherited the building many years before from Jacob Rise.

When the Foresters took over, the space became a clubhouse and a home for the insurance protection this group provided for member families.

An unsubstantiated use was discovered by the present owners during restoration work when many liquor bottles were uncovered and an older brick mason working on the job identified a roof structure as a "hooch house." He told the Joneses the building was a speak-easy during prohibition with the liquor supply stored in the rooftop hooch house where, it is presumed, local authorities never thought to look.

Duniway also mentions David McCully in the nomination form. He moved to Salem in 1858 and entered into partnership with J.L. Starkey in a general store on the present site of Ladd & Bush Bank.

In 1855 McCully obtained an interest in the *James Clinton*, one of the early steamboats on the Willamette. In 1862 he was one of the stockholders in the formation of the Peoples Transportation Company which obtained a monopoly on the river transportation and was sold in 1871 to Ben Holladay, who was building the Oregon and California Railroad.

In 1867 McCully began his second Salem store in the building he and Starkey had newly erected at 233 Commercial. He and his brother, Asa McCully, operated the Centennial Store, a grocery, until Asa sold his interest in 1878 to David's son-in-law, Andrew N. Gilbert. In 1884, David sold his interest to Sebastian C. Adams, who published a *Synchronological Chart of History*, the first major visual aid for teaching history. Adams, incidentally, was also the first president of what is now Linfield College and minister to the Christian Church in Salem.

---

[1] Others of similar vintage are Ladd & Bush Bank (1868); J.K. Gill Building (1868); Reed Opera House (1869); Willamette's Waller Hall (1867); Boon's Brick Store (1860); and The Dearborn Building (between 1868 and 1870).

Uptown Look In Downtown Salem

Historic restoration

By Jordis Schick

Previously published November 1994, Vol.32, No.4

When Mike and Angela Jones purchased part of the Starkey-McCully Block—at 231 and 233 Commercial NE in downtown Salem—from Robert and Nancy Gormsen in 1991, they bought it with every intention of seeking approval to restore the structure to include personal living quarters on the second floor in compliance with National Register of Historic Places guidelines.

The 1867 building had received approval for the national register in 1980, granted after David Duniway submitted extensive research verifying its historical significance (which qualified it for 15 years of frozen tax assessments). The whole purpose of Phase I approval is to encourage Phase II, which consists of a federal tax credit against any historic restoration and improvements made to the building.

And even though the Joneses soon realized there would be lots of obstacles blocking their path before plans could get off the ground floor, they still had stars in their eyes and the indomitable enthusiasm of the young about the challenge they were undertaking.

Now that the transformation has been completed and Mike and Angela are luxuriating in the spacious New York loft-like apartment they have carved out of the 2400-square-foot second story—and now that memories of the frustrations, time, and money involved are rapidly fading—they will tell you it was worth every minute. But don't let them fool you. There was a period in between when they (and everyone else involved) had major doubts.

For starters, who do you know willing to finance the restoration of a second floor full of pigeon droppings in a pretty decrepit old building? Pioneer Trust Bank is the institution the Joneses turned to, and they agreed to fund the project, albeit with some trepidation after original estimates escalated.

And wouldn't you be somewhat daunted if you discovered parts of your new building's ground floor were resting right on the ground, which meant a great deal of the foundation would have to be examined and restored (with the previous owner's participation) before you could even complete the purchase?

But the Joneses were pretty sophisticated, too. Wise enough to hire an architect familiar with historic restorations—Randy Saunders of Woodburn. And also smart enough to engage a top-rated local restorer, Robert Kraft of Kraft Carpentry, to work on the structure itself. Kraft's men hand cleaned all of the brick (no chemicals allowed). They also had to hand remove every bit of mortar to repoint the brick inside and out (using

The imposing arched entrance to the second floor apartment at 231 Commercial NE was installed when the space was converted to the Forester's Hall shortly after 1917. A recessed entertainment center is to its right; off the back hall are doorways leading to a bathroom and office. The streamlined kitchen is built on a separate platform.

JORDIS SCHICK PHOTO

the same mixture used originally), construct and replace all of the cornices and window eyebrows (to match the long-gone original ones), and install new gutters at the top. Kraft proved to be every bit as good as his reputation; his work was finished both on time and on budget.

Left photo taken before major work began. Below photo is after renovation of the entertainment center (with bottles from the rooftop "hooch house" on the shelves at left). Bottom photo is the new bath, where an oval jacuzzi tub is separated by glass brick. Another alcove encloses the shower and water closet; a third contains storage and utilities.

JORDIS SCHICK PHOTO

JORDIS SCHICK PHOTO

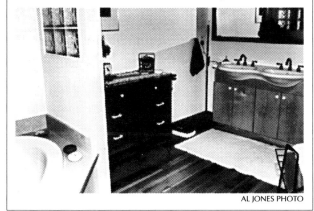

AL JONES PHOTO

The Joneses' first setback came after they submitted a proposal covering twenty-two different situations to State Historic Preservation Officer James Hamrick, the local agent for the National Trust. He came back with some thoughtful suggestions on ten of them; then the Trust's San Francisco office asked the Joneses to rethink three more details.

According to Mike and Angela, this was a blessing in disguise. The suggestions made lots of sense, especially the one that proposed unifying the 11.5-foot high "great room" expanse by only building partial 8-foot free-standing walls around the entertainment center (to the left of the entrance) and the bedroom and study at the far end toward the street.

The next big hassle came when they discovered the city's fire code dictated a fire wall between the first and second floors of the building. This took more time and expense—to painstakingly remove and replace the tin ceiling on the first floor so a one hour sheetrock barrier could be added.

Yet another major delay occurred when the original plaster walls were deemed too damaged to be saved. Every wall had to be replastered (using the same type plaster mixture and methods used originally).

Doug Lethine of C & R Builders, who restored the foundation, also served as general contractor for the interior part of the project, with Mike Skelton of Northwinds as the electrical contractor.

Now that the work is completed, the grand sweep of space inside looks anything but old. In fact, it looks exactly like a page in *Architectural Digest*, even though the original baseboards, floors, doors, and moldings have been used. The replastered walls are painted dark green with a diluted light green sponged on top (it took 15 gallons of base paint). Pale cream-colored woodwork offsets the dark walls.

The carefully crafted new kitchen opposite the front door is built on a platform constructed of an African purple-heart hardwood (the only new flooring). It sports an open serving bar; a generous pantry; suspended boxed beams to hold the lighting; counters of clear-coated concrete; and stainless steel appliances including a restaurant-sized gas stove, Subzero refrigerator, dishwasher, industrial garbage disposal, and twin sinks with a Grohe faucet.

The schoolhouse-type globes used for the hanging lights in the main space had to be replaced when they were all inadvertently broken by the construction crew, but the original ceiling caps and chains are in use. And the frames for the casement window copies are also original to the building.

The thoroughly modern bathroom sports a door with its original wooden peephole; double sinks with a large, framed mirror to tie them together; a cut-down version of the original window; an oval jacuzzi tub; a separate shower; storage space, and even a utility room tucked around the corner. The bathroom also has linoleum flooring from Italy, the same dark spongy green color as the great room's walls.

The entertainment center and kitchen cabinets are beautifully constructed of birch—an obvious departure from the old. The old leaky skylight has also been completely replaced, as well as many of the window panes surrounding the entrance door that was added when the space became the Forester's Hall.

There is an additional office next to the bath at the west end of the apartment, and up four steps beyond this is a door to a small deck at the rear that has a partial view of West Salem as well as a complete view of the rooftop "hooch house" that came with the territory—the legacy of the speakeasy that occupied the space during prohibition. A larger deck and new roofing were put on hold due to budget constraints.

The stairway from the street level is carpeted in a multi-colored leaf pattern. The window at the top (which opens into the front study) is original.

Mike and Angela are hard pressed to find any drawbacks now that they have been living in their loft for over two months. They point out the easy access to downtown restaurants and shopping, the quiet ambience after five o'clock (at least until the buses all run by at 5 a.m.), the self-containment, the low downtown crime rate. They did have to get a TV satellite because there is no cable downtown. And, at night, they do have to park their personal cars in the street rather than the alley due to minor vandalism. But that's it. They rate everything else as an A+ —exactly the same grade we would give these two young people for accomplishing such a top-drawer restoration in their first effort!

JORDIS SCHICK PHOTO

Above photo is Kraft's workmen hand cleaning exterior brick. Left photo is a view of the "great room" with the kitchen at left and partial walls at the far end, used to divide the space into a streetside bedroom at left, and a study at the right. The folding doors at the room's center date back to the time of the Forester's Hall.

JORDIS SCHICK PHOTO

It's Still Survival of the Fittest

The dandy dandelion

By Jordis Schick
Previously published May 1994, Vol.32, No.2

It's just amazing how tenaciously dandelions thrive and multiply—no matter what the conditions.

A member of the Sunflower Family, Tribe: Chicory, these tolerant little plants are just as happy living in the cracks of sidewalks as in the most expensive flowerbeds in town. And they react no differently to a deer, a lawnmower, a goat, or a merciless gardener.

Maybe that's why they got such a ferocious name, which comes from the French *dent de lion*, a literal rendering of the plant's medieval Latin name, *dens leonis* or "lion's tooth." The name refers to the way a dandelion's leaves resemble the toothy snarl of a lion and, according to *A Garden of Words*,[1] for several hundred years the plant also went by the English nickname "lion's tooth."

Curiously, the French have abandoned the lion name and now call the plant a "pissenlit." In French, *lit* means "bed" and word columnist Michael Gartner[2] says "we don't need to get into the rest of the word except to say that the French think the dandelion is such a strong diuretic that it can cause you to wet the bed." (He also says you can look the word up yourself if you have a big enough dictionary).

Some botanists say dandelions originated in the Himalayas and were introduced in Europe by the ancient Romans and consequently were taken to other continents by the immigrants.

And almost all botanists say dandelions aren't all bad. Fur trappers and traders used dandelions as "garden sass"—the first greens of spring that could be eaten to add essential vitamins and minerals to their diets.

Pioneers brought dandelion seeds west because the leaves and flowers had many uses, as did the milky juice in the stalks, roots and leaves. The leaves were, then as now, eaten for greens (it's remarkable how they have been "rediscovered" recently by the nouveau salad chefs). Pioneers also made the flowers into dandelion wine just as we do now. The root was used as both a coffee substitute and a laxative, so it appears the French may know something we don't.

Unlike most creatures, most dandelions are asexual, although pollination is needed to activate the ovules. The result, according to Rob Marvin,[3] is massive patches of clones in a neighborhood with one dandelion exactly like every other. They are subtly different from dandelions down the road, which will be from a different clone.

The dandelion's tiny seeds float down and settle wherever they land, many times right where you just pulled one out. When you cut off the dandelion's head, it supposedly senses the wound and grows its next generation of seeds even closer to the ground out of harm's way so it can spring up just when it's ready to go to seed. Sometimes it will even produce just a button of a blossom to really trick you.

But remember, the dandelion did have an important role in the history of the west, even though we Oregonians may feel right about now that its main mission is to conquer the world.

---

[1] Martha Barnette, *A Garden of Words*, 1992, published by Time Books, a division of Random House, Inc.
[2] Michael Gartner, "Blossoming Uses for the Dandelion," *Statesman Journal*, August 31, 1992.
[3] Rob Marvin, "What in the World," *The Oregonian*, May 28, 1992.

Windows

Historic Notes by Bonnie Hull
Previously published February 1994, Vol.32, No.1

In the mid-1980s when our neighborhood group was working on the historic district nomination for the Court-Chemeketa Residential Historic District, I had an evening session at the State Historic Preservation office with Elisabeth Walton Potter. It was an interesting session, yielding one of my favorite preservationist quotes, which is "Windows are one of the most character-defining features of a building."

There is a real beauty in an old window with wavy glass, with wooden "frames" framing the view in as well as the view out. But more than beauty is at stake for historic structures. Windows tell us things about a building and its style, and its period of construction. The size and location of window openings, the number of panes and their configuration, the type of woodwork framing the window inside and out, all offer clues to the time and place of construction. They make a statement—about how the architect or builder meant the building to look and also what other buildings of the same era probably looked like as well.

Sadly, windows are the first things changed in "remodeling" projects, as they are often easy and inexpensive to change. In our current era of weatherization many a structure has been irretrievably muddled by the insertion of a 1990s aluminum window in an 1890 or 1910 or 1920 structure. Old windows needing care can be repaired (in our case wooden storm windows were milled to our specifications for half the lowest bid from the aluminum companies). Salem has a number of qualified and talented carpenters who can repair old windows.

As I write this I am trying to think of a positive example to point to—to say here is a building that has had its old windows put back—but I can't think of a single one. I can, though, think of a long list of buildings that have had their windows removed. Currently the Justice Building at the corner of Court and Waverly Streets is slated for window remodeling, the windows to be replaced with metal-wrapped frames.

This building, designed by the well-known architect, W.C. Knighton, was built in 1929 with the large double-hung windows it currently has. Changes in fenestration essentially efface the historic qualities of a building. I suggest you drive by the Justice Building and look up at its lovely windows while you still can. Take a peek at Collins Hall on Willamette's campus and see if you can remember the wonderful many-paned windows that added a graceful note to the building (these have been replaced). Look up at the building on the southeast corner of State and High. A few of its large double-hung windows are still in place, but the rest have been replaced by single sheets of mirrored glass. Single sheets of mirrored glass are okay, but relate more to a building built in 1984 than to one built in 1926.

When you begin to really look at windows you revel in the huge variety of sizes and shapes they come in, and marvel at their interest and beauty. Becoming really aware of the built environment around us adds a wonderful dimension to every car trip, every walk through the neighborhood—and to our lives.

ILLUSTRATION BY BONNIE HULL

Volume XV Writers

Richard D. Barber

Richard was born in Corvallis, Oregon, on July 4, 1928, the son of Merrill L. and Doris L. Barber. After attending Salem schools, he spent the years 1946-48 on a U.S. Navy destroyer in the Western Pacific.

After his military service, Richard received his B.S. from the University of Oregon and his JD from the Willamette University Law School. Judge Barber is a past president of both the Marion County Bar Association and the Circuit Judges Association. He has served as a Circuit Judge since 1974.

Richard and wife Sallie have two daughters and three sons.

Mary Jane Chambers

Mary Jane was born in Portland, Oregon, to Willard and Phyllis Aker, lifetime residents and onion farmers at Brooks, Oregon.

She attended Brooks Elementary School and Gervais High School. She is a graduate of Oregon State University, taking a degree in Home Economics, featuring clothing and textiles.

In 1978 she started work at the Bank of Oregon, Brooks Office (which later became Key Bank) and was branch manager from 1984 until the branch closed in 1992.

Mary Jane was co-founder of the Brooks Historical Society and served as treasurer and president. She also helped organize the Farmworker Housing Development Corporation in Woodburn, and is currently involved in the Marion County Master Gardeners/OSU Extension Service.

Married to Roger in 1979, their "children" are the four-legged variety, a dog and two horses.

Lloyd Chapman

Lloyd Chapman is an Oregonian with special historical ties. His paternal grandparents followed the Oregon Trail to Sheridan in 1847. His great grandmother was Lorinda Bewley (who became Linda Chapman), one of the survivors of the Whitman massacre.

Lloyd's interest in history was additionally sparked by living in the late 19th century Erb House on 19th Street S. E. for more than a dozen years. He believes history is a valuable tool for bringing neighborhoods and the community together.

Lloyd graduated from Oregon State University in 1967, and received a masters degree in Public Administration from Syracuse University. He spent two years in Sri Lanka, Ceylon, with the Peace Corps and lived for several years in New York City. Lloyd has been back in Oregon since 1975, and is currently a network administrator for the Department of Land Conservation and Development.

His family includes his wife, Susan Lee Graves, and their daughter, Camas. Lloyd has been active with neighborhood associations for years, and currently serves on the Morningside board.

Ted Dethlefs

Ted was born in Chehalis, Washington. His father, Herman Edward Dethlefs, was born in Chicago, Illinois, and his mother, Opal Floy Phelps, was born in Gladwyn, Michigan.

Ted received a B.A. in Business Administration, and an M.A. in Recreation, both from Washington State

University. He served in the U.S. Navy as an aerial navigator. In his professional career he was involved in the recreation field in Idaho, and with the Fairview Hospital and Training Center and Oregon State Parks from 1952 to 1980.

He has previously written monthly articles for the Senior News Monthly.

Ted's civic activities include several years as a scoutmaster, a board member for Habitat for Humanity, and a 55 Alive Instructor. He is currently president of the Stained Glass Guild, and a board member of the Marion County Historical Society.

Ted and his wife Luella have five children and six grandchildren.

Maynard Charles Drawson

Maynard was born in Portland, Oregon, to Andrew N. and Violet D. Funston Drawson. In Salem he attended Richmond and Salem Heights Elementary Schools, Leslie Junior High and Salem High.

Maynard joined the Navy in World War II and served aboard the *U.S.S. Boston* CA69 as radar man in the Atlantic and Pacific from 1943 to 1946.

A retired barber, Maynard has authored books about the Pacific Northwest, *Treasures of the Oregon Country, Volumes 1–5,* and has written numerous articles about Oregon.

Maynard is well known for his unceasing efforts in promoting the Heritage Tree Program started in Marion County and now spread throughout Oregon. He is most generous, sharing his historic information through lectures, trips and other media.

Maynard is the father of seven children.

Adele Egan

Adele was obviously born to be the board secretary for Marion County Historical Society since she has served in that capacity for 20 years.

She is a fourth generation Oregonian, the daughter of Homer W. and Helen (Deckebach) Egan. The Deckebachs came to Salem in 1903, where Frank G. managed the Salem Brewery. After prohibition eliminated that as a legitimate business, he established the Marion Creamery.

The Egan family came to Oregon in 1852. Son Homer grew up on the family farm at Brooks and he and Helen raised their family there. Homer served as postmaster at the Brooks Post Office from 1941-1959, and Helen served as assistant postmaster and supervisor at the same post office, until 1965.

Adele attended Waconda Elementary, Parrish Junior High, and Salem High School, then received a B.A. in economics from Willamette University. Her professional career spanned thirty–seven and one half years with the State of Oregon, 35 in the Highway Right of Way Department as a Right of Way agent.

Her civic activities include having served as secretary of Salem City Club and on the board of the Salem Audubon Society. She is active in the Marion County Historical Society and the Brooks Historical Society in addition to being a long time supporter of Mission Mill Museum and of Deepwood.

Mary E. Eyre

Born in Illinois on April 9, 1897, Mary's parents were George and Ida Eyre. She had three brothers and a sister.

Mary attended Salem elementary schools and high school, and graduated from Willamette University in 1918. In 1976 Mary was the first woman to deliver a commencement address at Willamette University, and was awarded an honorary doctorate.

She retired in 1962 after forty years with the Salem High School social studies department. The Mary Eyre School is named in honor of her many years as a teacher.

Her civic activities have included League of Women Voters, American Association of University Women, Oregon United Nations Association and many others.

Mary is a founder of the Marion County Historical Society, Mission Mill Museum Association and Friends of Deepwood. Along with serving on their boards, she has been a contributor of published historical articles.

Leland Gilsen

Dr. Gilsen was born in San Francisco, California, in1942 and earned his doctorate at the University of Arizona in 1976. A career of field work, including an excavation in Guatemala, historic archaeology, and teaching led him to his current position as Oregon State Historic Preservation Archaeologist.

His wide-ranging activities include founding Oregon Archaeology Week, development of teaching and training materials, and a directory of Oregon flintknappers and artifact (replica) makers. Dr. Gilsen is a maker of replica artifacts and has made valuable contributions to the MCHS museum exhibits and educational materials.

Doctor and Mrs. Gilsen live in Salem. Their children are grown.

Mary A. Grant

Mary was born in Baker, Oregon, to William C. and Evelyn Witham Grant, both native Oregonians and still living in Baker City. Both of her grandfathers were important builders in Baker City and County.

She has her B.A. degree from Portland State University and M.L.S. from the University of Oregon.

Mary was Archivist for Georgia-Pacific Corp. until they moved to Atlanta, then became Archivist for the Catholic Archdiocese of Portland in Oregon. She also has made three trips to Ireland, pursuing an interest in Irish archaeology.

Her civic activities include giving guest lectures with the Historic Preservation League of Oregon, and also volunteering for other organizations.

Barbara Hanneman

Barbara Hanneman, who presented the David Duniway Memorial Service remarks, was a founding member of the Salem area Unitarian-Universalist Church along with David, and they and their families were long time friends.

Barbara worked in state government for thirty-three years, with the legislature and three governors.

She is presently on the boards of Salem City Club and the Garten Foundation.

The widow of Gene Hanneman, she has three grown children. Son Craig and daughter Laurie Speight live in Salem, and daughter Linda Batty lives in Colorado.

Reid Hanson

Reid, a home town boy, graduated from Salem High School in 1933, but was born in Oregon City. He has been an active member of the Marion County Historical Society since 1985 and has served on the board of directors.

Military service in Europe for three years interrupted his education until after World War II when he graduated with a Bachelor of Science degree in Engineering from Oregon State College. Reid is a registered professional engineer.

His work career took him overseas with U.S. contractors for seven years. He spent two years with an engineering firm in Salem, and twenty-two years with the State of Oregon as a Supervising Engineer. At the request of the mayor, he served two terms on the city Building Code Hearing Committee.

Reid has four grown children, two sons and two daughters.

Malissa Duniway-Holland

Malissa was born in Washington, D.C., in 1945, then during that year became an Oregonian when her parents returned to this state.

She has one B.A. in English and literature, and another B.A. in history from the University of Washington. Her teaching certificate is from Oregon College of Education, now Western Oregon University. She currently is teaching a combined 3rd, 4th and 5th grade class at Bethel School.

Malissa as a co-organizer of the Northeast Neighbors (NEN) and served on that neighborhood association's board and committees for several years. Additionally, she has served on the City of Salem's Housing Dispersal Committee, and on a traffic planning committee. Malissa is a member of and former Religious Education Director for the Unitarian-Universalist Congregation of Salem.

Malissa's family includes her husband, Stephen Holland; daughter, Eden Duniway Rogland; mother, Prines Ellen Conner; stepmother, Frances Duniway; and sister, Sancha Duniway Alley.

Bonnie Decker Hull

Bonnie has literally come a long way. She was born in Evanston, Illinois. She earned a degree in Art History at Michigan State University in 1966. She has been a practicing and exhibiting artist in Portland and the Willamette Valley as well as providing graphics for numerous Salem Public Library publications, and doing freelance graphic design as My House Graphics for numerous small groups.

After working at the Salem Public Library and the Willamette University Library, Bonnie is currently co-owner of the Arbor Cafe in downtown Salem.

Bonnie, with her husband Roger, researched and wrote the nomination document for the Court–Chemeketa Residential Historic District in Salem. In addition, she has researched historic structures in Salem, including the Capitol Theatre and the Carlton Smith House.

Her historical writings include: *The Disappearance and Revival of the Waller House in Old East Salem, The Willamette Journal of Liberal Arts* (with Roger Hull), and *Historic Notes* for the *Historic MARION* quarterly, 1993 to present.

Service on many civic and historic committees has long been a major activity for her, and she is currently the chair person of the Historic Landmarks Advisory Commission. Her husband is a Professor of Art at Willamette University. They have one son, Zachary, of Portland.

Robert Wilson Humphreys

A true Oregonian, Bob, with his wife Marjorie (Gries), still lives on the Century Farm where he was born.

The son of Orlo and Jennie (King) Humphreys, his grand, great and great great grandparents were early Oregon pioneers.

Bob attended Oak Grove Elementary, a one-room school, and graduated from Silverton High School.

Bob has served on many boards and commissions for the county and state. He is a past president of the Oregon School Boards Association, past chairman of the Oregon State Board of Agriculture, past president of the Oregon Seed Growers League, is a 31 year member of the Silverton Union High School Board, and is a past president of the Oregon Association of Intermediate Education Districts. In addition, Bob has been appointed to various boards and commissions by four Oregon Governors.

Membership in Oregon, Silverton Country, Santiam and Marion County Historical Societies reflects his long-time interest in local history.

Years of involvement in farming, agri-business, county and school organizations have given Bob a first–hand knowledge of the Waldo Hills communities and Marion County from which come his interesting articles.

The Humphreys have two sons, two daughters and twelve grandchildren all here in the Willamette Valley, a tribute to the Bob and Marjorie Humphreys.

Ann Lossner

An author well known to many local history buffs, Ann Lossner has written two books: *Looking Back at People and Places in Early Keizer,* and *More Looking Back,* as well as numerous articles related to the local area.

Ann was born and raised in Cleveland, Ohio, where she attended Cleveland College. Her family includes her husband of sixty years, three children, and seven grandchildren. Ann and Chester came to Salem in 1938, settling in Keizer in 1963.

Among her many activities in addition to writing, Ann served on the first Keizer Heritage Board, on its first museum committee, and still works on fund raisers. She has also been a Marion County Historical Society member and has attended Chemeketa Community College.

William Lucas

Bill was born in Winterset, Iowa, on April 24, 1929. After attending Salem public schools, he served in the U.S. Army from 1951 to 1953.

Bill has been associated with the food processing industry since 1945.

He serves on the Mission Mill Museum Board of Directors and is a past president of that board.

Bill and wife Jerie have three children and two grandchildren.

Jim Martin

Jim Martin was born in Eugene, Oregon. He graduated with a B.A. degree from the University of Santa Clara, Santa Clara, California, in 1971. Always interested in history, he has been a member and supporter of the Oregon Historical Society, Friends of the Salem Public Library and the Marion County Historical Society.

Jim has contributed articles on state history to the *Oregon Territory Magazine* of the Sunday *Statesman–Journal*, the *Oregonian*, the *Eugene Register Guard*, and the *Oregon Business Magazine*. He authored and published *A Bit of a Blue: The Life and Work of Frances Fuller Victor* in 1992.

John H. McMillan

Born in White Plains, New York, in 1931, John received a B.A. from Hamilton College in 1952, then served in the U.S. Army from 1952-1954.

John retired as publisher of the *Statesman Journal* and, since retirement, has been active in many local volunteer projects.

John and wife Carolyn have two adult daughters.

Eleanor Morgan

Eleanor came to Salem by the long way around. She was born in Alabama and received her B.A. degree in anthropology/art from the University of Alaska where she worked on a number of archaeology projects.

She has been an Oregon resident for a number of years and has served on the Oregon Archaeological Week committee for two years, is a past president of the Cherry City Art Guild, and has been a very productive volunteer for MCHS with a special interest in researching, planning and mounting exhibits.

Eleanor has a teen–age daughter.

Robert M. Ohling

From a rural one room school, through Albany High School, Bob went on to a B.S. degree in Agricultural Economics from Oregon State University. He served in the U.S. Navy from 1943 to 1946.

His career has kept him busy with such things as the OSU Extension Service, resident farm manager, the food processing industry, and work as a banking and agricultural consultant. He is especially interested in the relationship between agriculture and history.

Bob has served his church, United Methodist Home, 4–H Foundation, Oregon Fruit Products Company, Agricultural Market Development, as well as being a past president of the board of directors of the Mission Mill Museum. Also a historian, he has a special interest in the Oregon Electric Railway.

Bob and his wife Velda have three grown daughters, six grandchildren, and two great grandchildren.

Elisabeth Walton Potter

Elisabeth is a staff member of the State Historic Preservation Office, and is Coordinator of National Register Nominations. She was born in Salem and attended Salem public schools. After earning a B.A. degree in Art and Architectural History at the University of Oregon, she went on to earn M.A. degrees from Pennsylvania State University and University of Delaware.

Elisabeth has given freely of her time to serve on many boards and committees; secretary and member of the board of directors, Mission Mill Museum Association; board member of Marion County Historical Society; Salem Art Association, and Historic Preservation League of Oregon, to name only a few. She is also secretary and founding member of Friends of Pioneer Cemetery.

A long list of conference participation and published articles in professional journals is to her credit.

Elisabeth lives in Salem and has one brother.

Annabell Prantl

Annabell, though born in Sheridan, graduated from the High School of Commerce in Portland in 1941. She is the author of two books, *The Gervais Centennial Booklet*, and *The Gold On The Pudding*.

Annabell's career in retail merchandising, which she recounts in one of her articles, was brought to a close when she and Carl married in 1956.

With an interest in young people she has worked as a 4–H leader in horse projects and on FFA projects in Gervais. She and husband Carl have a son, Frank, and two daughters, Carla and Linda.

Jordis Benke Schick

Jordis Benke was born in Portland, Oregon. She and her husband Hal Schick have three grown children and three grown grandchildren.

Jordis graduated from the University of Oregon with a B.S. in Journalism. She did free lance advertising and copy writing, and was editor of the *Oregon Blue Book* and of the *Oregon Voters' Pamphlet 1978-1986*.

Her many civic activities include serving on the boards for the Marion County Historical Society (and as *Historic Marion* Editor), the Mission Mill Museum Association (and as Secretary), the Assistance League (and as Vice President), the Salem Art Association, the Salem General Hospital, plus Salem Boy's Club Cookbook editor, a Camp Fire Girl leader, South Salem High volunteer teaching assistant and ESL volunteer.

Jacqueline Schulte

"Jackie" was born in Taylorville, Illinois. Her parents, Richard and Myrna Simpson Glover, remained in Illinois.

Jackie received a nursing diploma from St. Louis City Hospital, then a B.S. and M.S. from Western Oregon University. She was an "army wife" from 1952 to 1959 while husband John was a captain in the Medical Corps. They are the parents of six children and eleven grandchildren.

Jackie has participated in a variety of activities connected with history and the senior population. She was director of Support Services for the Council on Aging, was an instructor for Chemeketa Community College's Program for Older Adults, which included Salem history, classes on writing life histories, and a variety of field trips to historic places.

She was founder of the Salem Chapter of Compassionate Friends, served on boards for Foster Grandparents, Mid–Willamette Hospice, Marion County Historical Society as president, and has filled various roles with schools, Marion–Polk Medical Auxiliary, Widows Support Group, and MCHS's video/oral history projects.

Suzanne W. Stauss

Suzanne was born during a short-term family residence in Chicago, Illinois, in 1947. Oklahoma is her family heritage. In 1949 her family joined her maternal grandparents in Corvallis, Oregon.

After high school, Suzanne departed Oregon to pursue academics and a career in commercial art and publishing. In 1976 she returned to Oregon, accepting graphic design vocation with the *Oregon Statesman* and *Capitol Journal* in Salem.

Suzanne now owns and operates Exhibit A Graphics, Inc. You may recognize the studio's tiny, yellow house restoration on 12th Street south, built in 1922 along a Salem trolley route.

Sybil Westenhouse

Sybil was born in Eugene, Oregon. Her maternal family has lived in the Salem, Dallas, Independence areas since the turn of the century. Her paternal family settled on a farm east of Scio in 1894.

Sybil attended Englewood Elementary for three years while in Salem and graduated from Scio High School. She earned her B.S. degree in Elementary Education from Oregon State College.

Sybil frequently researched material for classroom history projects. Retired from the teaching profession, she has especially appreciated having the time and opportunity to pursue historical information in depth.

Besides being a dedicated MCHS board member, Sybil gives generously of her time to the Salem Public Library Advisory Board and the Northeast Neighbors Neighborhood Association Board.

Directors, Board Members & Officers

Marion County Historical Society ◆ 1985-1998

1984 -1985

Director-Curator: Dan McElhinney

Officers
President: Addie Dyal
Vice President: Eric Olsen
Secretary: Adele Egan
Treasurer: Jean Andrews

Directors
Reid Hanson, Rebecca Hassman, Jerry Miller,
Dell Phillips, Carlile Roberts, Dick Slater

1985 -1986

Director-Curator: Dan McElhinney

Officers
President: Eric Olsen
Vice President: Robert Humphreys
Secretary: Adele Egan
Treasurer: Jean Andrews

Directors
John Evans, Reid Hanson, Rebecca Hassman,
Jerry Miller, Dell Phillips, Carlile Roberts,
Dick Slater

1986 -1987

Director-Curator: Dan McElhinney

Officers
President: Eric Olsen
Vice President: Robert Humphreys
Secretary: Adele Egan
Treasurer: Jean Andrews

Directors
John Evans, Reid Hanson, Rebecca Hassman,
Elisabeth Potter, Vesper Rose, Dick Slater

1987-1988

Director-Curator: Dan McElhinney

Officers
President: Jackie Schulte
Vice President: Ernie Savage
Secretary: Adele Egan
Treasurer: Jean Andrews

Directors
John Evans, Robert French, Bonnie Hull,
Robert Humphreys, Elisabeth Potter, Vesper Rose

1988 -1989

Executive Director: Dan McElhinney

Officers
President: Jackie Schulte
Vice President: Ernie Savage
Secretary: Adele Egan
Treasurer: Jean Andrews

Directors
Patrick Bickler, Robert French, Bonnnie Hull,
Robert Humphreys, Elisabeth Potter
Donald Upjohn

1989 -1990

Executive Director: Audra Oliver

Officers
President: Donald Upjohn
Vice President: Ernie Savage
Secretary: Adele Egan
Treasurer: Jean Andrews

Directors
Patrick Bickler, Robert French, Bonnie Hull,
Robert Humphreys, Elisabeth Potter,
Sybil Westenhouse

1990 - 1991

Executive Director: Audra Oliver

Officers
President: Eric Olsen
Vice President: Patrick Bickler
Secretary: Adele Egan
Treasurer: Donald Upjohn

Directors
Edward Austin, Martha Blau, Bonnie Hull,
Robert Humphreys, Linnea Patrick,
Sybil Westenhouse

1991-1992
Officers
President: Patrick Bickler
Vice President: Edward Austin
Secretary: Adele Egan
Treasurer: Donald Upjohn

Directors
Martha Blau, Dave Gahlsdorf, Linnea Patrick,
Coralie Rhoten, Jordis Schick, Robert Tompkins,
Sybil Westenhouse

1992-1993
Officers
President: Patrick Bickler
Vice President: Edward Austin
Secretary: Adele Egan
Treasurer: Dave Gahlsdorf

Directors
Martha Blau, Linnea Patrick, Jordis Schick,
Robert Tompkins, Donald Upjohn,
Sybil Westenhouse

Directors Emeritus
David Duniway, Mary Eyre, Robert Humphreys

1993-1994
Officers
President: Edward Austin
Vice President: Robert Tompkins
Secretary: Adele Egan
Treasurer: Dave Gahlsdorf

Directors
Wendy Cloyd, John Kelsch, Joe Paiva,
Jordis Schick, Donald Upjohn, Janice Weide,
David Weiss, Sybil Westenhouse

Directors Emeritus
Mary Eyre, Robert Humphreys

1994 -1995
Officers
President: Edward Austin
Vice President: Wendy Cloyd
Secretary: Adele Egan

Directors
Dave Gahlsdorf, Ron LeBlanc, Joe Paiva,
Jordis Schick, Robert Tompkins, Donald Upjohn,
Janice Weide, David Weiss,
Sybil Westenhouse

Directors Emeritus
Robert Humphreys, Alfred Jones

1995 -1996
Officers
President: Robert Tompkins
Vice President: David Weiss
Secretary: Adele Egan
Treasurer: Donna Butler

Directors
Robert Bergstrom, Scott Gavin,
Donald Upjohn, Sybil Westenhouse,
Steve Zielinski

Directors Emeritus
Robert Humphreys, Alfred Jones

1996-1997
Executive Director: Kyle R. Jansson

Officers
President: Robert Tompkins
Vice President: David Weiss
Secretary: Adele Egan
Treasurer: Donna Butler

Directors
Ted Dethlefs, Donald Upjohn,
Sybil Westenhouse, Steve Zielinski

Directors Emeritus
Robert Humphreys, Alfred Jones

1997-1998
Executive Director: Kyle R. Jansson

Officers
President: Robert Tompkins
Vice President: David Weiss
Secretary: Adele Egan
Treasurer: Donna Butler

Directors
Ted Dethlefs, Donald Upjohn,
Sybil Westenhouse, Steve Zielinski

Directors Emeritus
Robert Humphreys, Alfred Jones

In Memoriam

It has been the tradition of MCHS to list members of the Society
who have passed away since the previous volume of *Marion County HISTORY*

1984
Warren Evans 1984

1985
Dr. Constance Weinman March 12, 1985
Myrtle E. Roberts April 30, 1985
Lois C. Byrd Upjohn July 18, 1985
Jeanne R. Purvine July 31, 1985
Ellen Savage Goodenough November 3, 1985
Orrin Bryan Goodenough November 11, 1985
Esther B. Downs November 16, 1985
James J. Walton November 17, 1985
Barbara L. Boyer November 19, 1985
Helen Foley November 1985
Madge Jones December 26, 1985
Frank Cross 1985
Brenda E.U. McKeon 1985

1986
Edith B. Strozut March 1, 1986
Evelyn Pearl Pearsall August 28, 1986
George Anderson 1986
Frank E. Caskey 1986
Joseph M. Reiman 1986
Mrs. Garlen L. Simpson 1986
Grace M. Ditter December 1986
Eva E. Updegraff December 1986

1987
Pearl Eyre Andrews January 3, 1987
Genevieve L. Mader February 22, 1987
Kathryn L. Gunnell March 9, 1987
Stephanie Gerson May 1987
Mary C. Minto June 1987
Lyndon J. Farwell July 1987
Ruth Esther Tveit November 5, 1987

1988
Robert D. Gregg January 5, 1988
Gladys K. Bohlig January 5, 1988
Arthur L. "Roy" Priem January 21, 1988
Florentine R. Greenwood January 28, 1988
Carl R. Fitts February 18, 1988
Margaret Ann Schweigert June 20, 1988
Roy Harland September 14, 1988
Charles West November 15, 1988

1990
Floyd K. Bowers May 5, 1990
Alfred W. Loucks June 3, 1990
Hugh G. Morrow July 20, 1990
Grace Holman Williams August 30, 1990
Ray Barkley Haines September 23, 1990
Francis L. DeHarpport November 6, 1990
Norman P. Humphrey November 8, 1990

1991
C. Carroll Waller January 2, 1991
Ivan B. White March 16, 1991
E. Grace Boden June 2, 1991
Connell C. Ward July 20, 1991
Geo. S. Rossman Jr. July 23, 1991
Norma S. Longley August 15, 1991
Edwin J. Stillings August 21, 1991
Elizabeth F. Dimon November 13, 1991
Ruth I. Houck 1991
Craig L. Clark 1991

1992
Edwin D. Culp January 23, 1992
Mrs. Walter Morse February 25, 1992
Savilla P. Busick March 25, 1992
Eugene A. Ditter April 25, 1992
Norman Winslow April 1992
Edith Bragg Carson May 26, 1992
Ellis A. Stebbins June 1, 1992
Katherine M. Jelderks August 7, 1992
Harry L. Oldenburg December 5, 1992
Marjorie Robertson December 25, 1992
Felix Wright 1992

1993

Stan H. Davey   April 6, 1993
Frank B. Bennett   May 7, 1993
Mr. & Mrs. Robert Casteel   May 1993
Ethel L. Aspinall   June 1, 1993
Florence S. Mulcahy   June 12, 1993
Ella M. Stebbins   July 3, 1993
Ralph W. Taylor   July 17, 1993
Carlisle B. Roberts   August 5, 1993
David C. Duniway   September 12, 1993
Dr. Kenneth H. Waters   December 13, 1993
Ida C. Oldenburg   December 14, 1993
Helen Bradley   December 14, 1993
Frederick Norman Phillips   December 30, 1993

1994

David W. Powers III   January 27, 1994
Sanford "Sandy" Blau   February 7, 1994
Emma Hynes   February 8, 1994
Dr. Ralph M. Gordon   February 23, 1994
Dr. Richard H. Upjohn   February 24, 1994
Paul Hans Anderson   May 3, 1994
Wm. H. "Bill" Egan   June 5, 1994
Mrs. F. C. Bowers   June 25, 1994
Roland Seeger   September 6, 1994
R. Vance MacDowell   September 9, 1994
Ruth G. Peyree   October 19, 1994
Martha Ellen Thurtell   October 16, 1994
Helen Boardman Hammond   November 14, 1994
Maurice D. Burchfield   November 29, 1994
Emma Judson Crouser   December 24, 1994
Charles Baker   1994

1995

Ellen Speerstra Foster   January 25, 1995
Ruth McBride Powers   January 26, 1995
Sarah "Sally" W. McDuffie   March 29, 1995
Marjorie E. Humphrey   July 16, 1995
Myron F. Butler   August 8, 1995
Louis Updegraff   November 11, 1995
Helen Fox   November 23, 1995
Grace A. Curtis   December 4, 1995
Richard Dudley Slater   December 15, 1995
Cecil L. Edwards   December 22, 1995
Vern Davis   December 1995
Norma Frazier   December 1995

1996

Katherine Gouley   January 1996
Eugene W. Crothers   January 30, 1996
Florence E. Duffy   February 3, 1996
Lucille Hirons   April 16, 1996
Alfred C. Laue   May 1, 1996
Elma Ray Money   May 26, 1996
Mary C. Schomus   June 3, 1996
Mabel E. Montenegro   June 12, 1996
Delia S. Jette   June 28, 1996
Lawrence "Bud" George   July 5, 1996
Robert D. Cahill   July 1996
Grace DeHarpport   August 8, 1996
Chas. "Stu" McElhinney   October 7, 1996
Mary V. Will   December 12, 1996

1997

G. Bingham Powell Sr.   February 13, 1997
Duane Ardon Frazier   February 14, 1997
Charles Bernard Isom   March 8, 1997
Leonard Spencer Moser   March 24, 1997
Catherine Zorn   April 21, 1997
Emery David Bartruff   April 23, 1997
Bernita Jones Sharp   May 1, 1997
Sybil Spears McLeod   May 12, 1997
Esther VanPelt Slusher   May 1997
Charles Sumner Campbell   July 11, 1997

Index